PROFESSIONAL DEVELOPMENT SCHOOLS

A Directory of Projects in the United States

Second Edition

1995
Clinical Schools Clearinghouse
American Association of Colleges for Teacher Education

The Clinical Schools Clearinghouse and the publication of this directory are supported by the Ford Foundation Clinical Schools Project.

The material in this publication does not necessarily reflect the views of the American Association of Colleges for Teacher Education or the Ford Foundation.

Cite as:
Abdal-Haqq, I. (Comp.). (1995). *Professional development schools: A directory of projects in the United States* (2nd ed.). Washington, DC: American Association of Colleges for Teacher Education.

Writing, layout, and design by Ismat Abdal-Haqq

Copies may be ordered from:
AACTE Publications
One Dupont Circle NW, Suite 610
Washington, DC 20036-1186
(202) 293-2450

Single Copy: $18 prepaid (plus shipping & handling)

Content

Acknowledgments vii

Introduction ix

Survey Highlights xviii

Tables & Charts xix

Data Summary: Section I
Data Summary: Section II
Comparison of Selected Data from Survey 1 & Survey 2
Figure 1: PDS Program Features
Figure 2: Teacher Education Faculty Participation in PDS
            Programs
Figure 3: Funding Sources
Figure 4: PDS Program Starting Date
Figure 5: Computer Technology Used in PDS Teacher Educa-
            tion Program to Facilitate Instruction &/or Staff
            Development
Figure 6: Computer Technology Used in PDS Teacher Educa-
            tion Program to Facilitate Collaboration Among PDS
            Partners
Figure 7: Computer Technology Included in Subject Matter of
            Teacher Education &/or Staff Development Curricu-
            lum of PDS Participants

Profiles of Professional Development School Partnerships 1

Professional Development School Characteristics 147

Appendices 265

Appendix 1: Data Collection Form
Appendix 2: College & University Partners Profiled in This
            Directory
Appendix 3: Professional Development School Sites
Appendix 4: Bibliography
Appendix 5: The Clinical Schools Clearinghouse
Appendix 6: Publications on Professional Development Schools
            from the Clinical Schools Clearinghouse, ERIC
            Clearinghouse on Teaching and Teacher Education,
            and AACTE

Acknowledgments

The effort and support of many institutions and individuals have contributed to this publication. Generous support from the Ford Foundation enabled AACTE to establish the Clinical Schools Clearinghouse (CSC), which produced this directory. College and school faculty members who devoted time and energy to supplying data about their professional development school programs are sincerely thanked with genuine gratitude.

Mary Dilworth, AACTE's senior director of research and information, provided valuable assistance in designing the survey and reviewing the findings. The editing skills of Judy Beck, associate director of the ERIC Clearinghouse on Teaching and Teacher Education, have been of great help in preparing the manuscript for publication. The task of producing this directory would have been much more arduous without the energy and effort of Tyler Bolden, CSC secretary, who tracked survey responses, input data, compiled reports, and prepared text files for desktop publishing.

CSC staff would like to thank the many individuals who made use of the first edition of this directory and encouraged us to produce an update. Finally, we wish to acknowledge the dedication, commitment, and perseverance of the many individuals from school and college faculties, teachers unions, foundations, school districts, and other institutions who have labored so intensely to bring PDSs to life and to nurture their growth.

Introduction

During the last decade, educators and policymakers have devoted considerable energy and resources to planning and implementing professional development schools (PDSs). The PDS concept gained national attention in the mid-eighties when the Carnegie Corporation in its 1986 report, *A Nation Prepared: Teachers for the 21st Century*, called for clinical schools to be established. Also in 1986, *Tomorrow's Teachers: A Report of the Holmes Group*, designated professional development schools as a key component of redesigned teacher professional development.

In these reports, the role of clinical schools or professional development schools in the professional development of educators was compared to the role of teaching hospitals in preparing health professionals. These schools were described as the institutional setting that would provide coherent, systematic, and legitimate practicum experiences for novice and veteran educators. The objective of these experiences would be developing and refining professional practice.

The initial focus of PDSs was the nation's public school teaching corps, and the proposal of clinical training sites was, in part, a reaction to what was perceived to be the lamentable character of traditional student teaching. Traditionally, preservice teacher preparation culminated in a practicum, student teaching, which generally lasted 9 to 13 weeks. While the majority of practicing teachers have consistently acknowledged that their student teaching experience was the most critical component of their preservice preparation, there is also considerable evidence that the quality of an individual's student teaching experience depends more on the expertise of the cooperating teacher than on the structure of the program itself.

Traditional student teaching has been characterized as idiosyncratic and unconnected to research-based principles of best pratice. In general, guidance and support are minimal (Levine, 1988). Furthermore, what guidance and support do exist traditionally disappear altogether when a new teacher begins employment. Consequently, novice teachers become socialized into the existing school culture and typically, spend their professional lives perpetuating practices that have been criticized for inadequately preparing the majority of students to cope successfully with the demands of life in the twenty-first century.

Although the shortcomings of the nation's public schools have not been laid entirely at the feet of the practicum component of teacher preparation, better clinical experiences are seen as a key element of a number of proposals for upgrading professional development for educators. Furthermore, better clinical experiences obviously rely on

Introduction

better clinical settings. In an address to the 1991 Annual Meeting of the American Association of Colleges for Teacher Education (AACTE), Judith Lanier (1991), former dean of the college of education at Michigan State University, rationalized the need for professional development schools when she stated, "We cannot educate tomorrow's teachers in today's schools."

Initially, the PDS was envisioned as an exemplary elementary or secondary school, generally a public school, with three primary missions: (1) professional development of preservice, beginning, and veteran teachers; (2) inquiry into and refinement of effective practice; and (3) maximization of student acheivement. An associated goal is dissemination of promising practices and structures to the education community beyond the walls of the PDS. In recent years, attention has also been given to the professional development of administrators, counselors, and other education specialists.

A central feature of PDSs is that they are developed and managed collaboratively by a partnership composed of one or more school districts; one or more higher education institutions; and often, one or more teachers unions. Another key feature is that PDS programs operate in existing, "real-world" schools, which reflect the demographic realities of the communities that house them.

It is the existence of these multiple goals and key characteristics that distinguishes PDSs from their forerunners. Although a model PDS incorporates elements of the laboratory school, demonstration school, partnership school, portal school, and others; the scope of its mission sets it apart.

While it both attracts and promises, the scope of the PDS mission also complicates implementation and quality control. Frequently, those who establish PDSs selectively adopt particular elements of the PDS model. For example, some educators see the PDS primarily as a vehicle for restructuring schools while others see it primarily as a clinical training setting for the preparation of new teachers. The chosen focus is often apparent in the activities and organization of the program. For instance, in some programs, teacher development structures and activities do not extend beyond preservice teachers to include beginning and veteran teachers while in other cases, just the opposite occurs, and little or no programmatic activity exists for preservice teachers. Systematic inquiry, which is one of the core characteristics generally associated with these schools, is another PDS element

Introduction

that often seems to have no integral place in the program

Various reasons exist for this selectivity. One reason is that significant commitments of time and money are required to implement a comprehensive PDS model, and because these resources are not always immediately available to PDS planners, elements of the program are phased-in as resources become available. Even if resource availability is not a limiting factor, nurturing a PDS is acknowledged by both practitioners and theorists to be a long-term commitment. Thus, specific program components may be phased-in for strategic reasons. In addition, there are different interpretations of what a PDS should be and do. Since it is essentially a new and unregulated institution, it is pretty much open season for those who want to try their hand at establishing and running a PDS. To a large extent, any program that labels itself a PDS goes unchallenged.

For some time, there has been concern among PDS advocates about how to define the PDS mission, its structure, and its program is such a way that the education community has guidelines for establishing and operating PDSs, as well as some framework for quality control, but does not lose the flexibility to develop context-relevant programs. An attempt to develop such guidelines is being undertaken by the National Council for Accreditation of Teacher Education (NCATE), which recently received funds from the AT&T Foundation to support the PDS Standards Project.

Methodology

This directory is based on findings from the second national survey of PDSs conducted by the Clinical Schools Clearinghouse. Since 1991, CSC has been supported by the Ford Foundation and administered by the American Association of Colleges for Teacher Education (AACTE) and the ERIC Clearinghouse on Teaching and Teacher Education. Data from CSC's first national survey were collected during the fall and winter of 1991-1992, and findings were published in the first edition of *Professional Development Schools: A Directory of Projects in the United States* (Abdal-Haqq, 1992). Data from the present survey were collected during the fall and winter of 1993-1994 and are presented in this second edition of the PDS directory. Both surveys were conducted in order to: (1) identify existing PDSs; (2) collect information on the characteristics of these PDSs; (3) construct a database on PDSs, which can be used as a research and reference tool, and (4) produce a publication that presents the information collected.

Introduction

The survey instrument, Data Collection Form (Appendix 1), was developed by CSC staff. With the exception of items 6-13 in Section I, which were not present in the 1991-1992 survey instrument, the same Data Collection Form (DCF) was used in both surveys. A review of the PDS literature and conversations with educators involved in PDS development and implementation suggested data items.

DCFs were mailed to 106 individuals and institutions, primarily colleges and universities. CSC staff compiled an initial mailing list, which included institutions that participated in the 1991-1992 survey and other PDS programs identified later. In addition, an announcement and invitation to participate were placed in the AACTE newsletter, *Briefs*, and DCFs were mailed to those who responded to the announcement. Mail and phone follow-up were used to encourage response and to clarify unclear responses. Eventually, 66 usable responses were obtained, resulting in a response rate of 62%.

The PDS Database is a searchable database which was designed by CSC staff. Data from the DCFs were input into this database, which was also used to tabulate DCF data and to generate some of the that are used in this directory. As more PDSs are identified, this database will be expanded and updated.

Limitations

Before discussing results of the survey and the format of this directory, it is perhaps appropriate at this point to note that, in conducting the survey upon which this publication is based, the Clinical Schools Clearinghouse (CSC) relied upon self-reporting by respondents. No attempt was made by CSC to determine whether a program "qualified" as a PDS.

It should also be noted that throughout this publication, the term professional development schools is used by the writer. Survey respondents reflect the education literature in the variety of labels they use. Although the majority (69.8%) of schools profiled in this directory label themselves professional development schools, 13.6% refer to themselves as partner schools, 12.5% prefer clinical schools, and 2 % identify themselves as professional practice schools. Although these terms may not be considered completely interchangeable in all instances, the term professional development school is used in this publication as a generic label for institutions or entities that share goals and characteristics generally associated with the PDS model.

Introduction

PDS Growth

Results of this second national survey show a dramatic increase in the number of programs since 1991-1992. More than 50% of respondents indicated a start-up date between 1992 and 1994. The first edition of this directory, which was based on CSC's 1991-1992 survey, contained profiles of 80 elementary and secondary PDSs, established by 28 partnerships. The current directory (based on 1993-1994 survey data) includes profiles of 301 PDSs, established by 66 partnerships. Because some partnerships include more than one higher education institution, the total number of colleges represented is 78. The number of individual PDSs associated with a particular partnership ranges from 1 to 37. Approximately 21% of the respondents in the current survey also participated in the survey.

Unions and Affiliations

Unions affiliated with either the American Federation of Teachers or the National Education Association are partners in approximately 20% of the programs; and 54.6% of the programs are affiliated with a network, consortium, or foundation sponsor. These affiliations include the AT&T Teachers for Tomorrow Program, Holmes Group, Michigan Partnership for New Education, National Network for Educational Renewal, St. Louis Professional Development Schools Collaborative, and Texas Education Agency's Centers for Professional Development and Technology.

Funding

The three largest categories of financial support are colleges and universities (71.4%); foundations, corporations, and other private sources (63.5%); and school districts (52.4%). Support also comes from states (23.8%), teachers unions (3.2%) and the federal government (3.2%). However, a majority of the respondents (63.1%) that receive college support indicate that this support consists of grants, discretionary funds, or other types of "soft money."

Institutionalization

The proportion of soft money contributions to college funds for PDS development and implementation may be regarded as one clue to the level of institutionalization. Other indicators may be the number of colleges (69.7%) that provide release time or reduced course loads for college faculty who work with these very labor-intensive programs and the number of colleges (65.2%) with reward structures that acknowledge PDS-related activity on the part of faculty.

Introduction

The proportion of education department faculty who participate in planning or implementing the PDS program may also contribute to the picture of the institutionalization level. Typically, the college partner in a PDS program is represented by a small core of overburdened faculty. The broader the level of faculty involvement, the greater the potential for continuity and for the program's ability to survive the loss of one or two individuals. The segment of those responding to this item (36.4%) indicated that less than 20% of their department's faculty are involved in PDS planning or implementation.

Cohorts

Because the PDS strives to be an exemplary setting for both student and teacher learning, one expects to find present many of the effective practices, structures, and components supported by educational research. The placement of student teachers in cohorts for the practicums is one of these practices and is employed by 86.36% of the respondents.

Computer Technology

Less encouraging are the findings about how PDS programs are utilizing computer technology. Several investigations into the use of computer technology in education suggest that three primary elements must be present if students are to acquire an adequate level of familiarity with this technology (Bosch & Cardinale, 1993; Office of Technology Assessment, 1995). First, students should have exposure to a variety of computer applications. Secondly, computer technology should be integrated throughout the curriculum and not just limited to one or two courses. Finally, instructors must model the kind of usage they are attempting to promote. Vocknell and Sweeney (1994) also suggest that the key to effective classroom use of computer technology is teachers who are prepared to incorporate these elements into their own practice.

Survey respondents indicated that computer-related topics are included in their teacher education curriculums in varying degrees. Most include computer assisted instruction (78.7%), but only slightly more than half include telecommunications (55%) or interactive video (52.5%), both of which are becoming increasing meaningful as tools and subjects of instruction.

Just as public school students model their teachers, teacher education students model teacher educators. Responses to items related to the employment of computer applications to facilitate teacher education instruction suggest that modeling is at a moderate level

Introduction

in the teacher education programs surveyed. Computer assisted instruction is used to facilitate teacher education instruction in 60.3% of the PDS programs, telecommunications is used in 58.7%, and interactive video in 37.3%.

Start Date and Grade Level

Most respondents (51.9%) indicated a starting date between 1992 and 1994; 25.6%) began in 1993. The individual PDSs have a number of grade level configurations. Typical elementary configurations (i.e., PreK-6, K-5, K-6) represented 64% of the reported schools. Middle schools (grades 6-8), junior high schools (grades 7-9), and high schools (grades 9-12 and 10-12) account for 24.9% of the schools. The remaining 11.5% of reported schools included more atypical grade configurations (e.g., 3-8; PreK-12; PreK-K).

College/School Cooperation

In 81.7% of the PDSs, school and college faculty collaborate on research projects. School faculty members hold joint college/school appointments in 32.% of the PDSs surveyed. School faculty assist in planning the preservice curriculum at 92.9% of the schools, and at 93.2% of the schools, school faculty also assist in planning the inservice curriculum.

Teacher Development

Preservice teachers have courses on-site at 63.4% of the schools and mentor teachers at 90.9%. They are assigned to more than one cooperating teacher at 68.7% of the PDSs and participate in educational research at 47.9% of the PDS sites.

Beginning teacher induction programs are in place at 42.4% of the PDSs and at 43.8% mentors are assigned to beginning teachers. The inservice program is characterized by on-site courses for inservice teachers at 60.1% of the schools. While 59.1% of the schools designate experienced teachers as master teachers, only 9.9% of master teachers, cooperating teachers, and mentors have reduced course loads and only 25.3% of them have release time. Inservice teachers are involved in educational research at the school site at 56.2% of the PDSs, and at 83%, they are involved in curriculum development.

Multicultural Issues

Preservice teachers participate in structured learning experiences that address issues related to educating minority group students at 82.4% of the schools, and at 69.7% of the PDSs, inservice teachers participate in such experiences. A majority (43.8%) of PDSs have minority student populations of 0-19% while only 17.5% have minority

Introduction

student enrollment of 80-100%. At 75.8% of the PDSs, 0-19% of preservice teachers are from minority groups, but only 2.4% of the surveyed schools have 80-100% of their preservice teachers coming from minority groups.

Statistical summaries of survey findings, as well as graphical representations of selected program characteristics, are presented in the Tables & Charts section of the directory. Included is a table that compares selected data from the first and second surveys.

Directory Format

Survey highlights and a series of tables and charts follow the introduction. The tables and charts summarize selected survey findings. Profiles of the surveyed programs and schools are arranged alphabetically, by state. Characteristics of the 301 PDSs are presented in tables, which follow the profiles. In the tables, individual schools are listed alphabetically by state, college partner, and school.

Six appendices conclude the directory. Appendix 1 contains the Data Collection Form (DCF), used as the survey instrument. Alphabetical listings of college and university partners profiled in the directory and the individual PDSs are found in Appendix 2 and Appendix 3, respectively.

Seventy-eight colleges and university partners are listed in Appendix 2. Some of the PDS programs have more than one college or university partner. In these cases, only one profile is provided in the profiles section, and that profile is presented under the name of the institution that submitted the DCF. Appendix 2 includes cross-references to the appropriate profile where needed.

Appendix 4 contains the college and university partners of PDSs that were profiled in the 1992 edition of this directory but not in the current edition because they did not submit DCFs from the 1993-1994 survey. As mentioned earlier, only slightly more than 21% of the respondents who supplied data for this directory were also profiled in the first edition. Appendix 5 is a bibliography, which features resources related to the programs and schools that are profiled. Appendix 6 is a fact sheet that describes the purposes and activities of the Clinical Schools Clearinghouse, and Appendix 7 is a list of PDS-related publications produced by CSC, AACTE, and the ERIC Clearinghouse on Teaching and Teacher Education.

Introduction

References

Abdal-Haqq, I. (Comp.). (1992). *Professional development schools. A directory of projects in the United States*. Washington, DC: American Association of Colleges for Teacher Education.

Bosch, K. A., & Cardinale, L. (1993). Preservice teachers' perceptions of computer use during a field experience. *Journal of Computing in Teacher Education, 10*(1), 23-27. (ERIC Document Reproduction Service No. EJ492121)

Carnegie Corporation of New York. (1986). *A nation prepared: Teachers for the 21st century.* New York, NY: Author (ERIC Document Reproduction Service No. ED268120)

Holmes Group. (1986) *Tomorrow's teachers: A report of the Holmes Group*. East Lansing, MI: Author. (ERIC Document Reproduction Service No.ED270454).

Lanier, J. (Speaker). (1991). *Renewing teacher education: Postulates and paradigms* (Audio Cassette Recording No. TE127). Chicago, IL: Teach'em.

Levine, M. (Ed.). (1988). *Professional practice schools: Building a model. Volume 1*. Washington, DC: American Federation of Teachers. (ERIC Document Reproduction Service No. ED313344)

Vocknell, E., & Sweeney, J. (1994). How do teachers who use computers competently differ from other teachers? *Journal of Computing in Teacher Education, 10*(2), 24-31.

Survey Highlights

❑ Nationally, college-school partnerships, which include 78 colleges and universities, have established more than 300 professional development schools (PDSs).

❑ Approximetely 75% of the PDSs are in elementary grade settings.

❑ Nearly 20% of the surveyed programs have a teachers union partner.

❑ Foundations, corporations, and other private sources contribute funds to approximately 63.5% of the programs.

❑ Between 37% and 60% of the partnerships use computer technology to facilitate teacher education instruction. The level of use varies with the kind of computer application (e.g., telecommunications, computer assisted instruction).

❑ Nearly 52% of the PDSs surveyed were established between 1992 and 1994.

❑ About 55% of the programs have national or local network, consortium, or foundation affiliations.

❑ Approximately 86% of the surveyed PDS programs place student teachers in cohorts.

❑ About 65% of the PDS programs have college reward structures that acknowledge PDS-related work.

❑ The minority student enrollment is less than 40% at about 64% of the PDSs; and in almost 88% of the PDSs, less than 40% of the preservice teachers are from minority groups.

❑ Nearly 73% of the surveyed PDSs have activities and structures related to preservice teachers; about 42% have activities and structures related to beginning teachers; and almost 57% have activities and structures related to inservice teachers.

❑ In approximately 76% of the PDSs, structured learning experiences related to the education of minority group students exist for preservice and/or inservice teachers.

Tables & Charts

Data Summary: Section I xxi

Data Summary: Section II xxiii

Comparison of Selected Data from Survey 1 & Survey 2 xxvi

Figure 1: PDS Program Features xxix

Figure 2: Teacher Education Faculty Participation in PDS Programs xxx

Figure 3: Funding Sources xxxi

Figure 4: PDS Program Starting Date xxxii

Figure 5: Computer Technology Used in PDS Teacher Education
Program to Facilitate Instruction &/or Staff Development xxxiii

Figure 6: Computer Technology Used in PDS Teacher Education
Program to Facilitate Collaboration Among PDS Partners xxxiv

Figure 7: Computer Technology Included in Subject Matter of Teacher
Education &/or Staff Development Curriculum of PDS
Participants xxxv

Data Summary
Section I

Feature	% of PDSs Responding
respondents who participated in 1991-1992 PDS national survey	21.21%
union partner	19.70%
consortium, foundation, or other network affiliation	54.55%
student teacher cohorts	86.36%
college funding - "soft money"	63.08%
release time or reduced load for college faculty	69.70%
college reward structure acknowledges PDS-related work	65.15%
Faculty Participation	
0-19%	36.36%
20-39%	30.30%
40-59%	4.55%
60-79%	9.09%
80-100%	19.70%
Funding Sources	
school district	52.38%
university/college	71.43%
state	23.81%
foundations, corporations, & other private sources	63.49%
unions	3.17%
federal	3.17%

Feature	% of PDSs Responding
Computer Technology - to facilitate teacher education instruction	
telecommunications (e-mail, bulletin boards, etc.)	58.73%
computer-assisted instruction	60.32%
interactive video	37.29%
desktop publishing	53.97%
Computer Technology - to facilitate PDS partners' collaboration	
telecommunications (e-mail, bulletin boards, etc.)	55.17%
computer-assisted instruction	35.71%
interactive video	20.00%
desktop publishing	45.00%
Computer Technology - included in teacher education curriculum	
telecommunications (e-mail, bulletin boards, etc.)	55.00%
computer assisted instruction	78.69%
interactive video	52.54%
programming	30.51%
authoring systems	32.20%
desktop publishing	55.00%

Items indicated in the Feature column of this table, as well as in the two data summary tables which follow, correspond to items found on the Data Collection Form (Appendix 1) used in the survey.

Data Summary
Section II

Feature	% of PDSs Responding[a]
Start Date	
1994	2.96%
1993	25.56%
1992	23.33%
1991	21.48%
1990	12.59%
1989	7.78%
1988	2.59%
1987	1.48%
1986	0.74%
1984	0.74%
1983	0.74%
Grade Level	
K-6	42.09%
7-9	4.71%
10-12	5.05%
Other:[b]	
6-8	7.41%
K-5	8.08%
9-12	7.41%
PreK-6	13.80%
School Type	
clinical school	12.54%
professional development school	69.83%
professional practice school	2.03%
partner school	13.56%
Other	2.03%

Feature	% of PDSs Responding[a]
College/School Cooperation	
school faculty members hold joint school/college teaching appointments	32.03%
college faculty teach school students	42.76%
school faculty assist in planning preservice teacher education curriculum	92.91%
school faculty assist in planning inservice teacher education curriculum	93.20%
collaborative research involving school & college faculty	81.72%
Preservice Teachers Program	
on-site (school) courses for preservice teachers	63.41%
mentor teachers for preservice teachers	90.94%
clinical supervision of student teachers'	91.28%
each preservice teacher assigned to more than one cooperating teacher	68.66%
preservice teachers involved in educational research conducted at the school site	47.90%
Beginning Teachers Program	
beginning teacher induction program	42.39%
mentor teachers for beginning teachers	43.73%
clinical supervision of beginning teachers	39.86%
Inservice Teachers Program	
on-site (school) courses for inservice teachers	60.14%
cooperating teacher training provided to practicing teachers	87.28%
experienced teachers designated as master teachers	59.14%
mentor, master, and/or cooperating teachers have reduced course load	9.85%
mentor, master, and/or cooperating teachers have release time	25.27%
practicing teachers involved in curriculum development	82.99%

Feature	% of PDSs Responding[a]
Inservice Teachers Program, *continued*	
practicing teachers actively involved in decision making with regard to organizational/structural changes within the school	70.73%
inservice teachers involved in educational research conducted at the school site	56.18%
Multicultural Issues	
preservice teachers participate in structured learning experiences that address issues related to educating minority group students	82.41%
inservice teachers participate in structured learning experiences that address issues related to educating minority group students	69.76%
approximate percentage of student enrollment from minority groups	
0-19%	43.84%
20-39%	20.55%
40-59%	12.33%
60-79%	5.82%
80-100%	17.47%
approximate percentage of teacher interns (preservice teachers) from minority groups	
0-19%	75.78%
20-39%	12.11%
40-59%	3.81%
60-79%	5.88%
80-100%	2.42%

[a]Totals for some categories may exceed 100% due to rounding.
[b]A number of grade level configurations were reported in the Other option on the data collection form. The four that are listed were the most frequently indicated.

Comparison of Selected Data from Survey 1 & Survey 2

Feature	% of PDSs Responding	
	Survey 2	Survey 1[a]
Start Date		
1994	2.96%	n/a
1993	25.56%	n/a
1992	23.33%	n/a
1991	21.48%	37.00%
1990	12.59%	28.00%
1989	7.78%	16.00%
1988	2.59%	12.00%
1987	1.48%	7.00%
1986	0.74%	n/a
1984	0.74%	n/a
1983	0.74%	n/a
Grade Level		
K-6	42.09%	29.00%
7-9	4.71%	9.00%
10-12	5.05%	4.00%
Other:[b]		
6-8	7.41%	n/a
K-5	8.08%	n/a
9-12	7.41%	13.00%
PreK-6	13.80%	n/a
School Type		
clinical school	12.54%	2.00%
professional development school	69.83%	82.00%
professional practice school	2.03%	8.00%
partner school	13.56%	n/a

Feature	% of PDSs Responding	
	Survey 2	Survey 1[a]
Other	2.03%	n/a
College/School Cooperation		
school faculty members hold joint school/college teaching appointments	32.03%	45.00%
college faculty teach school students	42.76%	67.00%
school faculty assist in planning preservice teacher education curriculum	92.91%	99.00%
school faculty assist in planning inservice teacher education curriculum	93.20%	96.00%
collaborative research involving school & college faculty	81.72%	97.00%
Preservice Teachers Program		
on-site (school) courses for preservice teachers	63.41%	66.00%
mentor teachers for preservice teachers	90.94%	88.00%
clinical supervision of student teachers	91.28%	91.00%
each preservice teacher assigned to more than one cooperating teacher	68.66%	70.00%
preservice teachers involved in educational research conducted at the school site	47.90%	75.00%
Beginning Teachers Program		
beginning teacher induction program	42.39%	69.00%
mentor teachers for beginning teachers	43.73%	75.00%
clinical supervision of beginning teachers	39.86%	55.00%
Inservice Teachers Program		
on-site (school) courses for inservice teachers	60.14%	79.00%
cooperating teacher training provided to practicing teachers	87.28%	87.00%
experienced teachers designated as master teachers	59.14%	50.00%
mentor, master, and/or cooperating teachers have reduced course load	9.85%	19.00%
mentor, master, and/or cooperating teachers have release time	25.27%	74.00%

Feature	% of PDSs Responding	
	Survey 2	Survey 1[a]
practicing teachers involved in curriculum development	82.99%	89.00%
practicing teachers actively involved in decision making with regard to organizational/structural changes within the school	70.73%	91.00%
inservice teachers involved in educational research conducted at the school site	56.18%	75.00%
Multicultural Issues		
preservice teachers participate in structured learning experiences that address issues related to educating minority group students	82.41%	97.00%
inservice teachers participate in structured learning experiences that address issues related to educating minority group students	69.76%	73.00%
approximate percentage of student enrollment from minority groups		
0-19%	43.84%	23.00%
20-39%	20.55%	35.00%
40-59%	12.33%	14.00%
60-79%	5.82%	13.00%
80-100%	17.47%	14.00%
approximate percentage of teacher interns (preservice teachers) from minority groups		
0-19%	75.78%	78.00%
20-39%	12.11%	14.00%
40-59%	3.81%	6.00%
60-79%	5.88%	0.00%
80-100%	2.42%	2.00%

Note: Totals for some categories may not equal 100% due to rounding.

[a] Survey 1 data were collected during 1991-1992 and published in the first edition of *Professional Development Schools: A Directory of Projects in the United States* (1992). Survey 2 data, which are the basis of the current directory, were collected during 1993-1994.

[b] For both surveys, numerous grade level configurations were reported in the Other response to this item. The four that are listed were most frequently reported in Survey 2.

Figure 1
PDS Program Features

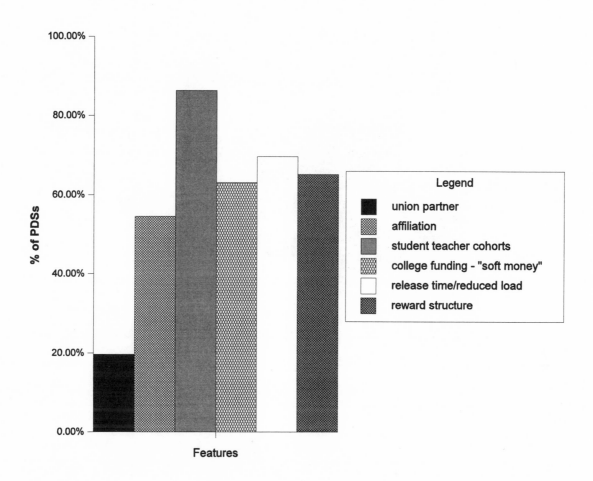

Note: See data collection form (p. 267) for specific items referenced above

Figure 2
Teacher Education Faculty Participation in PDS Programs

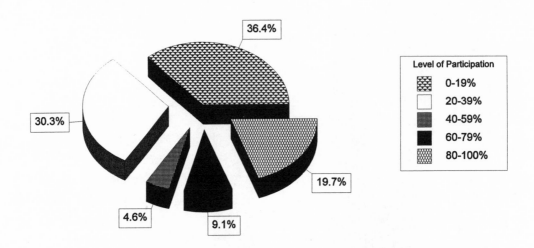

Note: See data collection form (p. 267) for specific items referenced above

Figure 3
Funding Sources

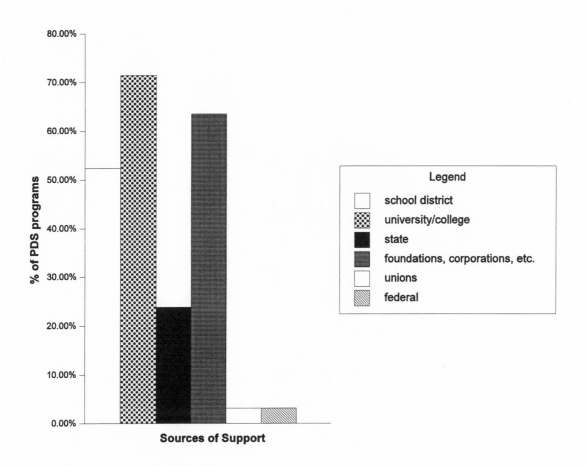

Note: See data collection form (p. 267) for specific items referenced above

Figure 4
PDS Program Starting Date

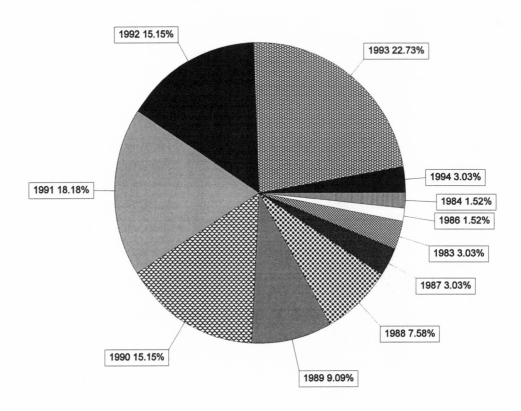

Note: See data collection form (p. 267) for specific items referenced above

Figure 5
Computer Applications Used in PDS Teacher Education Program
to Facilitate Instruction &/or Staff Development

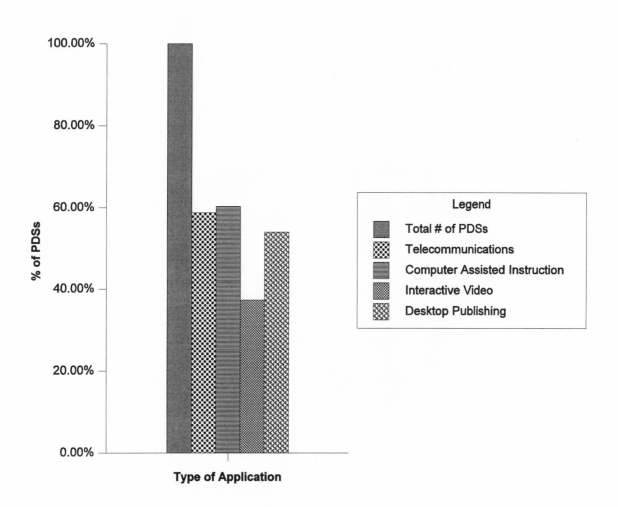

Note: See data collection form (p. 267) for specific items referenced above

Figure 6
Computer Technology Used in PDS Teacher Education Programs to Facilitate Collaboration Among PDS Partners

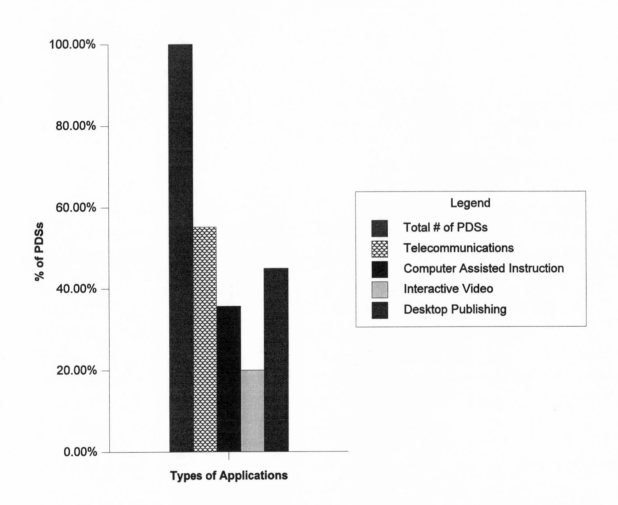

Note: See data collection form (p. 267) for specific items referenced above

Figure 7
Computer Technology Included in Subject Matter of Teacher Education &/or Staff Development Curriculum of PDS Participants

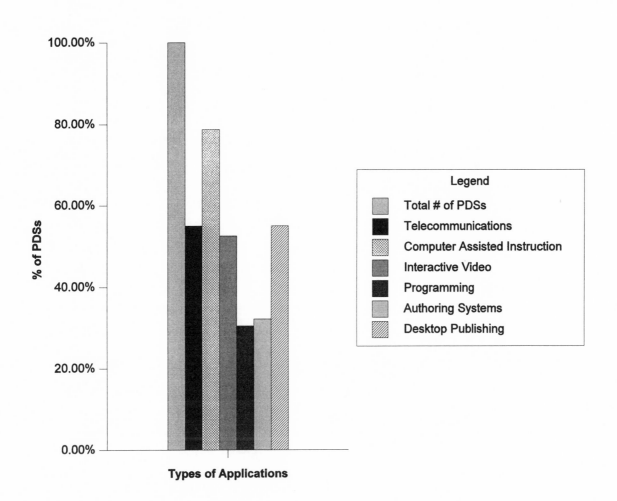

Note: See data collection form (p. 267) for specific items referenced above

Profiles of Professional Development School Partnerships

This section contains profiles of 66 PDS partnerships. Most profiles consist of at least two pages. The first page includes contact information for the partnership, partners, funding sources, affiliations, starting date, individual PreK-12 PDSs associated with the partnership, and program features. The data given in the first section of each profile represent responses to items in Section I of the Data Collection Form (Appendix 1) and relate to the overall PDS program. Only those program features to which positive responses were given by the respondent are listed.

The second section of each profile, which is generally the second page, provides a brief profile of **each** PDS associated with the respective partnership. Some partnerships operate just one PDS while others may operate over 30. More than 300 individual PDSs are profiled. In a few cases, the first section of the partnership profile is given, but no profiles of individual PDSs are provided. In these instances an explanation of this omission is included in the note field of the profile.

ARKANSAS

College/University	*University of Arkansas - Fayetteville*
Contact	Roderick J. McDavis, Dean University of Arkansas 324 Graduate Education Building Fayetteville, AR 72701 (501) 575-3208
Partners	University of Arkansas - Fayetteville Springdale School District
Funding	university; school district; Southwestern Bell Foundation
Starting Date	1992, August
PDS Sites	George Elementary School; Jefferson Elementary School; Woodland Junior High School;
Program Features	

- ❑ College funding for PDS program from grants, discretionary funds, or other types of "soft money"
- ❑ Release time, reduced course load, or other related arrangement made for college faculty actively involved with PDS sites
- ❑ Computer technology included in **subject matter** of teacher education &/or staff development curriculum of PDS participants:
  - ■ desktop publishing
- ❑ Approximately 0-19% of department faculty participate in PDS-related work (planning or implementation)

ARKANSAS

University of Arkansas - Fayetteville

School	George Elementary School
	2878 South Powell Street
	Springdale, AR 72764
	Phone: (501) 751-8710
Site Coordinator	Jim Lewis, Principal
Starting Date	1992, August
Grade Level	K-6
School Type	Partner School
School	Jefferson Elementary School
	612 South College
	Fayetteville, AR 72701
	Phone: (501) 444-3087
Site Coordinator	John Colbert
Starting Date	1989, August
Grade Level	K-6
School Type	Partnership School
School	Woodland Junior High School
	Poplar/Woodland Streets
	Fayetteville, AR 72702
	Phone: (501) 444-3067
Site Coordinator	David Hunt
Starting Date	1989, August
Grade Level	7-9
School Type	Partnership School

CALIFORNIA

College/University	*California State University - Fullerton*
Contact	Dr. Hallie Yopp Slowik; Dr. Andrea Guillaume; Dr. Tom Savage Department of Elementary & Bilingual Education California State University, Fullerton Fullerton, CA 92634 (714) 773-3411
Partners	California State University, Fullerton Fullerton, Placentia-Yorba Linda Unified, La Habra, Corona-Norco, and Santa Ana Unified School Districts
Starting Date	1990, September
PDS Sites	Golden Hill School; Highland School; Ladera Palma School; Linda Vista School; Monte Vista School; Raymond School; Sierra Vista School; Tynes School; Vicentia School;

Program Features	❑ Preservice teachers assigned to PDSs in cohorts
	❑ Computer technology used in PDS teacher education program to **facilitate instruction** &/or staff development:
	  ■ telecommunications (e.g., e-mail, bulletin boards)
	  ■ computer assisted instruction
	❑ Computer technology used to **facilitate collaboration** among PDS partners:
	  ■ telecommunications (e.g., e-mail, bulletin boards)
	❑ Computer technology included in **subject matter** of teacher education &/or staff development curriculum of PDS participants:
	  ■ computer assisted instruction
	  ■ interactive video
	❑ Policies of college with regard to hiring, tenure, promotion, or other aspects of college's reward structure, acknowledge PDS-related work
	❑ Approximately 20-39% of department faculty participate in PDS-related work (planning or implementation)

CALIFORNIA

California State University - Fullerton

School	Golden Hill School 732 Barris Drive Fullerton, CA 92632 Phone: (714) 447-7715	Raymond School 517 N. Raymond Fullerton, CA 92631 Phone: (714) 447-7740
Site Coordinator	Susan Formanek, Principal	Carolee Michael, Principal
Starting Date	1990, Fall	1990, Fall
Grade Level	K-6	K-6
School Type	Professional Development School	Professional Development School

School	Highland School 2301 Alhambra Norco, CA 91720 Phone: (909) 736-3308	Sierra Vista School 1800 E. Whittier La Habra, CA 90631 Phone: (310) 690-2359
Site Coordinator	Sandy Hamilton, Principal	Rick Snyder, Principal
Starting Date	1992, Fall	1993, Spring
Grade Level	K-5	3-5
School Type	Professional Development School	Professional Development School

School	Ladera Palma School 2151 E. Brookdale Avenue La Habra, CA 90631 Phone: (310) 690-2348	Tynes School 735 Stanford Drive Placentia, CA 92670 Phone: (714) 996-5550
Site Coordinator	Judy Wolfe, Principal	Beth Berndt, Principal
Starting Date	1993, Spring	1990, Fall
Grade Level	K-2	K-6
School Type	Professional Development School	Professional Development School

School	Linda Vista School 5600 S. Ohio Yorba Linda, CA 92686 Phone: (714) 779-2221	Vicentia School 2005 S. Vicentia Corona, CA 91720 Phone: (909)736-3228
Site Coordinator	Ann Test, Principal	Jason Scott
Starting Date	1990, Fall	1992, Fall
Grade Level	K-5	K-6
School Type	Professional Development School	Professional Development School

School	Monte Vista School 2116 Monte Vista Santa Ana, CA 92704 Phone: (714) 558-5831
Site Coordinator	Jacquin Terry, Principal
Starting Date	1992, Fall
Grade Level	K-5
School Type	Professional Development School

College/University	*San Diego State University*
Contact	George L. Mehaffey School of Teacher Education San Diego State University San Diego, CA 92182 (619) 594-5777
Partners	San Diego State University San Diego City Schools; La Mesa/Spring Valley District; Cajon Valley District; Chula Vista Elementary District
Funding	university; school district
Starting Date	1983
PDS Sites	Alliance for Excellence; Chula Vista Professional Development School; Kennedy Lab School; Marshall Professional Development School; Model Education Center; Partners in Education;

Program Features	❑ Preservice teachers assigned to PDSs in cohorts
	❑ Release time, reduced course load, or other related arrangement made for college faculty actively involved with PDS sites
	❑ Computer technology used in PDS teacher education program to **facilitate instruction** &/or staff development:
	  ■ telecommunications (e.g., e-mail, bulletin boards)
	  ■ computer assisted instruction
	  ■ interactive video
	❑ Computer technology used to **facilitate collaboration** among PDS partners:
	  ■ telecommunications (e.g., e-mail, bulletin boards)
	  ■ interactive video
	❑ Computer technology included in **subject matter** of teacher education &/or staff development curriculum of PDS participants:
	  ■ telecommunications (e.g., e-mail, bulletin boards)
	  ■ interactive video
	❑ Policies of college with regard to hiring, tenure, promotion, or other aspects of college's reward structure, acknowledge PDS-related work
	❑ Approximately 60-79% of department faculty participate in PDS-related work (planning or implementation)

San Diego State University

School	Alliance for Excellence School of Teacher Education San Diego State University* San Diego, CA 92182 Phone: (619) 594-5899	Model Education Center School of Teacher Education San Diego State University San Diego, CA 92182 Phone: (619) 594-1378
Site Coordinator	Anne Nagel, Professor	Marlowe Berg, Professor
Starting Date	1984	1983
Grade Level	K-6	K-6
School Type	Professional Development School	Professional Development School
School	Chula Vista Professional Development School School of Teacher Education San Diego State University San Diego, CA 92182 Phone: (619) 594-5777	Partners in Education School of Teacher Education San Diego State University San Diego, CA 92182 Phone: (619) 594-6086
Site Coordinator	George L. Mehaffy, Director	Cliff Bee, Professor
Starting Date	1991	1986
Grade Level	K-6	6-8
School Type	Professional Development School	Professional Development School
School	Kennedy Lab School School of Teacher Education San Diego State University San Diego, CA 92182 Phone: (619) 594-1370	
Site Coordinator	Nadine Bezuk, Associate Professor	
Starting Date	1984	
Grade Level	K-6	
School Type	Professional Development School	
School	Marshall Professional Development School School of Teacher Education San Diego State University San Diego, CA 92182 Phone: (619) 594-6128	
Site Coordinator	Judy Bippert, Coordinator of Field Experiences	
Starting Date	1993	
Grade Level	K-6	
School Type	Professional Development School	
Note	The respondent did not supply the addresses of individual PDSs.	

CALIFORNIA

College/University

University of California - Riverside

Contact

Judith H. Sandholtz, Director
Comprehensive Teacher Education Institute
School of Education
University of California - Riverside
Riverside, CA 92521
(909) 787-5798

Partners

University of California - Riverside
Jurupa School District

Funding

California State Department of Education Fund for Improvement of Secondary
Education (USDE)

Starting Date

1989

PDS Sites

Ribidoux High School

Program Features

- ❑ Preservice teachers assigned to PDSs in cohorts
- ❑ College funding for PDS program from grants, discretionary funds, or other types of "soft money"
- ❑ Computer technology used in PDS teacher education program to **facilitate instruction** &/or staff development:
  - ■ computer assisted instruction
  - ■ desktop publishing
- ❑ Computer technology included in **subject matter** of teacher education &/or staff development curriculum of PDS participants:
  - ■ computer assisted instruction
  - ■ desktop publishing
- ❑ Approximately 0-19% of department faculty participate in PDS-related work (planning or implementation)

CALIFORNIA

University of California,
Riverside

School	Ribidoux High School
	4250 Opal Street
	Riverside, CA 92509
	Phone: (909) 360-2863
Site Coordinator	Ben Bunz, Assistant Principal
Starting Date	1989
Grade Level	9-12
School Type	Professional Development School

College/University	*University of Delaware*
Contact	Karl Powers, Principal Thurgood Marshall Elementary School 101 Barrett Run Newark, DE 19720 (302) 454-4700
Partners	University of Delaware Christina School District
Affiliation	Holmes Group
Funding	university; school district; Eisenhower Act Funds
Starting Date	1993, September
PDS Sites	Thurgood Marshall Elementary School
Program Features	

- ❑ College funding for PDS program from grants, discretionary funds, or other types of "soft money"
- ❑ Release time, reduced course load, or other related arrangement made for college faculty actively involved with PDS sites
- ❑ Computer technology used in PDS teacher education program to **facilitate instruction** &/or staff development:
  - ■ telecommunications (e.g., e-mail, bulletin boards)
  - ■ computer assisted instruction
  - ■ desktop publishing
- ❑ Computer technology used to **facilitate collaboration** among PDS partners:
  - ■ telecommunications (e.g., e-mail, bulletin boards)
  - ■ desktop publishing
- ❑ Computer technology included in **subject matter** of teacher education &/or staff development curriculum of PDS participants:
  - ■ telecommunications (e.g., e-mail, bulletin boards)
  - ■ computer assisted instruction
- ❑ Policies of college with regard to hiring, tenure, promotion, or other aspects of college's reward structure, acknowledge PDS-related work
- ❑ Approximately 20-39% of department faculty participate in PDS-related work (planning or implementation)

DELAWARE

University of Delaware

School	Thurgood Marshall Elementary School 101 Barrett Run Newark, DE 19702 Phone: (302)454-4700
Site Coordinator	Dr. Betty Weir, Assistant to the Dean
Starting Date	1993, September
Grade Level	K-3
School Type	Professional Development School

FLORIDA

College/University	*University of South Florida*
Contact	Dr. Hilda Rosselli Dept. of Special Education, HMS 404 University of South Florida Tampa, FL 33620 (813) 974-3410
Partners	University of South Florida Pasco County Schools
Funding	school district; university
Starting Date	1990, August
PDS Sites	Thomas E. Weightman Middle School

Program Features

- ❑ Preservice teachers assigned to PDSs in cohorts
- ❑ College funding for PDS program from grants, discretionary funds, or other types of "soft money"
- ❑ Release time, reduced course load, or other related arrangement made for college faculty actively involved with PDS sites
- ❑ Computer technology used in PDS teacher education program to **facilitate instruction** &/or staff development:
  - ■ telecommunications (e.g., e-mail, bulletin boards)
  - ■ computer assisted instruction
  - ■ interactive video
  - ■ desktop publishing
- ❑ Computer technology included in **subject matter** of teacher education &/or staff development curriculum of PDS participants:
  - ■ telecommunications (e.g., e-mail, bulletin boards)
  - ■ computer assisted instruction
  - ■ interactive video
  - ■ programming
  - ■ desktop publishing
- ❑ Policies of college with regard to hiring, tenure, promotion, or other aspects of college's reward structure, acknowledge PDS-related work
- ❑ Approximately 20-39% of department faculty participate in PDS-related work (planning or implementation)

13

FLORIDA

University of South Florida

School	Thomas E. Weightman Middle School 30649 Wells Road Zephyrhills, FL 33544 Phone: (813) 929-2689
Site Coordinator	Hilda Rosselli, Assistant Professor
Starting Date	1990, August
Grade Level	6-8
School Type	Professional Development School

College/University	*Armstrong State College*
Contact	Maryellen S. Cosgrove, Ph.D. Armstrong State College 11935 Abercorn Street, Ext. Savannah, GA 31419 (912) 927-5281
Partners	Armstrong State College Savannah - Chatham County School District
Funding	college
Starting Date	1993, January
PDS Sites	White Bluff Elementary School

Program Features

❑ Release time, reduced course load, or other related arrangement made for college faculty actively involved with PDS sites
❑ Computer technology included in **subject matter** of teacher education &/or staff development curriculum of PDS participants:
  ■ computer assisted instruction
❑ Policies of college with regard to hiring, tenure, promotion, or other aspects of college's reward structure, acknowledge PDS-related work
❑ Approximately 80-100% of department faculty participate in PDS-related work (planning or implementation)

GEORGIA

Armstrong State College

School

White Bluff Elementary School
9902 White Bluff Road
Savannah, GA 31406
Phone: (912) 921-3740

Site Coordinator Maryellen S. Cosgrove, Ph.D.
Starting Date 1993, January
Grade Level K-6
School Type Professional Development School

College/University	*DePaul University*
Contact	Roxanne Owens DePaul University 2320 N. Kenmore Chicago, IL 60614 (312) 362-6598
Partners	DePaul University Glenview School District
Funding	university; school district
Starting Date	1990, June
PDS Sites	DePaul/Glenview Teacher Preparation Program

Program Features

❑ Preservice teachers assigned to PDSs in cohorts
❑ College funding for PDS program from grants, discretionary funds, or other types of "soft money"
❑ Release time, reduced course load, or other related arrangement made for college faculty actively involved with PDS sites
❑ Computer technology used in PDS teacher education program to **facilitate instruction** &/or staff development:
   ■ telecommunications (e.g., e-mail, bulletin boards)
   ■ computer assisted instruction
   ■ interactive video
   ■ desktop publishing
❑ Computer technology used to **facilitate collaboration** among PDS partners: staff development:
   ■ telecommunications (e.g., e-mail, bulletin boards)
   ■ computer assisted instruction
   ■ desktop publishing
❑ Computer technology included in **subject matter** of teacher education &/or staff development curriculum of PDS participants:
   ■ computer assisted instruction
   ■ interactive video
   ■ authoring systems
   ■ desktop publishing
❑ Policies of college with regard to hiring, tenure, promotion, or other aspects of college's reward structure, acknowledge PDS-related work
❑ Approximately 0-19% of department faculty participate in PDS-related work (planning or implementation)

ILLINOIS

DePaul University

School	Glenview Teacher Preparation Program DePaul University School of Education 2320 N. Kenmore Chicago, IL 60614 Phone: (312) 362-6598
Site Coordinator	Jean Conyers & Roxanne Owens
Starting Date	1990, June
Grade Level	K-8
School Type	Partner School

College/University	*Elmhurst College*
Contact	Dr. Linda Tusin Director, Satellite Program Elmhurst College 190 Prospect Avenue Elmhurst, IL 60126 (708) 617-3546
Partners	Elmhurst College School Districts #: 4, 87, 95, 205, 62, 86, 212, 15, 16, 64, 26, 12, 88, 45, & 7
Funding	college; Consortium for Advancement of Private Higher Education
Starting Date	1990, Spring
PDS Sites	Bellwood Preschool; Brook Park School; Bryan Junior High School; Conrad Fischer School; Early Childhood Education Center; Emerson School; Euclid School; Field School; Gower West School; Grant School; Hinsdale Central High School; Indian Trail Junior High School; Jackson School; Jefferson School (Bellwood); Jefferson School (Elmhurst); Lake Park Elementary School; Leyden High School-East Campus; Leyden High School-West Campus; Lincoln Elementary School; Lincoln Primary School; McKinley School; Queen Bee School; Reskin School; Roosevelt Elementary School; Roosevelt Junior High School; Sandburg Junior High School; Schafer School; Spring Hills School; Stone Park Preschool; Stone School; Wesley School; Westmore School; York High School

Program Features

- ❑ College funding for PDS program from grants, discretionary funds, or other types of "soft money"
- ❑ Release time, reduced course load, or other related arrangement made for college faculty actively involved with PDS sites
- ❑ Computer technology used in PDS teacher education program to **facilitate instruction** &/or staff development:
  - ■ computer assisted instruction
  - ■ desktop publishing
- ❑ Computer technology included in **subject matter** of teacher education &/or staff development curriculum of PDS participants:
  - ■ computer assisted instruction
  - ■ interactive video
  - ■ desktop publishing
- ❑ Policies of college with regard to hiring, tenure, promotion, or other aspects of college's reward structure, acknowledge PDS-related work
- ❑ Approximately 80-100% of department faculty participate in PDS-related work (planning or implementation)

ILLINOIS

Elmhurst College

School

Bellwood Preschool
c/o Stone Park Preschool
1801 N. 36th Avenue
Stone Park, IL 60165
Phone: (708) 544-9553

Emerson School
400 North West
Elmhurst, IL 60126
Phone: (708) 834-5562

Site Coordinator Dorothy Smith, Principal — Dan Wachholz, Principal
Starting Date 1993, September — 1991, February
Grade Level Pre-K — K-6
School Type Clinical School — Clinical School

School

Brook Park School
30th & Raymond
La Grange Park, IL 60505
Phone: (708) 354-3740

Euclid School
1211 Wheeling Road
Mt. Prospect, IL 60056
Phone: (708) 259-3303

Site Coordinator Judy Kmak, Principal — Joe Wawak, Principal
Starting Date 1991, September — 1991, September
Grade Level K-6 — K-6
School Type Clinical School — Clinical School

School

Bryan Junior High School
111 W. Butterfield Road
Elmhurst, IL 60126
Phone: (708) 617-2350

Field School
295 Emroy
Elmhurst, IL 60126
Phone: (708) 834-5313

Site Coordinator Dick Stahl, Principal — Dr. Jenny Wojcik, Principal
Starting Date 1991, September — 1991, February
Grade Level 7-9 — K-6
School Type Clinical School — Clinical School

School

Conrad Fischer School
Wilson & Victory Parkway
Elmhurst, IL 60126
Phone: (708) 832-8601

Gower West School
7650 S. Clarendon Hills Road
Willowbrook, IL 60514
Phone: (708) 323-6446

Site Coordinator Pete Graber, Principal — Emily Robertson, Principal
Starting Date 1991, September — 1992, September
Grade Level K-6 — K-6
School Type Clinical School — Clinical School

School

Early Childhood Education Center
543 N. Wood Dale Road
Wood Dale, IL 60191
Phone: (708) 595-9510

Grant School
1300 N. 34th Avenue
Melrose Park, IL 60160
Phone: (708) 343-0410

Site Coordinator Barbara Kwit, Principal — Joe Pater, Principal
Starting Date 1992, September — 1991, September
Grade Level Pre-K — K-6
School Type Clinical School — Clinical School

ILLINOIS

Elmhurst College

School	Hinsdale Central High School 55th and Grant Streets Hinsdale, IL 60521 Phone: (708) 887-1340	Lake Park Elementary School 330 W. Lake Park Drive Addison, IL 60101 Phone: (708) 628-2525
Site Coordinator	Dr. James Polzin, Assistant Principal	Dr. John Young, Principal
Starting Date	1991, February	1991, February
Grade Level	10-12	K-6
School Type	Clinical School	Clinical School
School	Indian Trail Junior High School 222 North Kennedy Drive Addison, IL 60101 Phone: (708) 628-2514	Leyden High School-East Campus 3400 N. Rose Street Franklin Park, IL 60131 Phone: (708) 451-3025
Site Coordinator	Susan Liechti, Principal	Helmar Ehrke, Assistant Principal
Starting Date	1991, February	1991, February
Grade Level	7-9	10-12
School Type	Clinical School	Clinical School
School	Jackson School 925 Swain Elmhurst, IL 60126 Phone: (708) 834-4544	Leyden High School-West Campus c/o Leyden High School-East Campus 3400 N. Rose Street Franklin Park, IL 60131 Phone: (708) 451-3025
Site Coordinator	Dr. Ramona McNeese	Helmar Ehrke, Assistant Principal
Starting Date	1991, February	1991, February
Grade Level	K-6	10-12
School Type	Clinical School	Clinical School
School	Jefferson School Crescent and Poplar Avenue Elmhurst, IL 60126 Phone: (708) 834-6261	Lincoln Elementary School Jackson and Linden Avenue Bellwood, IL 60104 Phone: (708) 544-3373
Site Coordinator	Tad Ryan, Principal	Vernita Jones, Principal
Starting Date	no information available	1993, January
Grade Level	K-6	3-5
School Type	Clinical School	Clinical School
School	Jefferson School 225 S. 46th Street Bellwood, IL 60104 Phone: (708) 547-3065	Lincoln Primary School 3519 Wilcox Bellwood, IL 60104 Phone: (708) 544-2815
Site Coordinator	Eva Smith, Principal	Kathy Mitchell, Principal
Starting Date	1992, September	1993, January
Grade Level	K-6	K-2
School Type	Clinical School	Clinical School

ILLINOIS

Elmhurst College

School	McKinley School Eastern Avenue & Butterfield Bellwood, IL 60104 Phone: (708) 544-5230	Sandburg Junior High School 345 East St. Charles Road Elmhurst, IL 60126 Phone: (708) 834-4534
Site Coordinator	Phylistine Murphy, Principal	George Jacobs, Principal
Starting Date	1991, September	1991, September
Grade Level	K-6	7-9
School Type	Clinical School	Clinical School
School	Queen Bee School 2N655 Bloomingdale Road Glendale Heights, IL 60139 Phone: (708) 260-6155	Schafer School 700 E. Pleasant Lombard, IL 60148 Phone: (708) 932-6470
Site Coordinator	Anthony DeAngelis, Principal	Dianne Imenga, Instructional Consultant
Starting Date	1992, September	1991, February
Grade Level	K-6	K-6
School Type	Clinical School	Clinical School
School	Reskin School 1555 Ardmore Glendale Heights, IL 60139 Phone: (708) 469-0612	Spring Hills School 560 S. Pinecroft Roselle, IL 60172 Phone: (708) 529-1883
Site Coordinator	Judy Gerharz, Teacher	Susan Stuckey, Principal
Starting Date	1993, January	1991, February
Grade Level	K-6	K-6
School Type	Clinical School	Clinical School
School	Roosevelt Elementary School 27th Avenue & Oak Street Bellwood, IL 60104 Phone: (708) 544-6995	Stone Park Preschool 1801 N. 36th Avenue Stone Park, IL 60165 Phone: (708) 345-3625
Site Coordinator	Edward Hayes, Principal	Dorothy Smith, Principal
Starting Date	1993, January	1993, September
Grade Level	K-6	Pre-K
School Type	Clinical School	Clinical School
School	Roosevelt Junior High School 25th Avenue and Oak Street Bellwood, IL 60104 Phone: (708) 544-3318	Stone School 1404 West Stone Avenue Addison, IL 60101 Phone: (708) 628-2545
Site Coordinator	Dr. Vinston Birdin, Principal	James Frontier, Principal
Starting Date	1992, September	1991, February
Grade Level	7-9	K-6
School Type	Clinical School	Clinical School

ILLINOIS

Elmhurst College

School	Wesley School 1111 West Westwood Trail Addison, IL 60101 Phone: (708) 628-2550
Site Coordinator	Thomas Romano, Principal
Starting Date	1991, February
Grade Level	K-6
School Type	Clinical School
School	Westmore School 340 School Street Lombard, IL 60148 Phone: (708) 932-6490
Site Coordinator	Judy Kaminski, Principal
Starting Date	1991, February
Grade Level	K-6
School Type	Clinical School
School	York High School 355 W. St. Charles Road Elmhurst, IL 60126 Phone: (708) 617-2420
Site Coordinator	Dr. James Nelson, Principal
Starting Date	no information available
Grade Level	10-12
School Type	Clinical School

College/University	*National Louis University*
Contact	David Freitas, Ed.D., Associate Dean National Louis University College of Education 2840 Sheridan Road Evanston, IL 60201 (708) 475-1100
Partners	National Louis University Glenview/Northbrook District #30
Affiliation	St. Louis Regional Educational Partnership
Starting Date	1991
PDS Sites	Glenview/Northbrook National College of Education Professional Development School
Program Features	❑ Preservice teachers assigned to PDSs in cohorts ❑ Release time, reduced course load, or other related arrangement made for college faculty actively involved with PDS sites ❑ Approximately 20-39% of department faculty participate in PDS-related work (planning or implementation)

ILLINOIS

National Louis University

School   Glenview/Northbrook National
                          College of Education Professional
                          Development School
                          2840 Sheridan Road
                          Evanston, IL 60201
                          Phone: (708) 475-1100

Site Coordinator   David Freitas, Ed.D., Associate Dean
Starting Date   1991
Grade Level   K-9
School Type   Professional Development School

INDIANA

College/University	*Indiana State University*
Contact	Dr. Robert O. Williams Indiana State University School of Education Terre Haute, IN 47809 (812) 237-2862
Partners	Indiana State University Clay Community School Corporation; South Vermillion School Corporation; Southwest Parke Community School Corporation; & Vigo County School Corporation
Affiliation	Professional Development School Network (NCREST)
Funding	university; Lilly Endowment Inc.
Starting Date	1991, June
PDS Sites	Chauncey Rose Middle School; Fayette Elementary School; Meadows Elementary School; Rosedale Elementary School; South Vermillion High School; Staunton Elementary School; Terre Haute North Vigo High School; Terre Haute South Vigo High School; West Vigo High School; West Vigo School
Program Features	

- ❑ Preservice teachers assigned to PDSs in cohorts
- ❑ College funding for PDS program from grants, discretionary funds, or other types of "soft money"
- ❑ Release time, reduced course load, or other related arrangement made for college faculty actively involved with PDS sites
- ❑ Computer technology used in PDS teacher education program to **facilitate instruction** &/or staff development:
  - ■ telecommunications (e.g., e-mail, bulletin boards)
  - ■ computer assisted instruction
- ❑ Computer technology used to **facilitate collaboration** among PDS partners:
  - ■ desktop publishing
- ❑ Computer technology included in **subject matter** of teacher education &/or staff development curriculum of PDS participants:
  - ■ telecommunications (e.g., e-mail, bulletin boards)
  - ■ computer assisted instruction
  - ■ interactive video
  - ■ programming
  - ■ authoring systems
- ❑ Policies of college with regard to hiring, tenure, promotion, or other aspects of college's reward structure, acknowledge PDS-related work
- ❑ Approximately 40-59% of department faculty participate in PDS-related work (planning or implementation)

Indiana State University

School	Chauncey Rose Middle School 1275 Third Avenue Terre Haute, IN 47807 Phone: (812) 462-4474	Stauton Elementary School P.O. Box 217 Stauton, IN 47881 Phone: (812) 448-8270
Site Coordinator	Daniel Tanoos	Jane Pychinka, Principal
Starting Date	1991, June	1991, June
Grade Level	6-8	K-6
School Type	Professional Development School	Professional Development School
School	Fayette Elementary School R.R. 12 Box 135 West Terre Haute, IN 47885 Phone: (812) 462-4451	Terre Haute North Vigo High School 3434 Maple Avenue Terre Haute, IN 47804 Phone: (812) 462-4312
Site Coordinator	Guy Dillard, Principal	Mytron Lisby, Principal
Starting Date	1991, June	1991, June
Grade Level	K-5	9-12
School Type	Professional Development School	Professional Development School
School	Meadows Elementary School 55 S. Brown Avenue Terre Haute, IN 47803 Phone: (812) 462-4301	Terre Haute South Vigo High School 3737 S. 7th Street Terre Haute, IN 47802 Phone: (812) 462-4252
Site Coordinator	Alice Walker	David Cunfiff, Acting Principal
Starting Date	1991, June	1991, June
Grade Level	K-5	9-12
School Type	Professional Development School	Professional Development School
School	Rosedale Elementary School E. Central Rosedale, IN 47874 Phone: (812) 548-2454	West Vigo High School 4590 W. Sarah Myers Drive West Terre Haute, IN 47885 Phone: (812) 462-4282
Site Coordinator	Adrienne Gideon, Principal	James Jackson, Principal
Starting Date	1991, June	1991, June
Grade Level	K-6	9-12
School Type	Professional Development School	Professional Development School
School	South Vermillion High School R.R. 1 Clinton, IN 47842 Phone: (812) 832-3551	West Vigo School 500 Olive Street West Terre Haute, IN 47885 Phone: (812) 462-4419
Site Coordinator	Mark Kirby, Principal	David Lotter, Principal
Starting Date	1991, June	1991, June
Grade Level	9-12	K-5
School Type	Professional Development School	Professional Development School

College/University	*Indiana University - Northwest*
Contact	Pamela A. Sandoval Indiana University - Northwest Urban Teacher Education Program 217 Sycamore 3400 Broadway Gary, IN 46408 (219) 980-6588
Partners	Indiana University-Northwest School City of East Chicago; Gary Community School Corporation; School City of Hammond Gary Teachers Union; Hammond Teachers' Federation; East Chicago Federation of Teachers*
Funding	university; school districts; Lilly Foundation
Starting Date	1989, Fall
PDS Sites	Central High School; Eggers Elementary Middle School; Franklin Elementary School; Horace Mann High School; Lincoln Elementary School

Program Features

- ❑ Preservice teachers assigned to PDSs in cohorts
- ❑ College funding for PDS program from grants, discretionary funds, or other types of "soft money"
- ❑ Computer technology used in PDS teacher education program to **facilitate instruction** &/or staff development:
  - ■ computer assisted instruction
  - ■ desktop publishing
- ❑ Computer technology used to **facilitate collaboration** among PDS partners:
  - ■ computer assisted instruction
  - ■ desktop publishing
- ❑ Computer technology included in **subject matter** of teacher education &/or staff development curriculum of PDS participants:
  - ■ telecommunications (e.g., e-mail, bulletin boards)
  - ■ computer assisted instruction
  - ■ programming
  - ■ desktop publishing
- ❑ Policies of college with regard to hiring, tenure, promotion, or other aspects of college's reward structure, acknowledge PDS-related work
- ❑ Approximately 60-79% of department faculty participate in PDS-related work (planning or implementation)

Note

*Additional partners include the Northwest Indiana Forum, a business group, and the Parent Advisory Board.

Indiana University - Northwest

School	Central High School 1100 W. Columbus Drive East Chicago, IN 46312 Phone: (219) 391-4031
Site Coordinator	Kathleen Ann Kutie
Starting Date	1993, August
Grade Level	9-12
School Type	Professional Development School
School	Eggers Elementary Middle School 5825 Blaine Avenue Hammond, IN 46320 Phone: (219) 933-2449
Site Coordinator	Debra E. Maddox, PDC Coordinator
Starting Date	1990, September
Grade Level	K-8
School Type	Professional Development School
School	Franklin Elementary School 600 E. 35th Avenue Gary, IN 46409 Phone: (219) 980-6330
Site Coordinator	Stella Markovich, Coordinator
Starting Date	1993, August
Grade Level	K-5
School Type	Professional Development School
School	Horace Mann High School 524 Garfield Street Gary, IN 46402 Phone: - no information available
Site Coordinator	Faye Ison
Starting Date	1990, September
Grade Level	10-12
School Type	Professional Development School
School	Lincoln Elementary 2001 E. 135th East Chicago, IN 46312 Phone: (219) 391-4256
Site Coordinator	Lois Lukowski, PDC/UTEP Coordinator
Starting Date	1989, September
Grade Level	K-6
School Type	Professional Development School

College/University

Indiana University Purdue University Indianapolis

Contact

Dr. Joan Pedersen
Indiana University Purdue University Indianapolis
902 W. New York Street
Indianapolis, IN 46202-5155
(317) 274-6842

Partners

Indiana University Purdue University Indianapolis (IUPUI)
Franklin Township; Indianapolis Public Schools; Lawrence Township; &
Washington Township

Funding

university

Starting Date

1993

PDS Sites

Arsenal Technical High School; Franklin Central High School; Franklin
Township Middle School; Harcourt Elementary School; Indian Creek
Elementary School; James A. Garfield Elementary School; North Central
High School; Riverside Elementary School; Westlane Middle School

Program Features

❑ Preservice teachers assigned to PDSs in cohorts
❑ Computer technology used in PDS teacher education program to
   facilitate instruction &/or staff development:
   ■ telecommunications (e.g., e-mail, bulletin boards)
   ■ computer assisted instruction
   ■ interactive video
   ■ desktop publishing
❑ Computer technology used to **facilitate collaboration** among PDS
   partners:
   ■ desktop publishing
❑ Computer technology included in **subject matter** of teacher education
   &/or staff development curriculum of PDS participants:
   ■ telecommunications (e.g., e-mail, bulletin boards)
   ■ computer assisted instruction
   ■ interactive video
   ■ desktop publishing
❑ Policies of college with regard to hiring, tenure, promotion, or other
   aspects of college's reward structure, acknowledge PDS-related work
❑ Approximately 80-100% of department faculty participate in PDS-
   related work (planning or implementation)

INDIANA

Indiana University Purdue University Indianapolis

School	Arsenal Technical High School 1500 East Michigan Street Indianapolis, IN 46201 Phone: (317) 226-3922 Fax: (317) 226-3932	Indian Creek Elementary School 10833 East 56th Street Indianapolis, IN 46236 Phone: (317) 823-4497 Fax: (317) 823-0973
Site Coordinator	Les Wood, Professor & Ron Dehnke, Associate Professor	Mike Cohen, Professor
Starting Date	1993	1993
Grade Level	10-12	K-6
School Type	Professional Development School	Professional Development School
School	Franklin Central High School 6215 South Franklin Road Indianapolis, IN 46259 Phone: (317) 862-6646 Fax: (317) 862-7262	James A. Garfield Elementary School 307 Lincoln Street Indianapolis, IN 46225 Phone: (317) 226-4231 Fax: (317) 226-3336
Site Coordinator	Nels Gould, Associate Professor	Jacqueline Blackwell, Associate Professor
Starting Date	1994	1993
Grade Level	10-12	K-6
School Type	Professional Development School	Professional Development School
School	Franklin Township Middle School 6019 South Franklin Road Indianapolis, IN 46259 Phone: (317) 862-2446 Fax: (317) 862-7238	North Central High School 1801 East 86th Street Indianapolis, IN 46240 Phone: (317) 259-5301 Fax: (317) 259-5369
Site Coordinator	Janet Boyle, Associate Professor	Charlie Barman, Associate Professor
Starting Date	1994	1993
Grade Level	7-9	10-12
School Type	Professional Development School	Professional Development School
School	Harcourt Elementary School 7535 Harcourt Road Indianapolis, IN 46260 Phone: (317) 259-5458 Fax: (317) 259-5459	Riverside Elementary School 2033 Sugar Grove Avenue Indianapolis, IN 46202 Phone: (317) 226-6830 Fax: (317) 226-4634
Site Coordinator	Mary Gilchrist & Chris Leland, Associate Professors	Golam Mannan, Associate Professor
Starting Date	1993	1993
Grade Level	K-6	K-6
School Type	Professional Development School	Professional Development School

INDIANA

*Indiana University Purdue
University Indianapolis*

School	Westlane Middle School
	1301 West 73rd Street
	Indianapolis, IN 46260
	Phone: (317) 259-5412
	Fax: (317) 259-5409
Site Coordinator	Stuart Hart, Associate Professor
Starting Date	1993
Grade Level	7-9
School Type	Professional Development School

College/University	*Purdue University*
Contact	Marilyn J. Haring, Dean School of Education 1443 LAEB Purdue University West Lafayette, IN 47907-1443 (317) 494-2336
Partners	Purdue University Tippecanoe School Corporation; Lafayette School Corporation; & MSD Warren County
Funding	university
Starting Date	1993, Fall
PDS Sites	Klondike Elementary School; Lafayette School Corporation; Pine Village School
Program Features	❑ College funding for PDS program from grants, discretionary funds, or other types of "soft money" ❑ Approximately 20-39% of department faculty participate in PDS-related work (planning or implementation)

INDIANA

Purdue University

School	Klondike Elementary School
	3311 Klondike Road
	West Lafayette, IN 47906
	Phone: (317) 463-5505
Site Coordinator	Lorie Sparks, Assistant Principal
Starting Date	1993, Fall
Grade Level	K-5
School Type	Professional Development School

School	Lafayette School Corporation
	2300 Cason Street
	Lafayette, IN 47905
	Phone: (317) 449-3200
Site Coordinator	Robert Myers, Superintendent of Schools
Starting Date	1993, October
Grade Level	K-12
School Type	no information available

School	Pine Village School
	R. R. 1 Box 3
	Pine Village, IN 47975
	Phone: (317) 385-2651
Site Coordinator	Gretchen Leuenberger, Principal
Starting Date	1993, September
Grade Level	K-6
School Type	Professional Development School

IOWA

College/University	*Drake University*
Contact	Dr. Pamela Curtiss School of Education Drake University 3206 University Avenue Des Moines, IA 50311 (515) 271-3726
Partners	Drake University Des Moines Community School District
Funding	university; New Iowa School Development Corporation Grant
Starting Date	1993, April
PDS Sites	Moulton Elementary School

Program Features	❑ Preservice teachers assigned to PDSs in cohorts
	❑ College funding for PDS program from grants, discretionary funds, or other types of "soft money"
	❑ Release time, reduced course load, or other related arrangement made for college faculty actively involved with PDS sites
	❑ Computer technology used in PDS teacher education program to **facilitate instruction** &/or staff development:
	    ■ computer assisted instruction
	    ■ interactive video
	❑ Policies of college with regard to hiring, tenure, promotion, or other aspects of college's reward structure acknowledge PDS-related work
	❑ Approximately 40-59% of department faculty participate in PDS-related work (planning or implementation)

IOWA

Drake University

School	Moulton Elementary School
	3206 University Avenue
	Des Moines, IA 50311
	Phone: (515) 221-2599
Site Coordinator	Dr. Pamela Curtiss
Starting Date	1993, April
Grade Level	K-6
School Type	Professional Development School

IOWA

College/University	*Iowa State University*
Contact	Ann Thompson Iowa State University 157 N. Lagomarcino Ames, IA 50011 (515) 294-5287
Partners	Iowa State University Madrid Public School District; Des Moines Public School District
Funding	university
Starting Date	1992, September
PDS Sites	Madrid Community School; Project Opportunity (Des Moines)*

Program Features

- ❑ Preservice teachers assigned to PDSs in cohorts
- ❑ Release time, reduced course load, or other related arrangement made for college faculty actively involved with PDS sites
- ❑ Computer technology used in PDS teacher education program to **facilitate instruction** &/or staff development:
  - ■ telecommunications (e.g., e-mail, bulletin boards)
  - ■ computer assisted instruction
  - ■ interactive video
  - ■ desktop publishing
- ❑ Computer technology included in **subject matter** of teacher education &/or staff development curriculum of PDS participants:
  - ■ telecommunications (e.g., e-mail, bulletin boards)
  - ■ computer assisted instruction
  - ■ interactive video
  - ■ programming
  - ■ authoring systems
  - ■ desktop publishing
- ❑ Approximately 20-39% of department faculty participate in PDS-related work (planning or implementation)

Note

*Project Opportunity is a pilot program in which the university places cohorts of approximately 30 preservice students, beginning during students' sophmore year, in schools in a variety of geographic and demographic settings. The first cohort has been placed at the Madrid Community School, which is a rural school housing an elementary division and a combined junior and senior high division on the same campus. The second cohort has been placed at elementary and secondary partner schools in the urban setting of Des Moines. The third cohort will be placed in elementary and secondary partner schools in the suburban school district of Ames. The PDS profile for Project Opportunity (Des Moines), which can be found on p. 35, as well as the data provided on PDS characteristics (p. 155) and included in the statistical summaries, reflects information provided by the respondent on the entire set of partner schools within the district.

IOWA

Iowa State University

School

Madrid Community School
599 North Kennedy
Madrid, IA 50156
Phone: (515) 795-3241

Site Coordinator   Barry Green
Starting Date   1993, January
Grade Level   K-12
School Type   Professional Development School

School

Project Opportunity
N126 Lagomarcino
Iowa State University
Ames, IA 50010
Phone: (515) 294-8413, 294-7021

Site Coordinator   Kathy R. Connor, Director
Starting Date   1993, August
Grade Level   PreK-12
School Type   Partner School

IOWA

College/University	*University of Northern Iowa*
Contact	Linda A. Fernandez University of Northern Iowa Malcolm Price Laboratory School Cedar Falls, IA 50613 (319) 273-6171
Partners	University of Northern Iowa
Funding	Iowa Board of Regents
Starting Date	1883 (lab school founded)
PDS Sites	Malcolm Price Laboratory School
Program Features	

- ❑ Preservice teachers assigned to PDSs in cohorts
- ❑ Release time, reduced course load, or other related arrangement made for college faculty actively involved with PDS sites
- ❑ Computer technology used in PDS teacher education program to **facilitate instruction** &/or staff development:
  - ■ telecommunications (e.g., e-mail, bulletin boards)
  - ■ computer assisted instruction
  - ■ interactive video
  - ■ desktop publishing
- ❑ Computer technology used to **facilitate collaboration** among PDS partners:
  - ■ telecommunications (e.g., e-mail, bulletin boards)
  - ■ computer assisted instruction
  - ■ interactive video
  - ■ desktop publishing
- ❑ Computer technology included in **subject matter** of teacher education &/or staff development curriculum of PDS participants:
  - ■ telecommunications (e.g., e-mail, bulletin boards)
  - ■ computer assisted instruction
  - ■ interactive video
  - ■ programming
  - ■ authoring systems
  - ■ desktop publishing
- ❑ Policies of college with regard to hiring, tenure, promotion, or other aspects of college's reward structure, acknowledge PDS-related work
- ❑ Approximately 80-100% of department faculty participate in PDS-related work (planning or implementation)

IOWA

University of Northern Iowa

School   Malcolm Price Laboratory School
                                19th & Campus
                                Cedar Falls, IA 50613
                                Phone: (319) 273-6171
Site Coordinator   Linda A. Fernandez, Director
Starting Date   1883 (founded)
Grade Level   PreK-12
School Type   Clinical School

KANSAS

College/University	*Emporia State University*
Contact	Dr. Tes Mehring Emporia State University Box 4036, The Teachers College Emporia State University, 1200 Commercial Emporia, KS 66801 (316) 341-5782
Partners	Emporia State University Unified School District 233 Olathe, KS
Funding	university
Starting Date	1993, August
PDS Sites	Countryside Elementary School; Pleasant Ridge Elementary School

Program Features

- ❑ Preservice teachers assigned to PDSs in cohorts
- ❑ Release time, reduced course load, or other related arrangement made for college faculty actively involved with PDS sites
- ❑ Computer technology used in PDS teacher education program to **facilitate instruction** &/or staff development:
  - ■ computer assisted instruction
- ❑ Computer technology included in **subject matter** of teacher education &/or staff development curriculum of PDS participants:
  - ■ computer assisted instruction
  - ■ interactive video
  - ■ desktop publishing
- ❑ Policies of college with regard to hiring, tenure, promotion, or other aspects of college's reward structure, acknowledge PDS-related work
- ❑ Approximately 60-79% of department faculty participate in PDS-related work (planning or implementation)

KANSAS

Emporia State University

School	Countryside Elementary School
	15800 W. 124th Terrace
	Olathe, KS 66062-1116
	Phone: (913) 782-0859
Site Coordinator	Dr. Jean Morrow
Starting Date	1993, August
Grade Level	K-6
School Type	Professional Development School
School	Pleasant Ridge Elementary School
	12235 Rosehill Road
	Overland Park, KS 66213
	Phone: (913) 897-2783
Site Coordinator	Dr. Jean Morrow
Starting Date	1993, August
Grade Level	K-6
School Type	Professional Development School

College/University

Fort Hays State University

Contact

Germaine Taggart
O'Loughlin Project
Curriculum & Instruction Rarick 242
Fort Hays State University
Hays, KS 67601
(913) 628-5847

Partners

Fort Hays State University
Unified School District 489 Hays, KS

Funding

university; school district

Starting Date

1990, September

PDS Sites

O'Loughlin Elementary School

Program Features

❑ Preservice teachers assigned to PDSs in cohorts
❑ College funding for PDS program from grants, discretionary funds, or other types of "soft money"
❑ Release time, reduced course load, or other related arrangement made for college faculty actively involved with PDS sites
❑ Computer technology used in PDS teacher education program to **facilitate instruction** &/or staff development:
   ■ telecommunications (e.g., e-mail, bulletin boards)
   ■ computer assisted instruction
   ■ interactive video
   ■ desktop publishing
❑ Computer technology used to **facilitate collaboration** among PDS partners:
   ■ telecommunications (e.g., e-mail, bulletin boards)
   ■ computer assisted instruction
   ■ desktop publishing
❑ Computer technology included in **subject matter** of teacher education &/or staff development curriculum of PDS participants:
   ■ telecommunications (e.g., e-mail, bulletin boards)
   ■ computer assisted instruction
   ■ interactive video
   ■ programming
   ■ authoring systems
   ■ desktop publishing
❑ Policies of college with regard to hiring, tenure, promotion, or other aspects of college's reward structure, acknowledge PDS-related work
❑ Approximately 80-100% of department faculty participate in PDS-related work (planning or implementation)

KANSAS

Fort Hays State University

School	O'Loughlin Elementary School
	CUIN Rarick 242
	Fort Hays State University
	Hays, KS 67601
	Phone: (913) 628-5847
Site Coordinator	Tanya Channell, Principal &
	Germaine Taggart
Starting Date	1990, Fall
Grade Level	K-5
School Type	Professional Development School

College/University	*University of Kansas*
Contact	Dr. Fred Rodriguez Kansas Alliance of Professional Development Schools University of Kansas 214 Bailey Hall Lawrence, KS 66045 (913) 864-4435
Partners	University of Kansas Lawrence, Turner, Kansas City, & Topeka School Districts
Affiliation	Professional Development School Network (NCREST); Holmes Group
Funding	university; school district; state education department grants
Starting Date	1991
PDS Sites	New York Elementary School; Quincy Elementary School; Turner Grade School; *

Program Features	❑ Preservice teachers assigned to PDSs in cohorts
	❑ College funding for PDS program from grants, discretionary funds, or other types of "soft money"
	❑ Release time, reduced course load, or other related arrangement made for college faculty actively involved with PDS sites
	❑ Computer technology used in PDS teacher education program to **facilitate instruction** &/or staff development:
	   ■ telecommunications (e.g., e-mail, bulletin boards)
	   ■ desktop publishing
	❑ Computer technology used to **facilitate collaboration** among PDS partners:
	   ■ telecommunications (e.g., e-mail, bulletin boards)
	   ■ desktop publishing
	❑ Computer technology included in **subject matter** of teacher education &/or staff development curriculum of PDS participants:
	   ■ telecommunications (e.g., e-mail, bulletin boards)
	   ■ computer assisted instruction
	   ■ interactive video
	   ■ programming
	   ■ authoring systems
	   ■ desktop publishing
	❑ Policies of college with regard to hiring, tenure, promotion, or other aspects of college's reward structure, acknowledge PDS-related work
	❑ Approximately 0-19% of department faculty participate in PDS-related work (planning or implementation)

Note	*Although profiles of the 3 PDS sites are given on the next page, data related to these sites were not included in statistical tabulations or in the PDS characteristics tables, which begin on p. 145.

KANSAS

University of Kansas

School	New York Elementary School
	936 New York
	Lawrence, KS 66044
	(913) 832-5780
Site Coordinator	Sharen Steele, Principal
Starting Date	1993, Fall
Grade Level	K-6
School Type	Professional Development School
School	Quincy Elementary School
	1500 N. Quincy
	Topeka, KS 66608
	(913) 357-5348
Site Coordinator	Dean Martin, Principal
Starting Date	1993, Fall
Grade Level	K-6
School Type	Professional Development School
School	Turner Grade School
	831 S. 55th
	Kansas City, KS 66106
	(913) 287-7281
Site Coordinator	Dr. Shirley Trees, Principal
Starting Date	1992, Fall
Grade Level	K-6
School Type	Professional Development School

College/University	*University of New Orleans*
Contact	Dr. Marylou Dantonio University of New Orleans Lakefront College of Education New Orleans, LA 70148 (504) 286-7046
Partners	University of New Orleans Jefferson Parish & Orleans Parish School Districts
Funding	Louisiana State Quality Education Trust Support Fund
Starting Date	1990, Fall
PDS Sites	Grace King High School; H. C. Schaumburg School; J. J. Audubon Elementary School*; Jefferson Elementary School; John Dibert Elementary School; Paul J. Solis Elementary School; Warren Easton School

Program Features	❑ Preservice teachers assigned to PDSs in cohorts
	❑ Computer technology used in PDS teacher education program to **facilitate instruction** &/or staff development:
	   ■ telecommunications (e.g., e-mail, bulletin boards)
	   ■ computer assisted instruction
	   ■ desktop publishing
	❑ Computer technology used to **facilitate collaboration** among PDS partners:
	   ■ telecommunications (e.g., e-mail, bulletin boards)
	   ■ desktop publishing
	❑ Approximately 20-39% of department faculty participate in PDS-related work (planning or implementation)

Note	*Although J. J. Audubon Elementary School is included among the PDSs profiled on the following page, it was not included in statistical calculations or in the PDS characteristics tables, which begin on page 145.

University of New Orleans

School	Grace King High School 4301 Grace King Place Metairie, LA 70002 Phone: (504) 888-7334	Paul J. Solis Elementary School 2850 Mount Laurel Gretna, LA 70056 Phone: (504) 342-5205
Site Coordinator	Pat Blanchard, Liasion Mentor/Math Teacher	Belle Downs, Liasion Mentor
Starting Date	1991, August	1991, September
Grade Level	9-12	K-6
School Type	Professional Development School	Professional Development School
School	H. C. Schaumburg Elementary School 9440 Spring Wood New Orleans, LA 70127 Phone: (504) 242-1812	Warren Easton School 3019 Canal New Orleans, LA 70119 Phone: (504) 821-0844
Site Coordinator	Juanita Brandon	Jany Craddock, Teacher
Starting Date	1991	no information available
Grade Level	K-6	9-12
School Type	Professional Development School	Professional Development School
School	Jefferson Elementary School 4440 Jefferson Highway Jefferson, LA 70121 Phone: (504) 733-9461	
Site Coordinator	Carol Wells, Teacher	
Starting Date	no information available	
Grade Level	K-6	
School Type	Professional Development School	
School	J. J. Audubon Elementary School 200 W. Loyola Drive Kenner, LA 70065 Phone: (504) 454-8014	
Site Coordinator	Sydna Hansen & Ann Olvany	
Starting Date	no information available	
Grade Level	K-6	
School Type	no information available	
School	John Dibert Elementary School 4217 Orleans Avenue New Orleans, LA 70119 Phone: (504) 483-6126	
Site Coordinator	Linda Swindle, Teacher Liasion	
Starting Date	no information available	
Grade Level	K-6	
School Type	Professional Development School	

College/University

Anna Maria College

Contact

Dr. Thomas Delprete
Box 66
Anna Maria College
Sunset Lane
Paxton, MA 01612-1198
(508) 849-3435

Partners

Anna Maria College
Shrewsbury & Worcester Public Schools

Funding

Anna Maria College
Shrewsbury & Worcester Public Schools

Starting Date

1988

PDS Sites

City View Professional Development School; Coolidge Professional Development School

Program Features

❑ Preservice teachers assigned to PDSs in cohorts
❑ Release time, reduced course load, or other related arrangement made for college faculty actively involved with PDS sites
❑ Policies of college with regard to hiring, tenure, promotion, or other aspects of college's reward structure, acknowledge PDS-related work
❑ Approximately 80-100% of department faculty participate in PDS-related work (planning or implementation)

MASSACHUSETTS

Anna Maria College

School	City View Professional Development School 80 Prospect Street Worcester, MA 01605 Phone: (508) 799-3670
Site Coordinator	Anna Barrie, Magnet School Facilitator
Starting Date	1991, Fall
Grade Level	K-6
School Type	Professional Development School
School	Coolidge Professional Development School Florence Street Shrewsbury, MA 01545 Phone: (508) 792-1569
Site Coordinator	Joan Trainor, Mentor Teacher
Starting Date	1988, Fall
Grade Level	1-4
School Type	Professional Development School

College/University	*Assumption College*
Contact	Elizabeth Monticelli Flagg Street School 27 Laurel Drive Hudson, MA 01749 (508) 562-6897
Partners	Assumption College Worcester Public Schools
Funding	university; school district
Starting Date	1991, September
PDS Sites	Flagg Street School
Program Features	❑ Preservice teachers assigned to PDSs in cohorts ❑ College funding for PDS program from grants, discretionary funds, or other types of "soft money" ❑ Release time, reduced course load, or other related arrangement made for college faculty actively involved with PDS sites ❑ Policies of college with regard to hiring, tenure, promotion, or other aspects of college's reward structure, acknowledge PDS-related work ❑ Approximately 20-39% of department faculty participate in PDS-related work (planning or implementation)

Assumption College

School	Flagg Street School
	115 Flagg Street
	Worcester, MA 01602
	Phone: (508) 799-3522
Site Coordinator	Dr. Palatto-Fontaine
Starting Date	1991, September
Grade Level	K-6
School Type	Professional Practice School

College/University	*University of Massachusetts - Amherst*
Contact	Joyce Conlin East Longmeadow High School Maple Street East Longmeadow, MA 01028 (413) 525-5460
Partners	University of Massachusetts - Amherst East Longmeadow Public Schools
Funding	FIPSE Grant; McGinty Foundation
Starting Date	1986, Fall
PDS Sites	East Longmeadow High School
Program Features	❑ Preservice teachers assigned to PDSs in cohorts ❑ Policies of college with regard to hiring, tenure, promotion, or other aspects of college's reward structure, acknowledge PDS-related work ❑ Approximately 0-19% of department faculty participate in PDS-related work (planning or implementation)

MASSACHUSETTS

University of Massachusetts - Amherst

School	East Longmeadow High School
	Maple Street
	East Longmeadow, MA 01028
	Phone: (413) 525-5460
Site Coordinator	Joyce Conlin
Starting Date	1986, Fall
Grade Level	7-12
School Type	Professional Development School

College/University	*University of Massachusetts - Lowell*
Contact	Anna O'Brien Social Studies Department Reading Memorial High School Reading, MA 01867 (617) 944-8200
Partners	University of Massachusetts - Lowell Lowell Public Schools
Funding	university; school district
Starting Date	1993
PDS Sites	Reading Memorial High School
Program Features	

- ❑ Preservice teachers assigned to PDSs in cohorts
- ❑ College funding for PDS program from grants, discretionary funds, or other types of "soft money"
- ❑ Computer technology used in PDS teacher education program to **facilitate instruction** &/or staff development:
  - ■ telecommunications (e.g., e-mail, bulletin boards)
  - ■ interactive video
- ❑ Computer technology used to **facilitate collaboration** among PDS partners:
  - ■ telecommunications (e.g., e-mail, bulletin boards)
  - ■ interactive video
- ❑ Computer technology included in **subject matter** of teacher education &/or staff development curriculum of PDS participants:
  - ■ computer assisted instruction
  - ■ programming
  - ■ desktop publishing
- ❑ Approximately 20-39% of department faculty participate in PDS-related work (planning or implementation)

MASSACHUSETTS

University of Massachusetts - Lowell

School   Reading Memorial High School
                              62 Oakland Road
                              Reading, MA 01867
                              Phone: (617) 944-8200

Site Coordinator   Anna O'Brien
Starting Date   1993
Grade Level   9-12
School Type   Professional Development School

College/University	*Wheelock College*
Contact	Vivian Troen Brookline Public Schools/Wheelock College 4 Cataumet Street Jamaica Plains, MA 02130 (617) 522-7160
Partners	Wheelock College; Simmons College Brookline Public Schools; Boston Public Schools
Affiliation	National Network for Educational Renewal (NNER)
Funding	university; school district; F.I.R.S.T. Grant; private foundations
Starting Date	1987, September
PDS Sites	Edward Devotion School
Program Features	

- ❑ Preservice teachers assigned to PDSs in cohorts
- ❑ College funding for PDS program from grants, discretionary funds, or other types of "soft money"
- ❑ Computer technology used in PDS teacher education program to **facilitate instruction** &/or staff development:
  - ■ telecommunications (e.g., e-mail, bulletin boards)
  - ■ desktop publishing
- ❑ Computer technology used to **facilitate collaboration** among PDS partners:
  - ■ telecommunications (e.g., e-mail, bulletin boards)
  - ■ desktop publishing
- ❑ Policies of college with regard to hiring, tenure, promotion, or other aspects of college's reward structure, acknowledge PDS-related work
- ❑ Approximately 20-39% of department faculty participate in PDS-related work (planning or implementation)

MASSACHUSETTS

Wheelock College

School	Edward Devotion School 345 Howard Street Brookline, MA 02146 Phone: (617) 730-2520
Site Coordinator	Vivian Troen, Coordinator
Starting Date	1987, September
Grade Level	K-6
School Type	Professional Development School

MICHIGAN

College/University	*University of Michigan - Dearborn*
Contact	John Poster, Dean School of Education University of Michigan - Dearborn 4901 Evergreen Road Dearborn, MI 48128 (313) 593-5435
Partners	University of Michigan - Dearborn Detroit Public Schools
Affiliation	Michigan Partnership for New Education
Funding	Kellogg Foundation
Starting Date	1993, September
PDS Sites	Catherine B. White Elementary School
Program Features	

- ❑ College funding for PDS program from grants, discretionary funds, or other types of "soft money"
- ❑ Release time, reduced course load, or other related arrangement made for college faculty actively involved with PDS sites
- ❑ Computer technology included in **subject matter** of teacher education &/or staff development curriculum of PDS participants:
  - ■ computer assisted instruction
- ❑ Policies of college with regard to hiring, tenure, promotion, or other aspects of college's reward structure, acknowledge PDS-related work
- ❑ Approximately 0-19% of department faculty participate in PDS-related work (planning or implementation)

MICHIGAN

University of Michigan - Dearborn

School	Catherine B. White Elementary School
	5161 Charles Street
	Detroit, MI 48212
	Phone: (313) 252-3149
Site Coordinator	no information available
Starting Date	1993, September
Grade Level	K-6
School Type	no information available

MICHIGAN

College/University	*Western Michigan University*
Contact	Sandra J. Odell Director of Undergraduate Studies College of Education Western Michigan University Kalamazoo, MI 49008 (616) 387-2960
Partners	Western Michigan University; Michigan State University Lakeview & Battle Creek School Districts
Affiliation	Michigan Partnership for New Education
Funding	Kellogg Foundation; Michigan Partnership for New Education
Starting Date	1992, August
PDS Sites	Battle Creek Central High School; Prairieview Elementary School
Program Features	

❑ Preservice teachers assigned to PDSs in cohorts
❑ College funding for PDS program from grants, discretionary funds, or other types of "soft money"
❑ Release time, reduced course load, or other related arrangement made for college faculty actively involved with PDS sites
❑ Computer technology used to **facilitate collaboration** among PDS partners:
   ■ telecommunications (e.g., e-mail, bulletin boards)
❑ Computer technology included in **subject matter** of teacher education &/or staff development curriculum of PDS participants:
   ■ telecommunications (e.g., e-mail, bulletin boards)
   ■ computer assisted instruction
❑ Policies of college with regard to hiring, tenure, promotion, or other aspects of college's reward structure, acknowledge PDS-related work
❑ Approximately 0-19% of department faculty participate in PDS-related work (planning or implementation)

MICHIGAN

Western Michigan University

School   Battle Creek Central High School
                                        Battle Creek Public Schools
                                        100 W. Van Buren
                                        Battle Creek, MI 49016
                                        Phone: (616) 965-9526
Site Coordinator   Dr. Carl Woloszyk, Professor
Starting Date   1992, August
Grade Level   10-12
School Type   Professional Development School

School   Prairieview Elementary School
                                        Lakeview School District
                                        1765 Iroquois Avenue
                                        Battle Creek, MI 49015
                                        Phone: (616) 965-2683
Site Coordinator   Dr. Ronald Croweell, Associate
                                        Professor
Starting Date   1992, August
Grade Level   K-6
School Type   Professional Development School

College/University	*University of Minnesota*
Contact	Jean A. King College of Education, University of Minnesota 265 e/Peik Hall 159 Pillsbury Drive, SE Minneapolis, MN 55455 (612) 626-1614
Partners	University of Minnesota Minneapolis Public Schools Minneapolis Federation of Teachers (MFT)
Affiliation	American Federation of Teachers (1990-1993)
Funding	university; school district; Exxon Foundation; Minneapolis Federation of Teachers
Starting Date	1990
PDS Sites	Patrick Henry Professional Practice School
Program Features	❑ Release time, reduced course load, or other related arrangement made for college faculty actively involved with PDS sites ❑ Computer technology used in PDS teacher education program to **facilitate instruction** &/or staff development: ■ telecommunications (e.g., e-mail, bulletin boards) ❑ Computer technology used to **facilitate collaboration** among PDS partners: ■ telecommunications (e.g., e-mail, bulletin boards) ❑ Computer technology included in **subject matter** of teacher education &/or staff development curriculum of PDS participants: ■ computer assisted instruction ■ interactive video ❑ Policies of college with regard to hiring, tenure, promotion, or other aspects of college's reward structure, acknowledge PDS-related work ❑ Approximately 0-19% of department faculty participate in PDS-related work (planning or implementation)

MINNESOTA

University of Minnesota

School	Patrick Henry Professional Practice School
	2020 43rd Avenue, North
	Minneapolis, MN 55412-1699
	Phone: (612) 627-2897
Site Coordinator	Jean A. King & Linda Baker
	Trevorrow, Co-Coordinators
Starting Date	1990
Grade Level	9-12
School Type	Professional Practice School

College/University	***Harris-Stowe State College***
Contact	Emelda B. Harris, Director Harris-Stowe State College Teaching Scholars Program 3026 Laclede Avenue St. Louis, MO 63103 (314) 340-3649
Partners	Harris-Stowe State College St. Louis Public School District
Affiliation	National Network for Educational Renewal (NNER)
Funding	Danforth Foundation; Southwestern Bell Foundation
Starting Date	1993, June
PDS Sites	Shepard Accelerated School Partnership

Program Features

- ❏ Preservice teachers assigned to PDSs in cohorts
- ❏ College funding for PDS program from grants, discretionary funds, or other types of "soft money"
- ❏ Release time, reduced course load, or other related arrangement made for college faculty actively involved with PDS sites
- ❏ Computer technology used in PDS teacher education program to **facilitate instruction** &/or staff development:
  - ■ desktop publishing
- ❏ Computer technology used to **facilitate collaboration** among PDS partners:
  - ■ desktop publishing
- ❏ Computer technology included in **subject matter** of teacher education &/or staff development curriculum of PDS participants:
  - ■ desktop publishing
- ❏ Policies of college with regard to hiring, tenure, promotion, or other aspects of college's reward structure, acknowledge PDS-related work
- ❏ Approximately 0-19% of department faculty participate in PDS-related work (planning or implementation)

MISSOURI

Harris-Stowe State College

School	Shepard Accelerated School Partnership 3026 Laclede Avenue St. Louis, MO 63103 Phone: (314) 340-3649
Site Coordinator	Emelda B. Harris, PDS Coordinator
Starting Date	1993
Grade Level	PreK-5
School Type	Professional Development School

MISSOURI

College/University	*Maryville University*
Contact	Mary Ellen Finch, Dean School of Education Maryville University St. Louis, MO 63141 (314) 576-9466
Partners	Maryville University St. Louis Public School District; Parkway School District St. Louis Teachers Union
Affiliation	St. Louis Regional Educational Partnership; National Network for Educational Renewal (NNER); St. Louis Professional Development Schools Collaborative
Funding	university; school district; Southwestern Bell; Danforth Foundation; St. Louis Regional Educational Partnership (Monsanto Fund)
Starting Date	1988
PDS Sites	South High School; Wilkinson Early Childhood Center

Program Features	❑ Preservice teachers assigned to PDSs in cohorts
	❑ College funding for PDS program from grants, discretionary funds, or other types of "soft money"
	❑ Release time, reduced course load, or other related arrangement made for college faculty actively involved with PDS sites
	❑ Computer technology used in PDS teacher education program to **facilitate instruction** &/or staff development:
	    ■ telecommunications (e.g., e-mail, bulletin boards)
	    ■ computer assisted instruction
	    ■ desktop publishing
	❑ Computer technology used to **facilitate collaboration** among PDS partners:
	    ■ telecommunications (e.g., e-mail, bulletin boards)
	❑ Computer technology included in **subject matter** of teacher education &/or staff development curriculum of PDS participants:
	    ■ computer assisted instruction
	❑ Policies of college with regard to hiring, tenure, promotion, or other aspects of college's reward structure, acknowledge PDS-related work
	❑ Approximately 80-100% of department faculty participate in PDS-related work (planning or implementation)

MISSOURI

Maryville University

School	South High School 13550 Conway Road St. Louis, MO 63141 Phone: (314) 576-9466
Site Coordinator	Sheila Biranne
Starting Date	no information available
Grade Level	9-12
School Type	Professional Practice School
School	Wilkinson Early Childhood Center 13550 Conway Road St. Louis, MO 63141 Phone: (314) 576-9466
Site Coordinator	Sheila Morris
Starting Date	1988
Grade Level	PreK-2
School Type	Professional Development School

College/University	*Saint Louis University*
Contact	Linda Bufkin, Ph.D. Saint Louis University 3750 Lindell Boulevard St. Louis, MO 63108 (314) 658-2510
Partners	Saint Louis University St. Louis Public Schools
Starting Date	1993, January
PDS Sites	Wyman School
Program Features	

- ❏ Preservice teachers assigned to PDSs in cohorts
- ❏ Computer technology used in PDS teacher education program to **facilitate instruction** &/or staff development:
  - ■ computer assisted instruction
  - ■ interactive video
  - ■ desktop publishing
- ❏ Computer technology included in **subject matter** of teacher education &/or staff development curriculum of PDS participants:
  - ■ computer assisted instruction
  - ■ interactive video
  - ■ desktop publishing
- ❏ Policies of college with regard to hiring, tenure, promotion, or other aspects of college's reward structure, acknowledge PDS-related work
- ❏ Approximately 20-39% of department faculty participate in PDS-related work (planning or implementation)

MISSOURI

St. Louis University

School	Wyman School
	1547 South Theresa
	St. Louis, MO 63104
	(314) 772-9328
Site Coordinator	John Phillips
Starting Date	1993, January
Grade Level	K-6
School Type	Professional Development School

College/University	*University of Missouri - Kansas City*
Contact	Kathryn E. Loncar University of Missouri - Kansas City School of Education 5100 Rockhill Road Kansas City, MO 64110 (816) 235-2467
Partners	University of Missouri - Kansas City Center School District
Funding	university; school district
Starting Date	1991, September
PDS Sites	Center Elementary; Red Bridge Elementary
Program Features	❑ Preservice teachers assigned to PDSs in cohorts ❑ Approximately 0-19% of department faculty participate in PDS-related work (planning or implementation)

MISSOURI

University of Missouri - Kansas City

School   Center Elementary School
                                          8401 Euclid
                                          Kansas City, MO 64132
                                          Phone: (816) 523-3066
Site Coordinator   Gus Jacobs, Principal
Starting Date   1993, September
Grade Level   K-6
School Type   Professional Development School

School   Red Bridge Elementary School
                                          10781 Oak
                                          Kansas City, MO 64114
                                          Phone: (816) 942-7821
Site Coordinator   Debbie Lerner
Starting Date   1991, September
Grade Level   K-6
School Type   Partnership School

MISSOURI

College/University	*University of Missouri - St.Louis*
Contact	Thomas R. Schnell, Associate Dean University of Missouri - St. Louis 8001 Natural Bridge Road St. Louis, MO 63121 (314) 553-5791
Partners	University of Missouri - St.Louis Maplewood, Parkway, & St. Louis Public School Districts
Affiliation	St. Louis Regional Educational Partnership
Funding	university; school district; Danforth Foundation; Commerce Bank of St. Louis; St. Louis Regional Educational Partnership
Starting Date	1991, August
PDS Sites	Chaney Elementary School; Laclede Elementary School; Parkway Central Middle School; Parkway River Bend Elementary
Program Features	❑ College funding for PDS program from grants, discretionary funds, or other types of "soft money"

❑ Release time, reduced course load, or other related arrangement made for college faculty actively involved with PDS sites

❑ Computer technology used in PDS teacher education program to **facilitate instruction** &/or staff development:
   ▪ telecommunications (e.g., e-mail, bulletin boards)
   ▪ computer assisted instruction
   ▪ interactive video
   ▪ desktop publishing

❑ Computer technology used to **facilitate collaboratio**n among PDS partners:
   ▪ telecommunications (e.g., e-mail, bulletin boards)
   ▪ computer assisted instruction
   ▪ interactive video
   ▪ desktop publishing

❑ Computer technology included in **subject matter** of teacher education &/or staff development curriculum of PDS participants:
   ▪ telecommunications (e.g., e-mail, bulletin boards)
   ▪ computer assisted instruction
   ▪ interactive video
   ▪ authoring systems
   ▪ desktop publishing

❑ Policies of college with regard to hiring, tenure, promotion, or other aspects of college's reward structure, acknowledge PDS-related work

❑ Approximately 40-59% of department faculty participate in PDS-related work (planning or implementation)

MISSOURI

University of Missouri - St. Louis

School	Chaney Elementary School 1800 Princeton Place Richmond Heights, MO 63117 Phone: (314) 644-4403
Site Coordinator	Leonard Marks, Principal
Starting Date	1991, August
Grade Level	3-6
School Type	Professional Development School
School	Laclede Elementary School 5821 Kennerly Avenue St. Louis, MO 63112 Phone: (314) 385-0546
Site Coordinator	Joyce Roberts, Principal
Starting Date	1994, January
Grade Level	K-5
School Type	Professional Development School
School	Parkway Central Middle School 471 North Woods Mill Road Chesterfield, MO 63017 Phone: (314) 851-8265
Site Coordinator	Dan Natale, Principal
Starting Date	1992, August
Grade Level	6-8
School Type	Professional Development School
School	Parkway River Bend Elementary School 224 River Valley Drive Chesterfield, MO 63017
Site Coordinator	Phone: (314) 469-7500
Starting Date	Jill Ramsey, Principal
Grade Level	1994, January
School Type	K-5 Professional Development School

MISSOURI

College/University	*Washington University*
Contact	Marilyn Cohn Washington University Box 1183 St. Louis, MO 63130 (314) 935-6702
Partners	Washington University Kirkwood School District
Affiliation	St. Louis Regional Educational Partnership
Funding	Danforth Foundation
Starting Date	1992, Fall
PDS Sites	Kirkwood High School
Program Features	

- ❑ Preservice teachers assigned to PDSs in cohorts
- ❑ Computer technology included in **subject matter** of teacher education &/or staff development curriculum of PDS participants:
  - ■ computer assisted instruction
  - ■ desktop publishing
- ❑ Approximately 0-19% of department faculty participate in PDS-related work (planning or implementation)

MISSOURI

Washington University

School	Kirkwood High School
	801 West Essex
	Kirkwood, MO 63122
	Phone: (314) 984-4400
Site Coordinator	Suzanne Kirkpatrick
Starting Date	no information available
Grade Level	9-12
School Type	Professional Development School

College/University	*Rowan College of New Jersey*
Contact	Dr. David E. Kapel, Dean School of Education & Related Professional Studies 201 Mullica Hill Road Glassboro, NJ 08028-1701 (609) 863-5241 Fax: (609) 863-5018
Partners	Rowan College of New Jersey Camden City & Winslow Township School Districts
Funding	university; school district
Starting Date	1992, Septemeber
PDS Sites	Cooper's Point Professional Development Family School of Excellence; Winslow Professional Development District
Program Features	

- ❑ Preservice teachers assigned to PDSs in cohorts
- ❑ Release time, reduced course load, or other related arrangement made for college faculty actively involved with PDS sites
- ❑ Computer technology used in PDS teacher education program to **facilitate instruction** &/or staff development:
  - ■ computer assisted instruction
  - ■ desktop publishing
- ❑ Computer technology used to **facilitate collaboration** among PDS partners:
  - ■ desktop publishing
- ❑ Computer technology included in **subject matter** of teacher education &/or staff development curriculum of PDS participants:
  - ■ computer assisted instruction
  - ■ interactive video
  - ■ programming
  - ■ authoring systems
  - ■ desktop publishing
- ❑ Approximately 0-19% of department faculty participate in PDS-related work (planning or implementation)

Rowan College of New Jersey

School	Cooper's Point Professional Development Family School of Excellence 3rd & State Streets Camden, NJ 08102 Phone: (609) 966-5370
Site Coordinator	Dr. Carol Sharp, Associate Professor
Starting Date	1992, September
Grade Level	K-8
School Type	Professional Development School
School	Winslow Professional Development District Central Avenue, Box 213 Blue Anchor, NJ 08037-0213 Phone: (609) 561-5615
Site Coordinator	Drs. Marian Rilling & Jay Kuder
Starting Date	1992, September
Grade Level	K-6
School Type	Professional Development School

College/University	***Buffalo State College***
Contact	Dr. David E. Day Elementary Education & Reading Buffalo State College 1300 Elmwood Avenue Buffalo, NY 14222 (716) 878-5916
Partners	Buffalo State College Tonawanda Union Free School District; Lancaster Central School District; Buffalo Public School District
Funding	college
Starting Date	1992, September
PDS Sites	Charles Drew Science Magnet School; Como Park Elementary; Futures Academy; Hoover Elementary School
Program Features	

❑ Preservice teachers assigned to PDSs in cohorts
❑ Computer technology used in PDS teacher education program to **facilitate instruction** &/or staff development:
  ■ telecommunications (e.g., e-mail, bulletin boards)
  ■ interactive video
❑ Computer technology used to **facilitate collaboration** among PDS partners:
  ■ telecommunications (e.g., e-mail, bulletin boards)
❑ Computer technology included in **subject matter** of teacher education &/or staff development curriculum of PDS participants:
  ■ telecommunications (e.g., e-mail, bulletin boards)
  ■ computer assisted instruction
  ■ interactive video
❑ Approximately 20-39% of department faculty participate in PDS-related work (planning or implementation)

NEW YORK

Buffalo State College

School	Charles Drew Science Magnet School One Martin Luther King Jr. Park Buffalo, NY 14211 Phone: (716) 897-8050
Site Coordinator	Delcene West & Dr. Rosemary Lonberger
Starting Date	1993, January
Grade Level	PreK-8
School Type	Professional Development School
School	Como Park Elementary School 1985 Como Park Boulevard Lancaster, NY 14086 Phone: (716) 686-3235
Site Coordinator	Dr. Andrea Stein, Principal & Dr. Carol Hodges
Starting Date	1994, January
Grade Level	K-5
School Type	Professional Development School
School	Futures Academy 295 Carlton Street Buffalo, NY 14204 Phone: (716) 851-3800
Site Coordinator	Marva Daniel & Dr. Carol Stevens
Starting Date	1994, January
Grade Level	PreK-8
School Type	Professional Development School
School	Hoover Elementary School 199 Thorncliff Road Kenmore, NY 14223 Phone: (716) 874-8414
Site Coordinator	Francis Paskowitz & Dr. Sarah Weitler
Starting Date	1991, September
Grade Level	K-6
School Type	Professional Development School

College/University	*Columbia University*
Contact	Frank Schwartz P.O. Box 155 Teachers College Columbia University New York, NY 10027 (212) 678-3166
Partners	Columbia University New York City Community School District #3 United Federation of Teachers
Affiliation	Ford Foundation Clinical Schools Project
Funding	Ford Foundation; Lawrence Wein Foundation; Uris Brothers Foundation; Aaron Diamond Foundation
Starting Date	1988, September
PDS Sites	I.S. 44; P.S.87

Program Features

- ❑ Preservice teachers assigned to PDSs in cohorts
- ❑ College funding for PDS program from grants, discretionary funds, or other types of "soft money"
- ❑ Release time, reduced course load, or other related arrangement made for college faculty actively involved with PDS sites
- ❑ Computer technology used in PDS teacher education program to **facilitate instruction** &/or staff development:
  - ■ telecommunications (e.g., e-mail, bulletin boards)
  - ■ computer assisted instruction
  - ■ desktop publishing
- ❑ Policies of college with regard to hiring, tenure, promotion, or other aspects of college's reward structure, acknowledge PDS-related work
- ❑ Approximately 20-39% of department faculty participate in PDS-related work (planning or implementation)

NEW YORK

Columbia University

School	I.S. 44
	100 West 77th Street
	New York, NY 10024
	Phone: (212) 678-2817
Site Coordinator	Lisa Nelson
Starting Date	1988, September
Grade Level	6-8
School Type	Professional Development School
School	P.S. 87
	160 West 78th Street
	New York, NY 10024
	Phone: (212) 678-2828
Site Coordinator	Tom Andrews
Starting Date	1988, September
Grade Level	K-5
School Type	Professional Development School

College/University

Syracuse University

Contact

Gwen Yarger-Kane
Syracuse University
162 Huntington Hall
Syracuse, NY 13244
(315) 443-2684

Partners

Syracuse University
West Syracuse Central, Syracuse City, Jamesville-DeWitt, North Syracuse,
& Onondaga Central School Districts
West Genesee Teachers Association

Funding

university; school district; state

Starting Date

1989, Fall*

PDS Sites

Camillus Middle School; East Hill Elementary School; Edward Smith
Elementary School; Franklin Elementary School; Jamesville Elementary
School; Jamesville-DeWitt High School; Jamesville-DeWitt Middle School;
;Moses-DeWitt Middle School; Onondaga Road Elementary School; Split
Rock Elementary School; Stonehedge Elementary School; Tecumseh
Elementary School; Webster Elementary School; West Genesee Middle
School; West Genesee Senior High School

Program Features

❑ Preservice teachers assigned to PDSs in cohorts
❑ Release time, reduced course load, or other related arrangement made
for college faculty actively involved with PDS sites
❑ Computer technology used in PDS teacher education program to
facilitate instruction &/or staff development:
- telecommunications (e.g., e-mail, bulletin boards)
- computer assisted instruction
- desktop publishing
❑ Computer technology used to **facilitate collaboration** among PDS
partners:
- telecommunications (e.g., e-mail, bulletin boards)
- computer assisted instruction
- desktop publishing
❑ Computer technology included in **subject matter** of teacher education
&/or staff developmentcurriculum of PDS participants:
- telecommunications (e.g., e-mail, bulletin boards)
- computer assisted instruction
- interactive video
- authoring systems
- desktop publishing
❑ Policies of college with regard to hiring, tenure, promotion, or other
aspects of college's reward structure, acknowledge PDS-related work
❑ Approximately 80-100% of department faculty participate in PDS-
related work (planning or implementation)

Note

*In 1973, the West Genesee Schools and Syracuse University agreed
to establish a Teacher Development Center. Beginning in 1974-1975, the Center
coordinated clinical schools collaborations. Based on the success of these
collaboratives, the concept was expanded in 1989 to a Professional Development
School model and now includes schools from several districts.

Syracuse University

School	Camillus Middle School 5525 Ike Dixon Road Camillus, NY 13031-9621 Phone: (315) 672-3159	Jamesville-DeWitt High School Edinger Drive DeWitt, NY 13214 Phone: (315) 445-8340
Site Coordinator	Dean DeSantis, Principal	Barbara Goessling, Principal
Starting Date	1989	1989
Grade Level	6-8	9-12
School Type	Professional Development School	Professional Development School
School	East Hill Elementary School 401 Blackmore Road Camillus, NY 13031-2199 Phone: (315) 487-4648	Jamesville-DeWitt Middle School Randall Road Jamesville, NY 13078 Phone: (315) 445-8360
Site Coordinator	John Bome, Principal & Alma Clearwater,Building-Level Chair	Ron Ramsden, Principal & Nancy Sellmeyer
Starting Date	1989	1989
Grade Level	K-5	5-8
School Type	no information available	Professional Development School
School	Edward Smith Elementary School 1106 Lancaster Avenue Syracuse, NY 13210 Phone: (315) 435-4650	Moses-DeWitt Elementary School Jamesville Road Syracuse, NY 13214 Phone: (315) 445-8370
Site Coordinator	Mary Coughlin & Lori Keevil/Gay Burch, Building-Level Chair	Mary Duffin, Building-Level Chair
Starting Date	1992	1989
Grade Level	K-6	K-4
School Type	Professional Development School	Professional Development School
School	Franklin Elementary School 428 South Alvord Street Syracuse, NY 13208 Phone: (315) 435-4550	Onondaga Road Elementary School 703 Onondaga Road Syracuse, NY 13219-2999 Phone: (315) 487-4653
Site Coordinator	Dominick Sabatino, Principal & Lenore Metter	Barry Guinn, Principal
Starting Date	1989	1989
Grade Level	K-5	K-5
School Type	Professional Development School	Clinical School
School	Jamesville Elementary School East Seneca Turnpike Jamesville, NY 13078 Phone: (315) 492-8612	Split Rock Elementary School 4151 Split Rock Road Camillus, NY 13031-9722 Phone: (315) 487-4656
Site Coordinator	Juanita Ares, Building-Level Chair	Gary VanDeCarr, Principal
Starting Date	1989	1989
Grade Level	K-4	K-5
School Type	Professional Development School	Professional Development School

NEW YORK

Syracuse University

School	Stonehedge Elementary School 400 Sanderson Drive Camillus, NY 13031-1699 Phone: (315) 487-4631
Site Coordinator	Donald Stebbins, Principal & Mary Ann Mecca
Starting Date	1989
Grade Level	K-5
School Type	Professional Development School
School	Tecumseh Elementary School Nottingham & Waring Roads Jamesville, NY 13078 Phone: (315) 445-8320
Site Coordinator	Edwina Feldman, Building-Level Chair
Starting Date	1989
Grade Level	K-4
School Type	Professional Development School
School	Webster Elementary School 500 Wadesworth Syracuse, NY 13208 Phone: no information available
Site Coordinator	Maxine Williams, Principal & Judith Giacchi
Starting Date	1990
Grade Level	K-5
School Type	Professional Development School
School	West Genesee Middle School 500 Sanderson Drive Camillus, NY 13031-1698 Phone: (315) 487-4615
Site Coordinator	Joseph Pecori, Principal
Starting Date	1989
Grade Level	6-8
School Type	Professional Development School
School	West Genesee Senior High School 5201 West Genesee Street Camillus, NY 13031-2299 Phone: (315) 487-4601
Site Coordinator	Helen White, Principal
Starting Date	1989
Grade Level	9-12
School Type	Professional Development School

College/University	*University of North Carolina - Greensboro*
Contact	Dr. Mary Olson University of North Carolina - Greensboro School of Education 335 Curry Greensboro, NC 27412 (910) 334-5100
Partners	University of North Carolina - Greensboro Guilford County & Winston-Salem/Forsyth County School Districts
Funding	university
Starting Date	1991, September
PDS Sites	Archer Elementary School; Bluford Elementary School; Brightwood Elementary School; Greene Elementary School; Global Magnet School School; Guilford Middle School; Guilford Primary School; Jackson Middle School; Jamestown Middle School; Jesse Wharton Elementary School; Kernersville Elementary School; Kiser Middle School; Millis Road Elementary School; Oak View Elementary School; Oak Hill Elementary School; Piney Grove Elementary School; Rankin Elementary School; Sedgefield Elementary School; Shadybrook Elementary School; Western Guilford High School

Program Features

- ❑ Preservice teachers assigned to PDSs in cohorts
- ❑ Release time, reduced course load, or other related arrangement made for college faculty actively involved with PDS sites
- ❑ Computer technology used in PDS teacher education program to **facilitate instruction** &/or staff development:
  - ■ computer assisted instruction
- ❑ Computer technology included in **subject matter** of teacher education &/or staff development curriculum of PDS participants:
  - ■ computer assisted instruction
- ❑ Policies of college with regard to hiring, tenure, promotion, or other aspects of college's reward structure, acknowledge PDS-related work
- ❑ Approximately 80-100% of department faculty participate in PDS-related work (planning or implementation)

University of North Carolina - Greensboro

School	Archer Elementary School 2610 Four Seasons Boulevard Greensboro, NC 27407 Phone: (910) 294-7335	Guilford Middle School 401 College Road Greensboro, NC 27410 Phone: (910) 316-5833
Site Coordinator	John VanHoose	Sam Miller
Starting Date	1991, August	1991, August
Grade Level	K-5	3-8
School Type	Professional Development School	Professional Development School
School	Bluford Elementary School 1901 Tuscaloosa Street Greensboro, NC 27401 Phone: (910) 370-8120	Guilford Primary School 411 Friendway Road Greensboro, NC 27410 Phone: (910) 316-5844
Site Coordinator	Dee Irwin	Sam Miller
Starting Date	1992, August	1991, August
Grade Level	K-5	K-2
School Type	Professional Development School	Professional Development School
School	Brightwood Elementary School 2500 Lees Chapel Road Greensboro, NC 27405 Phone: (910) 375-2565	Jackson Middle School 2200 Ontario Street Greensboro, NC 27403 Phone: (910) 294-7350
Site Coordinator	Barbara Stoodt	John VanHoose
Starting Date	1992, August	1992, August
Grade Level	K-5	K-5
School Type	Professional Development School	Professional Development School
School	Global Magnet School 1215 Westover Terrace Greensboro, NC 27408 Phone: (910) 370-8228	Jamestown Middle School 4401 Vickery Chapel Road Jamestown, NC 27282 Phone: (910) 819-2100
Site Coordinator	Dee Irwin	David Strahan
Starting Date	1992, August	1993, August
Grade Level	K-5	6-8
School Type	Professional Development School	Professional Development School
School	Greene Elementary School 1501 Benjamin Parkway Greensboro, NC 27408 Phone: (910) 545-2015	Jesse Wharton Elementary School 116 Pisgah Church Road Greensboro, NC 27405 Phone: (910) 545-2030
Site Coordinator	Cathy Matthews	Barbara Stoodt
Starting Date	1992, August	1992, August
Grade Level	K-5	K-5
School Type	Professional Development School	Professional Development School

School	Kernersville Elementary School 512 West Mountain Street Kernersville, NC 27284 Phone: (910) 996-1080	Piney Grove Elementary School 1500 Piney Grove Road Kernersville, NC 27284 Phone: (910) 993-0372
Site Coordinator	A.C. Miller	A.C. Miller
Starting Date	1991, August	1992, August
Grade Level	K-5	K-5
School Type	Professional Development School	Professional Development School
School	Kiser Middle School 616 Benjamin Parkway Greensboro, NC 27408 Phone: (910) 370-8240	Rankin Elementary School 3301 Summit Avenue Greensboro, NC 27408 Phone: (910) 375-2545
Site Coordinator	David Strahan	no information available
Starting Date	1991, August	1991, August
Grade Level	6-8	K-5
School Type	Professional Development School	Professional Development School
School	Mills Road Elementary School 4310 Mills Road Jamestown, NC 27282 Phone: (910) 819-2125	Sedgefield Elementary School 3905 Germantown Road Greensboro, NC Phone: (910) 316-5858
Site Coordinator	Robin Smith	Sam Miller
Starting Date	1992, August	1993, August
Grade Level	K-5	K-5
School Type	Professional Development School	Professional Development School
School	Oak Hill Elementary School 320 Wrightberry Avenue High Point, NC 27260 Phone: (910) 819-2925	Shadybrook Elementary School 503 Shadybrook Drive High Point, NC 27265 Phone: (910) 819-2950
Site Coordinator	Robin Smith	Robin Smith
Starting Date	1992, August	1992, August
Grade Level	K-5	K-5
School Type	Professional Development School	Professional Development School
School	Oak View Elementary School 614 Oak View Road High Point, NC 26275 Phone: (910) 819-2935	Western Guilford High School 409 Friendway Road Greensboro, NC 27410 Phone: (910) 316-5800
Site Coordinator	Cathy Matthews	Brenda Cox
Starting Date	1991, August	1993, August
Grade Level	K-5	9-12
School Type	Professional Development School	Professional Development School

College/University	*University of North Dakota*
Contact	Mary McDonnell Harris University of North Dakota Center for Teaching & Learning Box 7189 Grand Forks, ND 58202 (701) 777-2674
Partners	University of North Dakota Grand Forks Public Schools
Funding	university; school district; Knight Foundation
Starting Date	1990, September
PDS Sites	Lake Agassiz Elementary School
Program Features	

- ❑ Preservice teachers assigned to PDSs in cohorts
- ❑ College funding for PDS program from grants, discretionary funds, or other types of "soft money"
- ❑ Release time, reduced course load, or other related arrangement made for college faculty actively involved with PDS sites
- ❑ Computer technology used in PDS teacher education program to **facilitate instruction** &/or staff development:
  - ■ computer assisted instruction
- ❑ Computer technology included in **subject matter** of teacher education &/or staff development curriculum of PDS participants:
  - ■ computer assisted instruction
  - ■ desktop publishing
- ❑ Policies of college with regard to hiring, tenure, promotion, or other aspects of college's reward structure, acknowledge PDS-related work
- ❑ Approximately 60-79% of department faculty participate in PDS-related work (planning or implementation)

NORTH DAKOTA

University of North Dakota

School	Lake Agassiz Elementary School
	Stanford Road and 6th Avenue North
	Grand Forks, ND 58202
	Phone: (701) 746-2275
Site Coordinator	Sharon Gates
Starting Date	1991, September
Grade Level	K-6
School Type	Professional Development School

OHIO

College/University	*The Ohio State University*
Contact	Don Cramer, PDS Coordinator The Ohio State University 127 Arps Hall 1945 North High Street Columbus, OH 43210-1172 (614) 365-5500
Partners	The Ohio State University Columbus Public Schools, Bexley City Schools, Grandview Heights City Schools, Reynoldsburg City Schools, Southwestern City Schools, Upper Arlington City Schools, Whitehall City Schools, Worthington City Schools, Hilliard City Schools
Affiliation	Holmes Group
Funding	university; school district; Columbus Foundation; Lilly Endowment
Starting Date	1989, August
PDS Sites	Etna Road Elementary School; Independence High School; Northland High School; Thomas Worthington High School *

Program Features

❑ Preservice teachers assigned to PDSs in cohorts
❑ College funding for PDS program from grants, discretionary funds, or other types of "soft money"
❑ Release time, reduced course load, or other related arrangement made for college faculty actively involved with PDS sites
❑ Computer technology used in PDS teacher education program to **facilitate instruction** &/or staff development:
  ■ telecommunications (e.g., e-mail, bulletin boards)
  ■ computer assisted instruction
  ■ interactive video
  ■ desktop publishing
❑ Computer technology used to **facilitate collaboration** among PDS partners:
  ■ telecommunications (e.g., e-mail, bulletin boards)
  ■ computer assisted instruction
  ■ interactive video
  ■ desktop publishing
❑ Computer technology included in **subject matter** of teacher education &/or staff developmentcurriculum of PDS participants:
  ■ telecommunications (e.g., e-mail, bulletin boards)
  ■ computer assisted instruction
  ■ interactive video
  ■ programming
  ■ authoring systems
  ■ desktop publishing
❑ Policies of college with regard to hiring, tenure, promotion, or other aspects of college's reward structure, acknowledge PDS-related work
❑ Approximately 20-39% of department faculty participate in PDS-related work (planning or implementation)

91

OHIO

The Ohio State University

Note

*In addition to the 4 PDSs indicated above, the university participates in 10 other collaborative projects with local teachers unions and school districts.

OHIO

Ohio State University

School

Etna Road Elementary School -
Project TEACH
4531 Etna Road
Whitehall, OH 43213
Phone: (614) 231-1291

Site Coordinator — Jean Tippitt
Starting Date — 1990
Grade Level — K-6
School Type — Clinical School

School

Independence High School - Project
TRI
5175 Refugee Road
Columbus, OH 43232
Phone: (614) 365-5372

Site Coordinator — Beth Carnate
Starting Date — 1992, Autumn
Grade Level — 9-12
School Type — Professional Development School

School

Northland High School - Northland
Teaching Academy
1919 Northcliff Drive
Columbus, OH 43229
Phone: (614) 365-5342

Site Coordinator — Gary Love & Rose King
Starting Date — 1990
Grade Level — 9-12
School Type — Professional Development School

School

Thomas Worthington High School
Worthington BESS PDS Program
Worthington, OH 43085
Phone: (614) 431-6565

Site Coordinator — Mark Maley
Starting Date — 1992, September
Grade Level — 9-10
School Type — Professional Development School

College/University

Bloomsburg University

Contact

Dr. Ann L. Lee
School of Education
3201 McCormick Center for Human Services
Bloomsburg University
Bloomsburg, PA 17815
(717) 389-4073

Partners

Bloomsburg University
Danville Area School District

Funding

Pennsylvania Department of Education Bureau of Special Education

Starting Date

1991, September

PDS Sites

Danville Elementary School

Program Features

❑ Preservice teachers assigned to PDSs in cohorts
❑ College funding for PDS program from grants, discretionary funds, or other types of "soft money"
❑ Approximately 0-19% of department faculty participate in PDS-related work (planning or implementation)

Bloomsburg University

School   Danville Elementary School
                                   401 East Front Street
                                   Danville, PA 17821
                                   Phone: (717) 275-7570

Site Coordinator   Charles Eckenroth
Starting Date   1991, September
Grade Level   K-6
School Type   Professional Development School

College/University	*Millersville University*
Contact	Dr. Cheryl T. Desmond 162 Stayer Educational Center Millersville University Millersville, PA 17551 (717) 872-3381
Partners	Millersville University Manheim Township School District; Conestoga Valley School District
Funding	university
Starting Date	1994, January
PDS Sites	Conestoga Valley Middle School; Manheim Township Middle School
Program Features	❑ Preservice teachers assigned to PDSs in cohorts ❑ Computer technology included in **subject matter** of teacher education &/or staff development curriculum of PDS participants: ■ programming ❑ Approximately 0-19% of department faculty participate in PDS-related work (planning or implementation)

PENNSYLVANIA

Millersville University

School	Conestoga Valley Middle School
	11 School Drive
	Leola, PA 17540
	Phone: (717) 656-2627
Site Coordinator	Judy Anthony
Starting Date	1994, January
Grade Level	7-9
School Type	Professional Practice School

School	Manheim Township Middle School
	Box 5134 School Road
	Lancaster, PA 17601
	Phone: (717) 569-8231
Site Coordinator	Cheryl T. Desmond
Starting Date	1994, January
Grade Level	7-9
School Type	Professional Practice School

College/University

Temple University

Contact

Jayminn Sanford
College of Education - C.I.T.E. Department
13th & Montgomery Avenue
Ritter Hall 339
Philadelphia, PA 19122
(215) 204-5205

Partners

Temple University
City of Philadelphia School District

Affiliation

Holmes Group

Funding

CIGNA Insurance Company; Carnegie Foundation

Starting Date

1991, September

PDS Sites

no information available*

Program Features

❑ Preservice teachers assigned to PDSs in cohorts
❑ College funding for PDS program from grants, discretionary funds, or other types of "soft money"
❑ Release time, reduced course load, or other related arrangement made for college faculty actively involved with PDS sites
❑ Computer technology used in PDS teacher education program to **facilitate instruction** &/or staff development:
　■ computer assisted instruction
　■ interactive video
❑ Computer technology used to **facilitate collaboration** among PDS partners: staff development:
　■ computer assisted instruction
❑ Computer technology included in **subject matter** of teacher education &/or staff development curriculum of PDS participants:
　■ telecommunications (e.g., e-mail, bulletin boards)
　■ computer assisted instruction
　■ interactive video
　■ programming
❑ Policies of college with regard to hiring, tenure, promotion, or other aspects of college's reward structure, acknowledge PDS-related work
❑ Approximately 0-19% of department faculty participate in PDS-related work (planning or implementation)

Note

*The data received about the PDS sites were not presented in a format that allowed for their inclusion in the profiles of individual PDSs.

College/University	*University of South Carolina*
Contact	Dale P. Scannell 201 Wardlaw College of Education University of South Carolina Columbia, SC 29208 (803) 777-3074
Partners	University of South Carolina Richland I, Richland II, Lexington I, Lexington II, & Fort Jackson School Districts
Affiliation	National Network for Educational Renewal; Holmes Group
Funding	university; school district; Bellsouth Foundation; South Carolina Center for Advancement of Teaching & School Leadership
Starting Date	1990
PDS Sites	Airport High School; Crayton Middle School; Hood Street School; Horrell Hill Elementary School; Hyatt Park School; Meadowfield Elementary School; Pierce Terrace School; Pinckney Elementary School; Pontiac Elementary School; Summit Parkway Middle School; White Knoll Elementary School
Program Features	❑ Preservice teachers assigned to PDSs in cohorts ❑ College funding for PDS program from grants, discretionary funds, or other types of "soft money" ❑ Computer technology used in PDS teacher education program to **facilitate instruction** &/or staff development: ■ telecommunications (e.g., e-mail, bulletin boards) ■ computer assisted instruction ■ desktop publishing ❑ Computer technology used to **facilitate collaboration** among PDS partners: ■ telecommunications (e.g., e-mail, bulletin boards) ■ computer assisted instruction ■ desktop publishing ❑ Computer technology included in **subject matter** of teacher education &/or staff development curriculum of PDS participants: ■ telecommunications (e.g., e-mail, bulletin boards) ■ computer assisted instruction ■ interactive video ■ authoring systems ■ desktop publishing ❑ Approximately 0-19% of department faculty participate in PDS-related work (planning or implementation)

SOUTH CAROLINA

University of South Carolina

School	Airport High School 1315 Boston Avenue W. Columbia, SC 29169 Phone: (803) 822-5600	Meadowfield Elementary School 525 Galway Lane Columbia, SC 29209 Phone: (803) 783-5549
Site Coordinator	Jimmy Taylor	Lynn Robertson
Starting Date	1990	1990
Grade Level	9-12	PreK-5
School Type	Planning Site (PS)	Planning Site (PS)
School	Crayton Middle School 5000 Clemson Avenue Columbia, SC 29206 Phone: (803) 738-7224	Pierce Terrace School 5715 Adams Court Columbia, SC 29206 Phone: (803) 782-1772
Site Coordinator	Ellen H. Cooper	Philip Booth
Starting Date	1990	1990
Grade Level	6-8	PreK-1
School Type	Professional Development School-PS	Professional Development School-PS
School	Hood Street School 5615 Hood Street Columbia, SC 29206 Phone: (803) 787-8266	Pinckney Elementary School 5900 Chestnut Road Columbia, SC 29206 Phone: (803) 787-6815
Site Coordinator	Carol George	Rick Tanner
Starting Date	1990	1990
Grade Level	2-3	4-6
School Type	Professional Development School	Professional Devleopment School
School	Horrell Hill Elementary School 517 Horrell Hil Road Hopkins, SC 29061 Phone: (803) 783-5545	Pontiac Elementary School 500 Spears Creek Church Road Elgin, SC 29045 Phone: (803) 699-2700
Site Coordinator	Parthenia Satterwhite	Richard Inabinet
Starting Date	1990	1990
Grade Level	K-6	K-6
School Type	Professional Development School-PS	Professional Development School-PS
School	Hyatt Park School 4200 Main Street Columbia, SC 29203 Phone: (803) 735-3421	Summitt Parkway Middle School 200 Summit Parkway Columbia, SC 29223 Phone: (803) 699-3580
Site Coordinator	Eugene George	Jo Hecker
Starting Date	1990	1990
Grade Level	K-6	6-8
School Type	Professional Development School-PS	Professional Development School-PS

SOUTH CAROLINA

University of South Carolina

School	White Knoll Elementary School
	132 White Knoll Way
	W. Columbia, SC 29170
	Phone: (803) 957-7700
Site Coordinator	W. Darrell Barringer
Starting Date	1990
Grade Level	PreK-5
School Type	Professional Development School

College/University

Contact

Partners

Funding

Starting Date

PDS Sites

Program Features

Austin Peay State University

Carl Stedman or Camille Holt
Box 4428
Austin Peay State University
Clarksville, TN 37044
(615) 648-7696

Austin Peay State University

university; South Central Bell

1993, Spring

Burt Elementary School

❑ Preservice teachers assigned to PDSs in cohorts
❑ Release time, reduced course load, or other related arrangement made for college faculty actively involved with PDS sites
❑ Computer technology used in PDS teacher education program to **facilitate instruction** &/or staff development:
  ■ telecommunications (e.g., e-mail, bulletin boards)
  ■ computer assisted instruction
  ■ interactive video
❑ Computer technology used to **facilitate collaboration** among PDS partners:
  ■ telecommunications (e.g., e-mail, bulletin boards)
  ■ computer assisted instruction
  ■ interactive video
❑ Computer technology included in **subject matter** of teacher education &/or staff development curriculum of PDS participants:
  ■ computer assisted instruction
  ■ interactive video
❑ Policies of college with regard to hiring, tenure, promotion, or other aspects of college's reward structure, acknowledge PDS-related work
❑ Approximately 20-39% of department faculty participate in PDS-related work (planning or implementation)

TENNESSEE

Austin Peay State University

School	Burt Elementary School
	110 Bailey Street
	Clarksville, TN 37040
	Phone: no information available
Site Coordinator	Mrs. Irene Godgeon
Starting Date	1993, Spring
Grade Level	K-6
School Type	Partner School

College/University	***Memphis State University***
Contact	Cindi Chance, Director of Undergraduate Curriculum College of Education Ball Hall - Room 200 Memphis State University Memphis, TN 38152 (901) 678-4177
Partners	Memphis State University Memphis City School District; Shelby County School District; Dyer County School District; Memphis Catholic Diocese
Funding	university; school district
Starting Date	1991, Fall
PDS Sites	Campus School; Coleman Elementary School; Dyer County Central Elementary School; Frayser Elementary School; Lipman School; Newberry Elementary School; Raleigh Egypt Middle School; Ross Elementary School

Program Features

- ❑ Preservice teachers assigned to PDSs in cohorts
- ❑ Release time, reduced course load, or other related arrangement made for college faculty actively involved with PDS sites
- ❑ Computer technology used in PDS teacher education program to **facilitate instruction** &/or staff development:
  - ■ telecommunications (e.g., e-mail, bulletin boards)
  - ■ computer assisted instruction
  - ■ interactive video
  - ■ desktop publishing
- ❑ Computer technology used to **facilitate collaboration** among PDS partners:
  - ■ interactive video
- ❑ Computer technology included in **subject matter** of teacher education &/or staff development curriculum of PDS participants:
  - ■ telecommunications (e.g., e-mail, bulletin boards)
  - ■ computer assisted instruction
  - ■ interactive video
  - ■ programming
- ❑ Policies of college with regard to hiring, tenure, promotion, or other aspects of college's reward structure, acknowledge PDS-related work
- ❑ Approximately 20-39% of department faculty participate in PDS-related work (planning or implementation)

TENNESSEE

Memphis State University

School	Campus School Memphis State University Memphis, TN 38152 Phone: (901) 678-2285	Newberry Elementary School 5540 Newberry Avenue Memphis, TN 38118 Phone: (901) 366-2530
Site Coordinator	Satomi Izumi Taylor	Marty Harrison, University Liasion
Starting Date	1993, Fall	1992, August
Grade Level	K-6	K-5
School Type	Professional Development School	Professional Development School
School	Coleman Elementary School 3210 Raleigh-Millington Memphis, TN 38128 Phone: (901) 385-4306	Raleigh Egypt Middle School 4215 Alice Ann Drive Memphis, TN 38128 Phone: (901) 385-4141
Site Coordinator	Lillian Whitney	Mrs. Bonnie Shields Cummings, University Liasion
Starting Date	1993, August	1992, August
Grade Level	K-6	6-8
School Type	Professional Development School	Professional Development School
School	Dyer County Central Elementary School 1400 Hornbrook Street Dyersburg, TN 38024 Phone: (901) 285-1337	Ross Elementary 4890 Ross Road Memphis, TN 38138 Phone: (901) 369-1990
Site Coordinator	Patricia Brooks	Dr. Lisa DeMeulle, Assistant Professor
Starting Date	1993, August	1993, September
Grade Level	K-6	K-5
School Type	Professional Development School	Professional Development School
School	Frayser Elementary School 1607 Dellwood Avenue Memphis, TN 38127 Phone: (901) 357-3840	
Site Coordinator	Dr. Vivian Gunn Morris	
Starting Date	1992, August	
Grade Level	K-6	
School Type	Professional Development School	
School	Lipman School Memphis State University Memphis, TN 38152 Phone: (901) 678-2285	
Site Coordinator	Satomi Izumi Taylor	
Starting Date	1993, Fall	
Grade Level	Infant-K	
School Type	Professional Practice School	

College/University	*Incarnate Word College*
Contact	Judith York, Ph.D., Director CEDE-Ctr. for Educational Development & Excellence Institute of Texan Cultures 801 South Bowie Street San Antonio, TX 78205 (210) 558-2313
Partners	Incarnate Word College ;Our Lady of the Lake University; St. Mary's University Trinity University; University of Texas - San Antonio Edgewood Independent School District (ISD); Harlandale ISD; North East ISD; Northside ISD; San Antonio ISD; South San Antonio ISD Alliance for Education; USAA
Affiliation	Texas Education Agency
Funding	university; school district; Texas Education Agency
Starting Date	1992, September
PDS Sites	Brewer Elementary School; Clark High School; Connell Middle School; Coronado Escobar Elementary School; Driscoll Middle School School; Emma Frey Elementary School; Gardendale Elementary School; Hawthorne Elementary School; Hutchins Elementary School; Jackson-Keller Elementary School; Kingsborough Middle School; Lamar Elementary School; Loma Park Elementary School; Mark Twain Middle School; Memorial High School; *Providence High School; Robert E. Lee High School; Rodriguez Elementary School; *St. Martin Hall School; *St. Peter Prince of the Apostles School; Travis Elementary School; Truman Middle School**

Program Features	❑ Preservice teachers assigned to PDSs in cohorts
	❑ College funding for PDS program from grants, discretionary funds, or other types of "soft money"
	❑ Release time, reduced course load, or other related arrangement made for college faculty actively involved with PDS sites
	❑ Computer technology used in PDS teacher education program to **facilitate instruction** &/or staff development:
	  ■ telecommunications (e.g., e-mail, bulletin boards)
	  ■ computer assisted instruction
	  ■ interactive video
	  ■ desktop publishing
	❑ Computer technology used to **facilitate collaboration** among PDS partners:
	  ■ telecommunications (e.g., e-mail, bulletin boards)
	  ■ computer assisted instruction
	  ■ interactive video
	  ■ desktop publishing

Incarnate Word College

Program Features

- ❑ Computer technology included in **subject matter** of teacher education &/or staff development curriculum of PDS participants:
  - ■ telecommunications (e.g., e-mail, bulletin boards)
  - ■ computer assisted instruction
  - ■ interactive video
  - ■ authoring systems
  - ■ desktop publishing
- ❑ Policies of college with regard to hiring, tenure, promotion, or other aspects of college's reward structure, acknowledge PDS-related work
- ❑ Approximate percentage of department faculty who participate in PDS-related work (planning or implementation):
  - ■ Incarnate Word College - 80-100%
  - ■ Our Lady of the Lake University - 80-100%
  - ■ St. Mary's University - 80-100%
  - ■ Trinity University - 80-100%
  - ■ University of Texas - San Antonio - 20-39%

Notes

* PDS sites that are private schools.

**Although Region 20 Education Service Center is also listed as a PDS site, the data received on this site were not presented in a format that allowed for either their inclusion in either the profiles of individual PDSs or in the statistical summaries.

Incarnate Word College

School	Brewer Elementary School 906 Merida Street San Antonio, TX 78207 Phone: (210) 433-2691	Emma Frey Elementary School 900 S. San Eduardo San Antonio, TX 78237 Phone: (210) 433-5673
Site Coordinator	Miriam Martinez	Sue Wortham
Starting Date	1992, September	1992, September
Grade Level	K-6	K-6
School Type	Professional Development School	Professional Development School
School	Clark High School 5150 Dezavala San Antonio, TX 78249 Phone: (210) 561-5150	Gardendale Elementary School 1731 Dahlgreen San Antonio, TX 78237 Phone: (210) 433-6552
Site Coordinator	Richard Diem	Gillian Cook
Starting Date	1993, September	1992, September
Grade Level	10-12	K-6
School Type	Professional Development School	Professional Development School
School	Connell Middle School 400 Hot Wells San Antonio, TX 78223 Phone: (210) 534-6511	Hawthorne Elementary School 115 W. Josephine San Antonio, TX 78212 Phone: (210) 733-1321
Site Coordinator	Rose Andrews	Bruce Frazee
Starting Date	1992, September	1992, September
Grade Level	6-8	K-6
School Type	Professional Development School	Professional Development School
School	Coronado Escobar Elementary School 5622 W. Durango Street San Antonio, TX 78237 Phone: (210) 433-5561	Hutchins Elementary School 1919 Hutchins Boulevard San Antonio, TX 78224 Phone: (210) 923-2521
Site Coordinator	Reynaldo Pierce	no information available
Starting Date	1992, September	1993, September
Grade Level	K-6	K-6
School Type	Professional Development School	Professional Development School
School	Driscoll Middle School 17150 Jones Maltsberger San Antonio, TX 78247 Phone: (210) 491-6450	Jackson-Keller Elementary School 1601 Jackson-Keller Road San Antonio, TX 78213 Phone: (210) 525-0971
Site Coordinator	Rose Andrews	Sharri Albright
Starting Date	1992, September	1992, September
Grade Level	6-8	K-5
School Type	Professional Development School	Professional Development School

Incarnate Word College

School	Kingsborough Middle School 422 Ashley San Antonio, TX 78221 Phone: (210) 921-4428	Providence High School 1215 N. St. Mary's San Antonio, TX 78215 Phone: (210) 224-6651
Site Coordinator	Gillian Cook	Jose Hernandez
Starting Date	1993, September	1992, September
Grade Level	7-9	10-12
School Type	Professional Development School	Partner School
School	Lamar Elementary School 201 Parland Place San Antonio, TX 78209 Phone: (210) 822-7823	Robert E. Lee High School 1400 Jacksonville-Keller Road San Antonio, TX 78213 Phone: (210) 341-7761
Site Coordinator	no information available	Laurie Bergner
Starting Date	1992, September	1992, September
Grade Level	K-6	9-12
School Type	Professional Development School	Professional Development School
School	Loma Park Elementary School 400 Aurora San Antonio, TX 78228 Phone: (210) 433-4141	Rodriguez Elementary School 3626 W. Durango San Antonio, TX 78205 Phone: (210) 433-4251
Site Coordinator	Laurie Stevens	Trace Mahbubani
Starting Date	1992, September	1992, September
Grade Level	K-5	K-6
School Type	Professional Development School	Professional Development School
School	Mark Twain Middle School 2411 San Pedro Avenue San Antonio, TX 78212 Phone: (210) 732-4641	St. Martin Hall 411 S W 24th San Antonio, TX 78207 Phone: (210) 434-6711
Site Coordinator	David Flinders	Walt Garrison
Starting Date	1992, September	1992, September
Grade Level	6-8	PreK-8
School Type	Professional Development School	Professional Development School
School	Memorial High School 1227 Memorial Drive San Antonio, TX 78228 Phone: (210) 433-9434	St. Peter Prince of the Apostles 112 Marcia Place San Antonio, TX 78209 Phone: (210) 824-3171
Site Coordinator	Tom Levine	Rose Andrews
Starting Date	1992, September	1992, September
Grade Level	9-12	K-8
School Type	Professional Development School	Parrtner School

Incarnate Word College

School	Travis Elementary School 1915 N. Main San Antonio, TX 78212 Phone: (210) 733-1911
Site Coordinator	Sue Wortham
Starting Date	1992, September
Grade Level	K-6
School Type	Professional Development School

School	Truman Middle School 1018 S W 34th Street San Antonio, TX 78228 Phone: (210) 433-8651
Site Coordinator	Wanda Leyva
Starting Date	1992, September
Grade Level	6-8
School Type	Partner School

College/University	*Lubbock Christian University*
Contact	Dr. Joyce Hardin Lubbock Christian University 5601 W. 19th Street Lubbock, TX 79407 Phone: (806) 796-8800 Fax: (806) 796-0048
Partners	Lubbock Christian University Lubbock Independent School District (ISD); Friendship ISD
Affiliation	Panhandle/South Plains Center for Professional Development & Technology
Funding	university; school district; Panhandle/South Plains Center for Professional Development & Technology
Starting Date	1992, Fall
PDS Sites	Brown Elementary School; Hardwick Elementary School; Parkway Elementary School

Program Features

- ❏ Preservice teachers assigned to PDSs in cohorts
- ❏ Computer technology used in PDS teacher education program to **facilitate instruction** &/or staff development:
  - ■ telecommunications (e.g., e-mail, bulletin boards)
  - ■ computer assisted instruction
  - ■ interactive video
  - ■ desktop publishing
- ❏ Computer technology used to **facilitate collaboration** among PDS partners:
  - ■ telecommunications (e.g., e-mail, bulletin boards)
  - ■ computer assisted instruction
  - ■ interactive video
  - ■ desktop publishing
- ❏ Computer technology included in **subject matter** of teacher education &/or staff development curriculum of PDS participants:
  - ■ telecommunications (e.g., e-mail, bulletin boards)
  - ■ computer assisted instruction
  - ■ interactive video
- ❏ Approximately 80-100% of department faculty participate in PDS-related work (planning or implementation)

TEXAS

Lubbock Christian University

School	Brown Elementary School 2315 36th Lubbock, TX 79412 Phone: (806) 766-0833
Site Coordinator	Linda Willett
Starting Date	1992, Fall
Grade Level	K-6
School Type	Professional Development School
School	Hardwick Elementary School 1420 Chicago Lubbock, TX 79416 Phone: (806) 766-0844
Site Coordinator	Dr. Sam Ayers
Starting Date	1992, Fall
Grade Level	K-6
School Type	Professional Development School
School	Parkway Elementary School 406 N. Zenith Lubbock, TX 79403 Phone: (806) 766-1811
Site Coordinator	Brenda Gipson
Starting Date	1992, Fall
Grade Level	K-6
School Type	Professional Development School

College/University	*McMurray University*
Contact	Dr. Lewis E. Lemmond McMurray Station Box 578 McMurray University Abilene, TX 79697 Phone: (915) 691-6407 Fax: (915) 691-6599
Partners	McMurray University, Abilene Christian University, Hardin-Simmons University; Howard Payne University Abilene Independent School District (ISD); Brown Wood ISD; Wylie ISD; Region 14 Education Service Center
Funding	state; Sid W. Richardson Foundation
Starting Date	1993, September
PDS Sites	no information available*

Program Features	❏ Preservice teachers assigned to PDSs in cohorts
	❏ College funding for PDS program from grants, discretionary funds, or other types of "soft money"
	❏ Release time, reduced course load, or other related arrangement made for college faculty actively involved with PDS sites
	❏ Computer technology used in PDS teacher education program to **facilitate instruction** &/or staff development:
	  ■ telecommunications (e.g., e-mail, bulletin boards)
	  ■ computer assisted instruction
	  ■ desktop publishing
	❏ Computer technology used to **facilitate collaboration** among PDS partners:
	  ■ telecommunications (e.g., e-mail, bulletin boards)
	  ■ computer assisted instruction
	  ■ desktop publishing
	❏ Computer technology included in **subject matter** of teacher education &/or staff development curriculum of PDS participants:
	  ■ telecommunications (e.g., e-mail, bulletin boards)
	  ■ computer assisted instruction
	  ■ programming
	  ■ desktop publishing
	❏ Approximately 0-19% of department faculty participate in PDS-related work (planning or implementation)

Note	*The data received about the PDS sites were not presented in a format that allowed for their inclusion in the profiles of individual PDSs.

TEXAS

College/University

Contact

Partners

Affiliation

Funding

Starting Date

PDS Sites

Program Features

Southwest Texas State University

Pat Curtin or Patrice Werner
Southwest Texas State University
Center for Professional Development & Technology
1225 Hwy 123
San Marcos, TX 78667
(512) 396-6878

Southwest Texas State University
San Marcos Consolidated Independent School District (ISD); Elgin ISD;
Austin ISD; Region 13 Education Service Center

Texas Education Agency

school district; Texas Education Agency; Century Telephone of San Marcos

1992, September

Bowie Elementary School; Elgin Middle School; Goodnight Junior High
School; Highland Park Elementary School

❏ Preservice teachers assigned to PDSs in cohorts
❏ College funding for PDS program from grants, discretionary funds, or
  other types of "soft money"
❏ Release time, reduced course load, or other related arrangement made
  for college faculty actively involved with PDS sites
❏ Computer technology used in PDS teacher education program to
  facilitate instruction &/or staff development:
  ■ telecommunications (e.g., e-mail, bulletin boards)
  ■ computer assisted instruction
  ■ interactive video
  ■ desktop publishing
❏ Computer technology used to **facilitate collaboration** among PDS
  partners:
  ■ telecommunications (e.g., e-mail, bulletin boards)
  ■ computer assisted instruction
  ■ interactive video
  ■ desktop publishing
❏ Computer technology included in **subject matter** of teacher education
  &/or staff development curriculum of PDS participants:
  ■ telecommunications (e.g., e-mail, bulletin boards)
  ■ computer assisted instruction
  ■ interactive video
  ■ programming
  ■ authoring systems
  ■ desktop publishing
❏ Policies of college with regard to hiring, tenure, promotion, or other
  aspects of college's reward structure, acknowledge PDS-related work
❏ Approximately 80-100% of department faculty participate in PDS-
  related work (planning or implementation)

114

TEXAS

Southwest Texas State University

School	Bowie Elementary School 1225 Highway 123 San Marcos, TX 78666 Phone: (512) 396-6880
Site Coordinator	Pat Curtin
Starting Date	1992, September
Grade Level	3-5
School Type	Professional Development School
School	Elgin Middle School 510 S. Avenue F Elgin, TX 78621 Phone: (512) 281-3382
Site Coordinator	Pat Curtin
Starting Date	1992, September
Grade Level	6-8
School Type	Professional Development School
School	Goodnight Junior High School P.O. Box 1087 San Marcos, TX 78667 Phone: (512) 353-6760
Site Coordinator	Pat Curtin
Starting Date	1992, September
Grade Level	7-8
School Type	Professional Development School
School	Highland Park Elementary School 4900 Fairview Austin, TX 78731 Phone: (512) 459-6313
Site Coordinator	Pat Curtin
Starting Date	1992, September
Grade Level	K-5
School Type	Professional Development School

College/University

Texas A&M International University

Contact

Dr. Irene Rodriguez
Texas A&M International University
1 West End Washington Street
Laredo, TX 78041
(210) 722-8001

Partners

Texas A&M International University; Laredo Community College
Laredo Independent School District (ISD); United ISD; Zapata ISD; Cotulla
ISD; Region 1 Education Service Center

Funding

university; school district; Texas Education Agency

Starting Date

1992, September

PDS Sites

No information available*

Program Features

❑ Preservice teachers assigned to PDSs in cohorts
❑ College funding for PDS program from grants, discretionary funds, or
other types of "soft money"
❑ Release time, reduced course load, or other related arrangement made
for college faculty actively involved with PDS sites
❑ Computer technology used in PDS teacher education program to
facilitate instruction &/or staff development:
  ■ telecommunications (e.g., e-mail, bulletin boards)
  ■ computer assisted instruction
❑ Computer technology used to **facilitate collaboration** among PDS
partners:
  ■ telecommunications (e.g., e-mail, bulletin boards)
  ■ computer assisted instruction
❑ Computer technology included in **subject matter** of teacher education
&/or staff development curriculum of PDS participants:
  ■ telecommunications (e.g., e-mail, bulletin boards)
  ■ computer assisted instruction
  ■ authoring systems
  ■ desktop publishing
❑ Approximately 0-19% of department faculty participate in PDS-related
work (planning or implementation)

Note

*The data received about the PDS sites were not presented in a format that
allowed for their inclusion in the profiles of individual PDSs.

116

College/University	*Texas A&M University*
Contact	Nancy James Learning to Teach in Inner-City Schools (LTICS) College of Education - Texas A&M University 2121 West Holcombe, Suite 214G Houston, TX 77030 (713) 677-7712
Partners	Texas A&M University; University of Houston Houston Independent School District
Affiliation	National Diffusion Network
Funding	university; school district
Starting Date	1988, Fall
PDS Sites	Houston Teaching Academy

Program Features

❑ Preservice teachers assigned to PDSs in cohorts
❑ College funding for PDS program from grants, discretionary funds, or other types of "soft money"
❑ Release time, reduced course load, or other related arrangement made for college faculty actively involved with PDS sites
❑ Computer technology used in PDS teacher education program to **facilitate instruction** &/or staff development:
  ■ computer assisted instruction
  ■ desktop publishing
❑ Computer technology used to **facilitate collaboration** among PDS partners:
  ■ desktop publishing
❑ Computer technology included in **subject matter** of teacher education &/or staff development curriculum of PDS participants:
  ■ computer assisted instruction
  ■ desktop publishing
❑ Approximately 0-19% of department faculty participate in PDS-related work (planning or implementation)

TEXAS

Texas A & M University

School	Houston Teaching Academy
	1101 Taft
	Houston, TX 77019
	Phone: (713) 529-1186
Site Coordinator	Loretta Henderson
Starting Date	1988, Fall
Grade Level	K-8
School Type	Professional Development School

TEXAS

College/University	*Texas Tech University*
Contact	Dr. Charles A. Reavis Texas Tech University College of Education Box 41071 Lubbock, TX 79409-1071 (806) 742-1956
Partners	Texas Tech University Lubbock Independent School District (ISD); Wilson ISD
Affiliation	West Texas Teacher Education Collaborative
Funding	Sid W. Richardson Foundation
Starting Date	1991, September
PDS Sites	Bayless Elementary School; Hutchinson Junior High School; Lubbock High School ; Mackenzie Junior High School; Ramirez Elementary School; Wilson Independent School District

Program Features

- ❑ Preservice teachers assigned to PDSs in cohorts
- ❑ College funding for PDS program from grants, discretionary funds, or other types of "soft money"
- ❑ Release time, reduced course load, or other related arrangement made for college faculty actively involved with PDS sites
- ❑ Computer technology used in PDS teacher education program to **facilitate instruction** &/or staff development:
  - ■ computer assisted instruction
- ❑ Computer technology included in **subject matter** of teacher education &/or staff development curriculum of PDS participants:
  - ■ computer assisted instruction
- ❑ Approximately 20-39% of department faculty participate in PDS-related work (planning or implementation)

TEXAS

Texas Tech University

School	Bayless Elementary School 2115 58th Street Lubbock, TX 79412 Phone: (806) 766-1655	Wilson ISD P.O. Box 9 Wilson, TX 79381 Phone: (806) 628-6201
Site Coordinator	David Doyle	Bob Williams (high school) Kelly Hirt (elementary)
Starting Date	1991, September	1991, September
Grade Level	K-6	K-12
School Type	Professional Development School	Professional Development School

School	Hutchinson Junior High School 3102 Canton Avenue Lubbock, TX 79410 Phone: (806) 766-0755
Site Coordinator	Neal Logan
Starting Date	1991, September
Grade Level	7-9
School Type	Professional Development School

School	Lubbock High School 2004 19th Street Lubbock, TX 79400 Phone: (806) 766-1444
Site Coordinator	Rose Mediano
Starting Date	1991, September
Grade Level	10-12
School Type	Professional Development School

School	Mackenzie Junior High School 5402 12th Street Lubbock, TX 79416 Phone: (806) 766-0777
Site Coordinator	Beth Fischenich
Starting Date	1991, September
Grade Level	7-9
School Type	Professional Development School

School	Ramirez Elementary School 702 Avenue T Lubbock, TX 79401 Phone: (806) 766-1833
Site Coordinator	Lucy Brown
Starting Date	1991, September
Grade Level	K-6
School Type	Professional Development School

TEXAS

College/University	*University of Houston*
Contact	W. Robert Houston University of Houston 466 Farrish Hall Houston, TX 77204-5874 Phone: (713) 743-5049 Fax: (713) 743-4989
Partners	University of Houston; University of St. Thomas; Houston Baptist University Alief Independent School District (ISD); Houston ISD; Spring Branch ISD; Region 4 Education Service Center; Harris County Dept. of Education
Affiliation	Texas Education Agency
Funding	Texas Education Agency
Starting Date	1993, October
PDS Sites	Ben Milam PDTC; Hamilton PDTC; Kennedy PDTC; Lockhart PDTC; Rufus Cage Professional Development & Technology Center (PDTC); Westwood PDTC; Woodview PDTC; Valley Oaks PDTC

Program Features

- ❑ Preservice teachers assigned to PDSs in cohorts
- ❑ College funding for PDS program from grants, discretionary funds, or other types of "soft money"
- ❑ Release time, reduced course load, or other related arrangement made for college faculty actively involved with PDS sites
- ❑ Computer technology used in PDS teacher education program to **facilitate instruction** &/or staff development:
    - ■ telecommunications (e.g., e-mail, bulletin boards)
    - ■ computer assisted instruction
    - ■ desktop publishing
- ❑ Computer technology used to **facilitate collaboration** among PDS partners:
    - ■ telecommunications (e.g., e-mail, bulletin boards)
    - ■ computer assisted instruction
    - ■ interactive video
    - ■ desktop publishing
- ❑ Computer technology included in **subject matter** of teacher education &/or staff development curriculum of PDS participants:
    - ■ telecommunications (e.g., e-mail, bulletin boards)
    - ■ computer assisted instruction
    - ■ interactive video
    - ■ programming
    - ■ authoring systems
- ❑ Approximately 20-39% of department faculty participate in PDS-related work (planning or implementation)

121

TEXAS

University of Houston

School	Ben Milam Professional Development & Technology Center 1100 Roy Houston, TX 77007 Phone: (713) 862-9482	Rufus Cage Professional Development & Technology Center 4528 Leeland Houston, TX 77023 Phone: (713) 926-9288
Site Coordinator	Frances Houser-Rogers	Steven Amstutz
Starting Date	1993, September	1993, September
Grade Level	K-6	K-6
School Type	Professional Development School	Professional Development School
School	Hamilton Professional Development & Technology Center 139 East 20th Street Houston, TX 77008 Phone: (713) 861-0913	Valley Oaks Professional Development & Technology Center 8390 Westview Houston, TX 77095 Phone: (713) 465-9119
Site Coordinator	Diana Mulet	Vicky Hardway
Starting Date	1993, September	1993, September
Grade Level	6-8	K-6
School Type	Professional Development School	Professional Development School
School	Kennedy Professional Devlopment & Technology Center 10200 Huntington Place Houston, TX 77099 Phone: (713) 983-8338	Westwood Professional Development & Technology Center 2100 Shadowdale Houston, TX 77043 Phone: (713) 486-2426
Site Coordinator	Mary Hosking	Alton Frailey
Starting Date	1993, September	1993, September
Grade Level	K-6	K-6
School Type	Professional Development School	Professional Development School
School	Lockhart Professional Development & Technology Center 3501 Southmore Houston, TX 77004 Phone: (713) 522-8593	Woodview Professional Development & Technology Center 9749 Cedardale Houston, TX 77055 Phone: (713) 465-7326
Site Coordinator	Mary Ann Wilson	Barbara Hadley
Starting Date	1993, September	1993, September
Grade Level	K-6	K-6
School Type	Professional Development School	Professional Development School

College/University	*University of Houston - Clear Lake*
Contact	Nolie Mayo University of Houston - Clear Lake Box 245, 2700 Bay Area Boulevard Houston, TX 77058 (713) 283-3579
Partners	University of Houston - Clear Lake Alvin Independent School District (ISD); Goose Creek ISD; Texas City ISD; Region 4 Education Service Center
Affiliation	Texas Education Agency
Funding	university; school district; IBM
Starting Date	1994, September
PDS Sites	Alvin Junior High School; Central Middle School; George Washington Carver Elementary School

Program Features

❑ Preservice teachers assigned to PDSs in cohorts
❑ College funding for PDS program from grants, discretionary funds, or other types of "soft money"
❑ Release time, reduced course load, or other related arrangement made for college faculty actively involved with PDS sites
❑ Computer technology used in PDS teacher education program to **facilitate instruction** &/or staff development:
  ■ telecommunications (e.g., e-mail, bulletin boards)
  ■ computer assisted instruction
  ■ interactive video
  ■ desktop publishing
❑ Computer technology used to **facilitate collaboratio**n among PDSpartners:
  ■ telecommunications (e.g., e-mail, bulletin boards)
  ■ computer assisted instruction
  ■ desktop publishing
❑ Computer technology included in **subject matter** of teacher education &/or staff development curriculum of PDS participants:
  ■ telecommunications (e.g., e-mail, bulletin boards)
  ■ computer assisted instruction
  ■ interactive video
  ■ authoring systems
  ■ desktop publishing
❑ Policies of college with regard to hiring, tenure, promotion, or other aspects of college's reward structure, acknowledge PDS-related work
❑ Approximately 20-39% of department faculty participate in PDS-related work (planning or implementation)

TEXAS

University of Houston - Clear Lake

School	Alvin Junior High School 2301 W. South Alvin, TX 77511 Phone: (713) 331-1416
Site Coordinator	Susan Cornell
Starting Date	1993, September
Grade Level	7-8
School Type	Professional Development School
School	Central Middle School 3014 Sealy Galveston, TX 77554 Phone: (409) 765-2102
Site Coordinator	Karen Whisnand
Starting Date	1993, September
Grade Level	7-9
School Type	Professional Development School
School	George Washington Carver Elementary School 800 Carver Baytown, TX 77520 Phone: (713) 420-4600
Site Coordinator	Annese Jones
Starting Date	1993, September
Grade Level	PreK-5
School Type	Professional Development School

College/University	*University of Texas - El Paso*
Contact	Dr. Deborah J. Miller-Wood El Paso Center for Professional Development & Technology University of Texas - El Paso College of Education - 500 West University Avenue El Paso, TX 79968-0569 (915) 747-5253
Partners	University of Texas - El Paso Socorro Independent School District (ISD); El Paso ISD; Ysleta ISD; Region 19 Education Service Center El Paso Collaborative for Academic Excellence
Affiliation	National Network for Educational Renewal; Texas Education Agency
Funding	school district; Coca-Cola; Exxon; PEW Charitable; Apple; Phillip Morris
Starting Date	1993, September
PDS Sites	H. D. Hilley Elementary School; Lamar Elementary School; Riverside High School; Wiggs Middle School; Ysleta Elementary School;
Program Features	

- ❑ Preservice teachers assigned to PDSs in cohorts
- ❑ College funding for PDS program from grants, discretionary funds, or other types of "soft money"
- ❑ Release time, reduced course load, or other related arrangement made for college faculty actively involved with PDS sites
- ❑ Computer technology used in PDS teacher education program to **facilitate instruction** &/or staff development:
  - ■ desktop publishing
- ❑ Computer technology used to **facilitate collaboration** among PDS partners:
  - ■ computer assisted instruction
  - ■ desktop publishing
- ❑ Computer technology included in **subject matter** of teacher education &/or staff development curriculum of PDS participants:
  - ■ desktop publishing
- ❑ Policies of college with regard to hiring, tenure, promotion, or other aspects of college's reward structure, acknowledge PDS-related work
- ❑ Approximately 20-39% of department faculty participate in PDS-related work (planning or implementation)

TEXAS

University of Texas - El Paso

School	H. D. Hiley Elementary School 693 N. Rio Vista El Paso, TX 79927 Phone: (915) 860-3770
Site Coordinator	Maria Luisa Niestas
Starting Date	1993, September
Grade Level	PreK-5
School Type	Professional Development School

School	Lamar Elementary School 1440 E. Cliff Street El Paso, TX 79902 Phone: (915) 533-9883
Site Coordinator	Sara Smith
Starting Date	1993, September
Grade Level	PreK-5
School Type	Professional Development School

School	Riverside High School 301 Midway Drive El Paso, TX 79915 Phone: (915) 778-5491
Site Coordinator	Ralph Ornelas
Starting Date	1993, September
Grade Level	9-12
School Type	Professional Development School

School	Wiggs Middle School 1300 Circle El Paso, TX 79902 Phone: (915) 544-6768
Site Coordinator	Carmen Stearns
Starting Date	1993, September
Grade Level	6-8
School Type	Professional Development School

School	Ysleta Elementary School 9009 Alameda Avenue El Paso, TX 79907 Phone: (915) 859-8121
Site Coordinator	Dolores DeAvila
Starting Date	1993, September
Grade Level	PreK-6
School Type	Professional Development School

UTAH

College/University

Brigham Young University

Contact

Robert S. Patterson, Dean
Brigham Young University
343 MCKB
Provo, UT 84602
(801) 378-3695

Partners

Brigham Young University
Wasatch, Alpine, Provo, Nebo, and Jordan School Districts

Affiliation

National Network for Educational Renewal

Funding

university; school district

Starting Date

1984

PDS Sites

Alpine Elementary School; Aspen Elementary School; Barratt Elementary School; Canyon Crest Elementary School; Cascade Elementary School; Copperview Elementary School; Cottonwood Heights Elementary School; Draper Elementary School; Edgemont Elementary School; Franklin Elementary School; Geneva Elementary School; Jordan Ridge Elementary School; Larsen Elementary School; Highland Elementary School; Jordan Ridge Elementary School; Larsen Elementary School; Lindon Elementary School; Manila Elementary School; Mapleton Elementary School; Maeser Elementary School; Parkview Elementary School; Rock Canyon Elementary School; Rees Elementary School; Sage Creek Elementary School; Salem Elementary School; Santaquin Elementary School; Shelley Elementary School; Southland Elementary School; Sprucewood Elementary School; Sunrise Elementary School; Sunset View Elementary School; Taylor Elementary School; Timpanogos Elementary School; Westmore Elementary School; Westridge Elementary School; Willow Canyon Elementary School; Wilson Elementary School*

Program Features

❑ Preservice teachers assigned to PDSs in cohorts
❑ College funding for PDS program from grants, discretionary funds, or other types of "soft money"
❑ Release time, reduced course load, or other related arrangement made for college faculty actively involved with PDS sites
❑ Computer technology used in PDS teacher education program to **facilitate instruction** & /or staff development:
　■ telecommunications (e.g., e-mail, bulletin boards)
　■ computer assisted instruction
　■ desktop publishing
❑ Computer technology used to **facilitate collaboration** among PDS partners:
　■ telecommunications (e.g., e-mail, bulletin boards)
　■ computer assisted instruction
　■ desktop publishing

127

Brigham Young University

Program Features

Note

❑ Computer technology included in **subject matter** of teacher education &/or staff development curriculum of PDS participants:
  ■ telecommunications (e.g., e-mail, bulletin boards)
  ■ computer assisted instruction
  ■ authoring systems
  ■ desktop publishing
❑ Policies of college with regard to hiring, tenure, promotion, or other aspects of college's reward structure, acknowledge PDS-related work
❑ Approximately 60-79% of department faculty participate in PDS-related work (planning or implementation)

*The university reported that there are 43 PDS sites in this partnership, but provided information for only 37 of them.

Brigham Young University

School	Alpine Elementary School 400 E 300 N Alpine, UT 84004 Phone: (801) 756-8525	Copperview Elementary School 8449 S 150 W Midvale, UT 84047 Phone: (801) 565-7440
Site Coordinator	Paul Rasband	Rick Dumont
Starting Date	1987, August	1993, August
Grade Level	K-6	K-6
School Type	Partner School	no information available

School	Aspen Elementary School 945 W 2000 N Orem, UT 84057 Phone: (801) 227-8700	Cottonwood Heights Elementary School 2515 E 7600 S Salt Lake City, UT 84121 Phone: (801) 944-2934
Site Coordinator	Stan Butler	Frank Shaw
Starting Date	1993, September	no information available
Grade Level	K-6	K-6
School Type	Partner School	Partner School

School	Barratt Elementary School 168 N 900 E American Fork, UT 84003 Phone: (801) 756-8528	Draper Elementary School 1080 E 12660 S Draper, UT 84020 Phone: (801)572-7005
Site Coordinator	John Jesse, Principal	Ron Jarrett
Starting Date	1987, August	no information available
Grade Level	K-6	K-6
School Type	Partner School	Partner School

School	Canyon Crest Elementary School 4664 N Canyon Road Provo, UT 84604 Phone: (801) 221-9873	Edgemont Elementary School 550 E 3600 S Provo, UT 34604 Phone: (801) 221-9984
Site Coordinator	Ray Morgan	Marjean Bingham
Starting Date	1987	no information available
Grade Level	K-6	K-6
School Type	Partner School	Partner School

School	Cascade Elementary School 160 N 800 E Orem, UT 84057 Phone: (801) 227-8707	Franklin Elementary School 355 S 700 W Provo, UT 84601 Phone: (801) 374-4925
Site Coordinator	Nancy Brooks	Marlin Palmer
Starting Date	1988, August	no information available
Grade Level	K-5	K-6
School Type	Partner School	Partner School

Brigham Young University

School	Geneva Elementary School 400 N 665 W Orem, UT 84057 Phone: (801) 227-8714	Larsen Elementary School 1175 E Flonette Spanish Fork, UT 84660 Phone: (801) 798-4035
Site Coordinator	Wayne Crabb	Sterling Argyle
Starting Date	1993, September	no information available
Grade Level	K-6	K-6
School Type	Partner School	Professional Development School
School	Goshen Elementary School 60 N Center Goshen, UT 84633 Phone: (801) 667-3361	Lindon Elementary School 30 N Main Lindon, UT 84062 Phone: (801) 785-8717
Site Coordinator	Garth Bird	Jeanne Holdaway
Starting Date	no information available	1992, August
Grade Level	K-7	K-6
School Type	Partner School	Partner School
School	Grant Elementary School 105 S 400 E Springville, UT 84663 Phone: (801) 489-2840	Maeser Elementary School 150 S 500 E Provo, UT 84601 Phone: (801) 374-4945
Site Coordinator	Mark Balzotti	Kim Langton
Starting Date	no information available	no information available
Grade Level	K-5	K-6
School Type	Partner School	Partner School
School	Highland Elementary School 10865 N 16000 W Highland, UT 84003 Phone: (801) 756-8537	Manila Elementary School 1726 N 600 W Pleasant Grove, UT 84062 Phone: (801) 785-8720
Site Coordinator	Kathy Whitbeck	John Burton
Starting Date	1991, August	no information available
Grade Level	K-5	K-6
School Type	Partner School	Partner School
School	Jordan Ridge Elementary School 2936 W 9800 S South Jordan, UT 84065 Phone: (801) 254-8025	Mapleton Elementary School 120 W Maple Mapleton, UT 84663 Phone: (801) 489-2850
Site Coordinator	Kreig Kelley	J. Lynn Jones
Starting Date	no information available	1989
Grade Level	K-6	K-5
School Type	Partner School	Partner School

Brigham Young University

School	Parkview Elementary School 360 S 1st E Payson, UT 84651 Phone: (801) 465-6010	Santaquin Elementary School 25 S 400 W Santaquin, UT 84655 Phone: (801) 754-3611
Site Coordinator	Ryan Creer	Kim Bartlow
Starting Date	no information available	no information available
Grade Level	K-5	K-7
School Type	Partner School	Partner School
School	Rees Elementary School 185 E 400 No Spanish Fork, UT 84660 Phone: (801) 798-4055	Shelley Elementary School 550 N 200 W American Fork, UT 84003 Phone: (801) 756-8540
Site Coordinator	Ray Mecham	Dennis Duffy
Starting Date	no information available	1993, August
Grade Level	K-6	K-5
School Type	Partner School	Partner School
School	Rock Canyon Elementary School 2405 N 650 E Provo, UT 84604 Phone: (801) 374-4935	Southland Elementary School 12675 S 2700 W Riverton, UT 84065 Phone: (801) 254-8047
Site Coordinator	Terry Shoemaker	Lyn Burningham
Starting Date	1990, September	no information available
Grade Level	K-6	K-6
School Type	Partner School	Partner School
School	Sage Creek Elementary School 1050 S 700 E Springville, UT 84663 Phone: -	Sprucewood Elementary School 12025 S 1000 E Sandy, UT 84092 Phone: (801) 572-7077
Site Coordinator	no information available	Susan Turner
Starting Date	no information available	no information available
Grade Level	K-5	K-6
School Type	Partner School	Partner School
School	Salem Elementary School 140 W 100 S Salem, UT 84653 Phone: (801) 423-1182	Sunrise Elementary School 1520 E 11265 S Sandy, UT 84092 Phone: (801) 572-7016
Site Coordinator	Brent Hawkins	Doree Strauss
Starting Date	no information available	1993, August
Grade Level	K-5	K-6
School Type	Partner School	Partner School

UTAH

Brigham Young University

School	Sunset View Elementary School 525 S 16th W Provo, UT 84604 Phone: (801) 374-4950	Willow Canyon Elementary School 9650 S 1700 E Sandy, UT 84092 Phone: (801) 572-7020
Site Coordinator	Cindy Wright, Principal	Spencer Young
Starting Date	no information available	no information available
Grade Level	no information available	K-6
School Type	no information available	Partner School
School	Taylor Elementary School 40 S 5th W Payson, UT 84651 Phone: (801) 465-6050	Wilson Elementary School 590 W 5th S Payson, UT 84651 Phone: (801) 465-6060
Site Coordinator	Lynette Neff	Roger Bushman
Starting Date	no information available	no information available
Grade Level	K-6	no information available
School Type	Partner School	no information available
School	Timpanogos Elementary School 449 N 5th W Provo, UT 84601 Phone: (801) 374-4955	
Site Coordinator	Rosemarie Smith	
Starting Date	no information available	
Grade Level	K-6	
School Type	Partner School	
School	Westmore Elementary School 1150 S Main Orem, UT 84058 Phone: (801) 227-8742	
Site Coordinator	Jim Melville	
Starting Date	1993, August	
Grade Level	no information available	
School Type	no information available	
School	Westridge Elementary School 1720 W 1460 N Provo, UT 84604 Phone: (801) 374-4870	
Site Coordinator	John Bone	
Starting Date	no information available	
Grade Level	K-6	
School Type	Partner School	

UTAH

College/University	*University of Utah*
Contact	Dr. Nedra A. Crow University of Utah GSE, 225 MBH Salt Lake City, UT 84112 (801) 581-8221
Partners	University of Utah Davis, Salt Lake City, Granite, Murray, and Jordan School Districts Utah Education Asssociation
Affiliation	Holmes Group
Funding	university; school district
Starting Date	1987, September
PDS Sites	Bountiful Elementary School; Eisenhower Junior High School; Granger High School; Highland High School; Nibley Park Elementary School; Washington Elementary School
Program Features	

❑ Preservice teachers assigned to PDSs in cohorts
❑ College funding for PDS program from grants, discretionary funds, or other types of "soft money"
❑ Release time, reduced course load, or other related arrangement made for college faculty actively involved with PDS sites
❑ Computer technology used in PDS teacher education program to **facilitate instruction** &/or staff development:
   ■ telecommunications (e.g., e-mail, bulletin boards)
   ■ computer assisted instruction
   ■ desktop publishing
❑ Computer technology used to **facilitate collaboration** among PDS partners:
   ■ telecommunications (e.g., e-mail, bulletin boards)
   ■ computer assisted instruction
   ■ desktop publishing
❑ Computer technology included in **subject matter** of teacher education &/or staff development curriculum of PDS participants:
   ■ telecommunications (e.g., e-mail, bulletin boards)
   ■ computer assisted instruction
   ■ interactive video
   ■ programming
   ■ authoring systems
   ■ desktop publishing
❑ Approximately 80-100% of department faculty participate in PDS-related work (planning or implementation)

UTAH

University of Utah

School	Bountiful Elementary School 1620 South 50 West Bountiful, UT 84010 Phone: (801) 299-2002	Washington Elementary School - Exemplary Practice School 420 N 200 W Salt Lake City, UT 84103 Phone: (801) 533-3072
Site Coordinator	Ellen Stantus, Principal	Dr. Carol Lubomudrov
Starting Date	1990, September	1991, September
Grade Level	K-6	K-6
School Type	Clinical School	Partner School

School	Eisenhower Junior High School 4351 S. Redwood Road Salt Lake City, UT 84123 Phone: (801) 263-6165
Site Coordinator	Larry Wilde
Starting Date	1990, September
Grade Level	7-9
School Type	Professional Development School

School	Granger High School 3690 South 3600 W West Valley City, UT 84119 Phone: (801) 964-7600
Site Coordinator	Danny Talbot, Principal
Starting Date	1990, September
Grade Level	10-12
School Type	Professional Development School

School	Highland High School 2166 South 1700 E Salt Lake City, UT 84106 Phone: (801) 484-4343
Site Coordinator	Hillary Bertinollie
Starting Date	1990, September
Grade Level	10-12
School Type	Professional Development School

School	Nibley Park Elementary School 2785 South 800 E Salt Lake City, UT 84106 Phone: (801) 481-4842
Site Coordinator	Jake Larson, Principal
Starting Date	1990, September
Grade Level	K-6
School Type	Professional Development School

VIRGINIA

College/University	*University of Virginia*
Contact	Greta Morine-Dershimer University of Virginia Curry School of Education 405 Emmett Street Charlottesville, VA 22901 (804) 924-0748
Partners	University of Virginia Charlottesville Public School District
Funding	Xerox Foundation
Starting Date	1989, September
PDS Sites	Jackson-Via Elementary School
Program Features	

- ❏ Preservice teachers assigned to PDSs in cohorts
- ❏ College funding for PDS program from grants, discretionary funds, or other types of "soft money"
- ❏ Release time, reduced course load, or other related arrangement made for college faculty actively involved with PDS sites
- ❏ Computer technology used in PDS teacher education program to **facilitate instruction** &/or staff development:
  - ■ telecommunications (e.g., e-mail, bulletin boards)
- ❏ Computer technology used to **facilitate collaboration** among PDS partners:
  - ■ telecommunications (e.g., e-mail, bulletin boards)
- ❏ Computer technology included in **subject matter** of teacher education &/or staff development curriculum of PDS participants:
  - ■ telecommunications (e.g., e-mail, bulletin boards)
  - ■ computer assisted instruction
- ❏ Policies of college with regard to hiring, tenure, promotion, or other aspects of college's reward structure, acknowledge PDS-related work
- ❏ Approximately 0-19% of department faculty participate in PDS-related work (planning or implementation)

135

VIRGINIA

University of Virginia

School	Jackson-Via Elementary School
	508 Harris Street
	Charlottesville, VA 22903
	Phone: (804) 295-3161
Site Coordinator	Nancy Lambert
Starting Date	1989, September
Grade Level	K-4
School Type	Professional Development School

College/University

Contact

Partners

Funding

Starting Date

PDS Sites

Program Features

Virginia Commonwealth University

Alan McLeod
Virginia Commonwealth University
Box 842020
Richmond, VA 23284-2020
(804) 367-1324

Virginia Commonwealth University
Richmond City Public School Districts

university; school district

1993, June

Whitcomb Model Elementary School

❑   Preservice teachers assigned to PDSs in cohorts
❑   College funding for PDS program from grants, discretionary funds, or
     other types of "soft money"
❑   Computer technology used in PDS teacher education program to
     facilitate instruction &/or staff development:
     ■   telecommunications (e.g., e-mail, bulletin boards)
❑   Computer technology used to **facilitate collaboration** among PDS
     partners:
     ■   telecommunications (e.g., e-mail, bulletin boards)
❑   Computer technology included in **subject matter** of teacher education
     &/or staff development curriculum of PDS participants:
     ■   telecommunications (e.g., e-mail, bulletin boards)
❑   Approximately 0-19% of department faculty participate in PDS-related
     work (planning or implementation)

VIRGINIA

Virginia Commonwealth University

School	Whitcomb Model Elementary School
	2100 Sussex Street
	Richmond, VA 23223-3622
	Phone: (804) 780-4318
Site Coordinator	Michael D. Davis, Ph.D.
Starting Date	1993, September
Grade Level	K-5
School Type	Professional Development School

College/University	*University of Washington*
Contact	University of Washington 201 Miller Hall, DQ-12 Seattle, WA 98195 (206) 543-1847
Partners	University of Washington Bellevue, Central Kitsop, Everett; Federal Way, Issaquah, Lake Washington, Renton, & Seattle City School Districts Washington Education Association
Affiliation	Ford Clinical Schools Project; National Network for Educational Renewal; Professional Development School Network (NCREST); AACTE-DeWitt Wallace Comprehensive Services Program
Funding	university; school district; Washington Education Association
Starting Date	1989
PDS Sites	Meany Middle School; Odle Middle School; Adelaide Elementary School; Cedar Wood Elementary School; Clear Creek Elementary School; Juanita Elementary School; Kennydale Elementary School; Maple Hills Elementary School

Program Features

- ❑ Preservice teachers assigned to PDSs in cohorts
- ❑ Computer technology used in PDS teacher education program to **facilitate instruction** &/or staff development:
    - ■ telecommunications (e.g., e-mail, bulletin boards)
- ❑ Computer technology used to **facilitate collaboration** among PDS partners:
    - ■ telecommunications (e.g., e-mail, bulletin boards)
- ❑ Computer technology included in **subject matter** of teacher education &/or staff development curriculum of PDS participants:
    - ■ telecommunications (e.g., e-mail, bulletin boards)
    - ■ computer assisted instruction
- ❑ Approximately 0-19% of department faculty participate in PDS-related work (planning or implementation)

University of Washington

School	Adelaide Elementary School 1635 S.W. 304th Federal Way, WA 98023 Phone: (206) 838-2306	Maple Hills Elementary School 15644 204th Avenue S.E. Renton, WA 98059-9018 Phone: (206) 228-5363
Site Coordinator	Diane Anderson	Mary Stolze
Starting Date	1992	1992
Grade Level	K-6	K-6
School Type	Professional Development School	Professional Development School
School	Cedar Wood Elementary School 3414 168th Street, S.E. Bothell, WA 98012 Phone: (206) 338-5165	Meany Middle School/Professional Development School 301 21st Avenue East Seattle, WA 98112 Phone: (206) 281-6160
Site Coordinator	Jan Daugherty	Shari James
Starting Date	1992	1989, September
Grade Level	K-6	6-8
School Type	Professional Development School	Professional Development School
School	Clear Creek Elementary School 3999 Sunde Road Silverdale, WA 98383 Phone: (206) 692-3160	Odle Middle School/Professional Development School 14401 Northeast 8th Street Bellevue, WA 98007 Phone: (206) 455-6211
Site Coordinator	Susan Quick	Chris Vall-Spinosa
Starting Date	1992	1989, September
Grade Level	K-6	6-8
School Type	Professional Development School	Professional Development School
School	Juanita Elementary School 9635 N.E. 132nd Street Kirkland, WA 98034 Phone: (206) 823-8136	
Site Coordinator	Kathy Marshall	
Starting Date	1992	
Grade Level	K-6	
School Type	Professional Development School	
School	Kennydale Elementary School 1700 N.E. 28th Street Renton, WA 98056 Phone: (206) 235-2303	
Site Coordinator	Jim Ventris	
Starting Date	1992	
Grade Level	K-6	
School Type	Professional Development School	

College/University	*Washington State University*
Contact	Bernard Oliver, Dean Washington State University College of Education Pullman, WA 99164-2114 (509) 335-4853
Partners	Washington State University Pullman School District #267
Funding	university; school district
Starting Date	1991, August
PDS Sites	Lincoln Middle School
Program Features	❑ College funding for PDS program from grants, discretionary funds, or other types of "soft money" ❑ Release time, reduced course load, or other related arrangement made for college faculty actively involved with PDS sites ❑ Computer technology used in PDS teacher education program to **facilitate instruction** &/or staff development: ■ computer assisted instruction ❑ Computer technology included in **subject matter** of teacher education &/or staff development curriculum of PDS participants: ■ computer assisted instruction ■ interactive video ■ desktop publishing ❑ Policies of college with regard to hiring, tenure, promotion, or other aspects of college's reward structure, acknowledge PDS-related work ❑ Approximately 0-19% of department faculty participate in PDS-related work (planning or implementation)

WASHINGTON

Washington State University

School
Lincoln Middle School
Southeast 315 Crestview
Pullman, WA 99163
Phone: (509) 334-3411

Site Coordinator Phyllis Vettrus
Starting Date 1991, August
Grade Level 6-8
School Type Professional Development School

College/University	*West Virginia University*
Contact	Sarah Steel, Associate Director/PDS The Benedum Project, West Virginia University College of Human Resources & Education 601 Allen Hall, P.O. Box 6122 Morgantown, WV 26506-6122 (304) 293-6762
Partners	West Virginia University Marion, Monogalia, and Taylor County School Districts
Affiliation	Professional Development School Network (NCREST); Holmes Group
Funding	university; school district; Claude Worthington Benedum Foundation
Starting Date	1990, February
PDS Sites	Central Elementary School; East Dale Elementary School; Grafton High School; Morgantown High School; Suncrest Primary School

Program Features

- ❏ Preservice teachers assigned to PDSs in cohorts
- ❏ College funding for PDS program from grants, discretionary funds, or other types of "soft money"
- ❏ Release time, reduced course load, or other related arrangement made for college faculty actively involved with PDS sites
- ❏ Computer technology used in PDS teacher education program to **facilitate instruction** &/or staff development:
  - ■ telecommunications (e.g., e-mail, bulletin boards)
  - ■ computer assisted instruction
  - ■ interactive video
  - ■ desktop publishing
- ❏ Computer technology used to **facilitate collaboration** among PDS partners:
  - ■ telecommunications (e.g., e-mail, bulletin boards)
  - ■ desktop publishing
- ❏ Computer technology included in **subject matter** of teacher education &/or staff development curriculum of PDS participants:
  - ■ telecommunications (e.g., e-mail, bulletin boards)
  - ■ computer assisted instruction
  - ■ interactive video
  - ■ programming
  - ■ authoring systems
  - ■ desktop publishing
- ❏ Policies of college with regard to hiring, tenure, promotion, or other aspects of college'sreward structure, acknowledge PDS-related work
- ❏ Approximately 60-79% of department faculty participate in PDS-related work (planning or implementation)

143

West Virginia University

School	Central Elementary School 475 Baird Street Morgantown, WV 26505 Phone: (304) 291-9258
Site Coordinator	Ruth Oaks & Frank Mrazek
Starting Date	1990, February
Grade Level	K-6
School Type	Professional Development School
School	East Dale Elementary School Route 3 Fairmont, WV 26554 Phone: (304) 367-2132
Site Coordinator	Janet Crescenzi & Etta Zasloff
Starting Date	1990, February
Grade Level	K-6
School Type	Professional Development School
School	Grafton High School Riverside Drive Grafton, WV 26534 Phone: (304) 265-3046
Site Coordinator	Diana Colebank & Greg Cartwright
Starting Date	1990, February
Grade Level	9-12
School Type	Professional Development School
School	Morgantown High School 109 Wilson Avenue Morgantown, WV 26505 Phone: (304) 291-9260
Site Coordinator	Gwen Rosenbluth & Tom Hart
Starting Date	1990, February
Grade Level	10-12
School Type	Professional Development School
School	Suncrest Primary School Junior Avenue Morgantown, WV 26505 Phone: (304) 291-9347
Site Coordinator	Joyce Lang & Suzanne Newbrough
Starting Date	1990, February
Grade Level	K-3
School Type	Professional Development School

College/University	*University of Wisconsin - Madison*
Contact	Dr. Cookie Miller or B. Robert Plbachinck University of Wisconsin - Madison 225 N. Mills Street Madison, WI 53706 (608) 262-6137
Partners	University of Wisconsin - Madison Madison Metropolitan School District Madison Teachers Incorporated
Funding	university; school district
Starting Date	1988, Summer
PDS Sites	Lincoln Elementary School
Program Features	❑ Preservice teachers assigned to PDSs in cohorts ❑ Computer technology included in **subject matter** of teacher education &/or staff development curriculum of PDS participants: ■ telecommunications (e.g., e-mail, bulletin boards) ❑ Policies of college with regard to hiring, tenure, promotion, or other aspects of college's reward structure, acknowledge PDS-related work ❑ Approximately 0-19% of department faculty participate in PDS-related work (planning or implementation)

WISCONSIN

University of Wisconsin - Madison

School	Lincoln Elementary School
	909 Sequoia Trail
	Madison, WI 53713-2599
	Phone: (608) 267-4262
Site Coordinator	Dr. Cookie Miller
Starting Date	1988, Summer
Grade Level	K-6
School Type	Professional Development School

Professional Development School Characteristics

Professional Development School Characteristics - Table 1 149
  College/School Cooperation
  Preservice Teachers Program

Professional Development School Characteristics - Table 2 178
  Preservice Teachers Program, *continued*
  Beginning Teachers Program

Professional Development School Characteristics - Table 3 208
  Beginning Teachers Program, *continued*
  Inservice Teachers Program

Professional Development School Characteristics - Table 4 237
  Inservice Teachers Program, *continued*
  Multicultural Issues

The tables in this section present respondents' answers to specific items in Section 2 of the Data Collection Form (Appendix 1). PDSs are listed alphabetically—by state, college or university partner, and individual school name.

Professional Development School Characteristics - Table 1

Professional Development School	College/School Cooperation					Preservice Teachers Program
	school faculty members hold joint school/college teaching appointments	college faculty teach school students	school faculty assist in planning preservice teacher education curriculum	school faculty assist in planning inservice teacher education curriculum	collaborative research involving school & college faculty	on-site (school) courses for preservice teachers
ARKANSAS University of Arkansas, Fayetteville						
George Elementary School	no	no	yes	yes	yes	yes
Jefferson Elementary School	no response	no response	no response	no response	yes	no response
Woodland Junior High School	no response	no response	yes	yes	yes	no response
CALIFORNIA California State University, Fullerton						
Golden Hill School	no	yes	yes	yes	yes	no
Highland School	no	yes	yes	yes	yes	no
Ladera Palma School	no	yes	yes	yes	yes	no
Linda Vista School	no	yes	yes	yes	yes	no
Monte Vista School	no	yes	yes	yes	yes	no
Raymond School	no	yes	yes	yes	yes	no
Sierra Vista School	no	yes	yes	yes	yes	no

Professional Development School Characteristics - Table 1

Professional Development School	College/School Cooperation					Preservice Teachers Program
	school faculty members hold joint school/college teaching appointments	college faculty teach school students	school faculty assist in planning preservice teacher education curriculum	school faculty assist in planning inservice teacher education curriculum	collaborative research involving school & college faculty	on-site (school) courses for preservice teachers
Tynes School	no	yes	yes	yes	yes	no
Vicentia School	no	yes	yes	yes	yes	no
CALIFORNIA **San Diego State University**						
Alliance for Excellence	no	yes	yes	no	no	yes
Chula Vista Professional Development School	yes	yes	yes	no	no	yes
Kennedy Lab School	no	yes	no	no	no	yes
Model Education Center	no	yes	yes	no	no	yes
Marshall Professional Development School	no	yes	yes	no	no	yes
Partners in Education	no	yes	yes	yes	yes	yes
CALIFORNIA **University of California, Riverside**						
Ribidoux High School	no response	no response	yes	yes	yes	yes
DELAWARE **University of Delaware**						
Thurgood Marshall Elementary School	yes	yes	yes	yes	yes	yes

Professional Development School Characteristics - Table 1

Professional Development School	College/School Cooperation					Preservice Teachers Program
	school faculty members hold joint school/college teaching appointments	college faculty teach school students	school faculty assist in planning preservice teacher education curriculum	school faculty assist in planning inservice teacher education curriculum	collaborative research involving school & college faculty	on-site (school) courses for preservice teachers
FLORIDA **University of South Florida**						
Thomas E. Weightman Middle School	yes	yes	yes	yes	yes	yes
GEORGIA **Armstrong State College**						
White Bluff Elementary School	no	no	yes	yes	no	yes
ILLINOIS **DePaul University**						
Glenview Teacher Preparation Program	yes	yes	yes	yes	yes	yes
ILLINOIS **Elmhurst College**						
Brook Park School	yes	no	yes	yes	yes	no
Bryan Junior High School	yes	no	yes	yes	yes	no
Conrad Fischer School	yes	no	yes	yes	yes	no
Early Childhood Education Center	yes	no	yes	yes	yes	no
Emerson School	yes	no	yes	yes	yes	no
Euclid School	yes	no	yes	yes	yes	no

151

Professional Development School Characteristics - Table 1

Professional Development School	College/School Cooperation					Preservice Teachers Program
	school faculty members hold joint school/college teaching appointments	college faculty teach school students	school faculty assist in planning preservice teacher education curriculum	school faculty assist in planning inservice teacher education curriculum	collaborative research involving school & college faculty	on-site (school) courses for preservice teachers
Field School	yes	no	yes	yes	yes	no
Gower West School	yes	no	yes	yes	yes	no
Grant School	yes	no	yes	yes	yes	no
Hinsdale Central High School	yes	no	yes	yes	yes	no
Indian Trail Junior High School	yes	no	yes	yes	yes	no
Jackson School	yes	no	yes	yes	yes	no
Jefferson School	yes	no	yes	yes	yes	no
Jefferson School	yes	no	yes	yes	yes	no
Lake Park Elementary School	yes	no	yes	yes	yes	no
Leyden High School-East Campus	yes	no	yes	yes	yes	no
Leyden High School-West Campus	yes	no	yes	yes	yes	no
Lincoln Elementary School	yes	no	yes	yes	yes	no
Lincoln Primary School	yes	no	yes	yes	yes	no

Professional Development School Characteristics - Table 1

Professional Development School	College/School Cooperation					Preservice Teachers Program
	school faculty members hold joint school/college teaching appointments	college faculty teach school students	school faculty assist in planning preservice teacher education curriculum	school faculty assist in planning inservice teacher education curriculum	collaborative research involving school & college faculty	on-site (school) courses for preservice teachers
McKinley School		yes	no	yes	yes	
Queen Bee School		yes	no	yes	yes	
Reskin School		yes	no	yes	yes	
Roosevelt Elementary School		yes	no	yes	yes	
Roosevelt Junior High School		yes	no	yes	yes	
Sandburg Junior High School		yes	no	yes	yes	
Schafer School		yes	no	yes	yes	
Spring Hills School		yes	no	yes	yes	no
Bellwood Preschool		yes	no	yes	yes	no
Stone Park Preschool		yes	no	yes	yes	no
Stone School		yes	no	yes	yes	no
Wesley School		yes	no	yes	yes	no
Westmore School	yes	no	yes	yes	yes	no

153

Professional Development School Characteristics - Table 1

Professional Development School	College/School Cooperation					Preservice Teachers Program
	school faculty members hold joint school/college teaching appointments	college faculty teach school students	school faculty assist in planning preservice teacher education curriculum	school faculty assist in planning inservice teacher education curriculum	collaborative research involving school & college faculty	on-site (school) courses for preservice teachers
York High School	yes	no	yes	yes	yes	no
ILLINOIS **National Louis University**						
Glenview/Northbrook	yes	no	no	yes	yes	yes
INDIANA **Indiana State University**						
Chauncey Rose Middle School	no	no	yes	yes	yes	yes
Fayette Elementary School	no	no	yes	yes	yes	yes
Meadows Elementary School	no	no	yes	yes	yes	yes
Rosedale Elementary School	no	no	yes	yes	yes	yes
South Vermillion High School	no	no	yes	yes	yes	yes
Stanton Elementary School	no	no	yes	yes	yes	yes
Terre Haute North Vigo High School	no	no	yes	yes	yes	yes
Terre Haute South Vigo High School	no	no	yes	yes	yes	yes
West Vigo High School	no	no	yes	yes	yes	yes

Professional Development School Characteristics - Table 1

Professional Development School	College/School Cooperation					Preservice Teachers Program
	school faculty members hold joint school/college teaching appointments	college faculty teach school students	school faculty assist in planning preservice teacher education curriculum	school faculty assist in planning inservice teacher education curriculum	collaborative research involving school & college faculty	on-site (school) courses for preservice teachers
West Vigo School	no	yes	yes	yes	yes	yes
INDIANA Indiana University Northwest						
Central High School	no	no	yes	yes	no	no
Eggers Elementary Middle School	no	no	yes	yes	yes	no
Franklin Elementary School	n/a	yes	yes	yes	no	yes
Horace Mann High School	yes	no	yes	yes	yes	yes
Lincoln Elementary	yes	no	yes	yes	yes	yes
INDIANA Indiana University Purdue University Indianapolis (IUPUI)						
Arsenal Technical High School	no	yes	yes	yes	yes	yes
Franklin Central High School	no	yes	yes	yes	yes	yes
Franklin Township Middle School	no	yes	yes	yes	yes	yes
Harcourt Elementary School	no	yes	yes	yes	yes	yes

Professional Development School Characteristics - Table 1

Professional Development School	College/School Cooperation					Preservice Teachers Program
	school faculty members hold joint school/college teaching appointments	college faculty teach school students	school faculty assist in planning preservice teacher education curriculum	school faculty assist in planning inservice teacher education curriculum	collaborative research involving school & college faculty	on-site (school) courses for preservice teachers
INDIANA Purdue University						
Westlane Middle School	no	yes	yes	yes	yes	yes
Riverside School	no	yes	yes	yes	yes	yes
North Central High School	no	yes	yes	yes	yes	yes
James A. Garfield	no	yes	yes	yes	yes	yes
Indian Creek Elementary School		yes	yes	yes	yes	yes
Klondike Elementary School	no	no	no	no	no	no
Lafayette School Corporation	no	yes	yes	yes	yes	yes
Pine Village School	no	no	no	no	yes	no
INDIANA Emporia State University						
Countryside Elementary School	no	yes	yes	yes	yes	yes
Pleasant Ridge Elementary School	no	yes	yes	yes	yes	yes
IOWA Drake University						

Professional Development School Characteristics - Table 1

Professional Development School	College/School Cooperation					Preservice Teachers Program
	school faculty members hold joint school/college teaching appointments	college faculty teach school students	school faculty assist in planning preservice teacher education curriculum	school faculty assist in planning inservice teacher education curriculum	collaborative research involving school & college faculty	on-site (school) courses for preservice teachers
Moulton Elementary School	no	yes	yes	yes	yes	yes
IOWA Iowa State University						
Madrid School System	no	no	yes	yes	yes	yes
Project Opportunity - ISU/Madrid Site	n/a	yes	yes	yes	yes	yes
IOWA University of Northern Iowa						
Malcolm Price Laboratory School	yes	yes	yes	yes	no response	no response
KANSAS Fort Hays State University						
O'Loughlin Elementary School	yes	no	yes	yes	yes	yes
LOUISIANA University of New Orleans						
Grace King High School	yes	no	no	no	yes	no
H.C. Schaumburg Elementary School	no	no	yes	yes	yes	yes
Jefferson Elementary School	no	yes	no	yes	yes	no
John Dibert Elementary School	no	no	yes	yes	no	no

Professional Development School Characteristics - Table 1

Professional Development School	College/School Cooperation					Preservice Teachers Program
	school faculty members hold joint school/college teaching appointments	college faculty teach school students	school faculty assist in planning preservice teacher education curriculum	school faculty assist in planning inservice teacher education curriculum	collaborative research involving school & college faculty	on-site (school) courses for preservice teachers
Paul J. Solis Elementary School	no	no	yes	no	no	no
Warren Easton	no	no	yes	no	no response	no
MASSACHUSETTS Anna Maria College						
City View Professional Development School	no	no	yes	yes	no	yes
Coolidge Professional Development School	no	no	yes	yes	no	yes
MASSACHUSETTS Assumption College						
Flagg Street School	yes	no	no	no	yes	yes
MASSACHUSETTS University of Massachusetts, Amherst						
East Longmeadow High School	yes	no	yes	yes	no	yes
MASSACHUSETTS University of Massachusetts, Lowell						
Reading Memorial High School	yes	yes	yes	yes	yes	yes
MASSACHUSETTS Wheelock College						

158

Professional Development School Characteristics - Table 1

Professional Development School	College/School Cooperation					Preservice Teachers Program
	school faculty members hold joint school/college teaching appointments	college faculty teach school students	school faculty assist in planning preservice teacher education curriculum	school faculty assist in planning inservice teacher education curriculum	collaborative research involving school & college faculty	on-site (school) courses for preservice teachers
Edward Devotion School	yes	yes	yes	yes	no	yes
MICHIGAN University of Michigan, Dearborn						
Catherine B. White Elementary School	no	yes	yes	yes	no	no
MICHIGAN Western Michigan University						
Battlecreek Central High School	no	no	yes	yes	yes	yes
Prairieview Elementary School	no	no	yes	yes	yes	yes
MINNESOTA University of Minnesota						
Patrick Henry Professional Practice School	no	no	yes	yes	yes	no
MISSOURI Harris-Stowe State College						
Shepard Accelerated School Partnership	yes	no	no	yes	yes	yes
MISSOURI Maryville University						
South High School	yes	yes	yes	yes	yes	yes
Wilkinson Early Childhood Center	yes	yes	yes	yes	yes	n/a

Professional Development School Characteristics - Table 1

Professional Development School	College/School Cooperation					Preservice Teachers Program
	school faculty members hold joint school/college teaching appointments	college faculty teach school students	school faculty assist in planning preservice teacher education curriculum	school faculty assist in planning inservice teacher education curriculum	collaborative research involving school & college faculty	on-site (school) courses for preservice teachers
MISSOURI Saint Louis University						
Wyman School	no	yes	no	no	no	yes
MISSOURI University of Missouri, Kansas City						
Center Elementary School	no	no	no	no	no	no
Red Bridge Elementary School	no response	yes	yes	yes	yes	no response
MISSOURI University of Missouri, St. Louis						
Chaney Elementary School	yes	yes	yes	yes	yes	yes
Laclede Elementary School	no	yes	yes	yes	yes	yes
Parkway Central Middle School	yes	yes	yes	yes	yes	yes
Parkway River Bend Elementary School	yes	yes	yes	yes	yes	no
MISSOURI Washington University						
Kirkwood High School	no	no	yes	yes	yes	yes

Professional Development School Characteristics - Table 1

Professional Development School	College/School Cooperation					Preservice Teachers Program
	school faculty members hold joint school/college teaching appointments	college faculty teach school students	school faculty assist in planning preservice teacher education curriculum	school faculty assist in planning inservice teacher education curriculum	collaborative research involving school & college faculty	on-site (school) courses for preservice teachers
NEW JERSEY Rowan College of New Jersey						
Cooper's Point Professional Development Family School of Excellence	no	yes	yes	yes	yes	yes
Winslow Professional Development District	no	yes	yes	yes	yes	yes
NEW YORK Buffalo State College						
Charles Drew Science Magnet School	yes	no	yes	no	n/a	yes
Como Park Elementary School	n/a	n/a	n/a	n/a	n/a	yes
Futures Academy	n/a	n/a	yes	n/a	n/a	yes
Hoover Elementary School	yes	no	yes	yes	n/a	yes
NEW YORK Columbia University						
I.S. 44	yes	no response	yes	yes	yes	yes
P.S. 87	yes	no response	yes	no response	yes	yes
NEW YORK Syracuse University						
Camillus Middle School	no	no	yes	yes	yes	no

Professional Development School Characteristics - Table 1

Professional Development School	College/School Cooperation					Preservice Teachers Program
	school faculty members hold joint school/college teaching appointments	college faculty teach school students	school faculty assist in planning preservice teacher education curriculum	school faculty assist in planning inservice teacher education curriculum	collaborative research involving school & college faculty	on-site (school) courses for preservice teachers
East Hill Elementary School	no	no	yes	yes	yes	yes
Edward Smith Elementary School	no	yes	yes	yes	yes	no
Franklin Elementary School	no	yes	yes	yes	yes	no
Jamesville Elementary School	no	yes	yes	yes	yes	no
Jamesville-DeWitt High School	no	yes	yes	yes	yes	no
Jamesville-DeWitt Middle School	no	yes	yes	yes	yes	no
Moses-DeWitt Elementary School	no	no	yes	yes	yes	no
Onondaga Road Elementary School	no	no	yes	yes	yes	no
Split Rock Elementary School	no	no	yes	yes	no	yes
Stonehedge Elementary School	no	yes	yes	yes	yes	yes
Tecumseh Elementary School	no	yes	yes	yes	yes	no
Webster Elementary School	no	yes	yes	yes	no	no
West Genesee Middle School	no	no	yes	yes	yes	no

Professional Development School Characteristics - Table 1

Professional Development School	College/School Cooperation — school faculty members hold joint school/college teaching appointments	college faculty teach school students	school faculty assist in planning preservice teacher education curriculum	school faculty assist in planning inservice teacher education curriculum	collaborative research involving school & college faculty	Preservice Teachers Program — on-site (school) courses for preservice teachers
West Genesee Senior High School	no	yes	yes	yes	yes	no
NORTH CAROLINA University of North Carolina, Greensboro						
Archer Elementary School	no	yes	yes	yes	yes	yes
Bluford Elementary School	n/a	yes	yes	yes	yes	yes
Brightwood Elementary School	n/a	yes	yes	yes	yes	yes
Global Magnet School	n/a	yes	yes	yes	yes	yes
Greene Elementary School	n/a	yes	yes	yes	yes	yes
Guilford Middle School	no	yes	yes	yes	yes	yes
Guilford Primary School	no	yes	yes	yes	yes	yes
Jackson Middle School	n/a	yes	yes	yes	yes	yes
Jamestown Middle School	n/a	yes	yes	yes	yes	yes
Jesse Wharton Elementary School	n/a	yes	yes	yes	yes	yes
Kernersville Elementary School	no	yes	yes	yes	yes	yes

Professional Development School Characteristics - Table 1

Professional Development School	College/School Cooperation					Preservice Teachers Program
	school faculty members hold joint school/college teaching appointments	college faculty teach school students	school faculty assist in planning preservice teacher education curriculum	school faculty assist in planning inservice teacher education curriculum	collaborative research involving school & college faculty	on-site (school) courses for preservice teachers
Kiser Middle School	no	yes	yes	yes	yes	yes
Mills Road Elementary School	n/a	yes	yes	yes	yes	yes
Oak Hill Elementary School	n/a	yes	yes	yes	yes	yes
Oak View Elementary School	no	yes	yes	yes	yes	yes
Piney Grove Elementary School	n/a	yes	yes	yes	yes	yes
Rankin Elementary School	no	yes	yes	yes	yes	yes
Sedgefield Elementary School	n/a	yes	yes	yes	yes	yes
Shadybrook Elementary School	n/a	yes	yes	yes	yes	yes
Western Guilford High School	n/a	yes	yes	yes	yes	yes
NORTH DAKOTA **University of North Dakota**						
Lake Agassiz Elementary School	no response	yes	yes	yes	yes	yes
OHIO **Ohio State University**						
Etna Road Elementary School - Project TEACH	no	no	yes	yes	yes	no

Professional Development School Characteristics - Table 1

Professional Development School	College/School Cooperation					Preservice Teachers Program
	school faculty members hold joint school/college teaching appointments	college faculty teach school students	school faculty assist in planning preservice teacher education curriculum	school faculty assist in planning inservice teacher education curriculum	collaborative research involving school & college faculty	on-site (school) courses for preservice teachers
Independence High School - Project TRI	yes	no	yes	yes	yes	yes
Northland High School - Northland Teaching Academy	no	no	no	no	no	yes
Thomas Worthington High School	yes	no	yes	yes	yes	yes
PENNSYLVANIA Bloomsburg University						
Danville Elementary School	no response	no response	yes	yes	yes	yes
PENNSYLVANIA Millersville University						
Conestoga Valley Middle School	yes	no	yes	yes	no	yes
Manheim Township Middle School	yes	no	yes	yes	no response	yes
SOUTH CAROLINA University of South Carolina						
Airport High School	no response	yes	yes	yes	no response	yes
Crayton Middle School	no response	no response	no response	yes	no response	no response
Hood Street School	yes	no response	yes	yes	no response	no response
Horrell Hill Elementary School	no response	no response	no response	yes	yes	no response

Professional Development School Characteristics - Table 1

Professional Development School	College/School Cooperation					Preservice Teachers Program
	school faculty members hold joint school/college teaching appointments	college faculty teach school students	school faculty assist in planning preservice teacher education curriculum	school faculty assist in planning inservice teacher education curriculum	collaborative research involving school & college faculty	on-site (school) courses for preservice teachers
Hyatt Park School	no response	yes	yes	yes	yes	no response
Meadowfield Elementary School	no response	no response	yes	yes	no response	yes
Pierce Terrace School	no response	no response	yes	yes	no response	no response
Pinckney Elementary School	no response	no response	no response	yes	yes	yes
Pontiac Elementary School	no response	no response	yes	yes	yes	no response
Summitt Parkway Middle School	no response	yes	yes	yes	no response	yes
White Knoll Elementary School	no response	no response	yes	yes	yes	no response
TENNESSEE Austin Peay State University						
Burt Elementary School	n/a	yes	yes	yes	n/a	n/a
TENNESSEE Memphis State University						
Campus School	no	no	no	yes	no	no
Coleman Elementary School	yes	yes	yes	yes	yes	yes
Dyer County Central Elementary School	no	no	no response	yes	yes	no

166

Professional Development School Characteristics - Table 1

Professional Development School	College/School Cooperation					Preservice Teachers Program
	school faculty members hold joint school/college teaching appointments	college faculty teach school students	school faculty assist in planning preservice teacher education curriculum	school faculty assist in planning inservice teacher education curriculum	collaborative research involving school & college faculty	on-site (school) courses for preservice teachers
Frayser Elementary School	no	yes	yes	yes	yes	yes
Lipman School	no	no	no	no	no	no
Newberry Elementary School	no	yes	no	yes	yes	no
Raleigh Egypt Middle School	no	yes	yes	yes	yes	yes
Ross Elementary	no	no	yes	yes	no	no
TEXAS Incarnate Word College						
Brewer Elementary School	no	no	yes	yes	yes	no
Clark High School	no	no	yes	yes	yes	no
Connell Middle School	no	no	yes	yes	no	no
Coronado Escobar Elementary School	yes	yes	no	no	no	yes
Driscoll Middle School	no	no	yes	yes	no	no
Emma Frey Elementary School	no	no	yes	yes	yes	no
Gadendale Elementary School	no	no	yes	yes	yes	no

Professional Development School Characteristics - Table 1

Professional Development School	College/School Cooperation					Preservice Teachers Program
	school faculty members hold joint school/college teaching appointments	college faculty teach school students	school faculty assist in planning preservice teacher education curriculum	school faculty assist in planning inservice teacher education curriculum	collaborative research involving school & college faculty	on-site (school) courses for preservice teachers
Hawthorne Elementary School	yes	no	yes	yes	yes	yes
Hutchins Elementary School	no	no	yes	yes	yes	no
Jackson-Keller Elementary School	yes	no	yes	yes	yes	yes
Kingsborough Middle School	no	no	yes	yes	yes	no
Lamar Elementary School	no	no	yes	yes	yes	no
Loma Park Elementary School	no	no	yes	yes	no	yes
Mark Twain Middle School	yes	no	yes	yes	yes	yes
Memorial High School	no	no	yes	yes	no	yes
Providence High School	no	no	no	no	no	no
Robert E. Lee High School	yes	no	yes	yes	yes	yes
Rodriguez Elementary School	no	no	yes	yes	yes	yes
St. Martin Hall	no	no	no	yes	yes	yes
St. Peter Prince of the Apostles	no	no	yes	yes	no	no

Professional Development School Characteristics - Table 1

Professional Development School	College/School Cooperation					Preservice Teachers Program
	school faculty members hold joint school/college teaching appointments	college faculty teach school students	school faculty assist in planning preservice teacher education curriculum	school faculty assist in planning inservice teacher education curriculum	collaborative research involving school & college faculty	on-site (school) courses for preservice teachers
Travis Elementary School	no	no	yes	yes	yes	no
Truman Middle School	no	no	yes	no	no	yes
TEXAS Lubbock Christian University						
Parkway Elementary School	no	yes	yes	yes	no	yes
Hardwick Elementary School	no	yes	yes	yes	no	yes
Brown Elementary School	no	yes	yes	yes	no	yes
TEXAS Southwest Texas State University						
Bowie Elementary School	yes	yes	yes	yes	yes	yes
Elgin Middle School	yes	yes	yes	yes	yes	yes
Goodnight Junior High School	yes	yes	yes	yes	yes	yes
Highland Park Elementary School	yes	yes	yes	yes	yes	yes
TEXAS Texas A&M University						
Houston Teaching Academy	yes	no response	no response	no response	yes	yes

Professional Development School Characteristics - Table 1

Professional Development School	College/School Cooperation					Preservice Teachers Program
	school faculty members hold joint school/college teaching appointments	college faculty teach school students	school faculty assist in planning preservice teacher education curriculum	school faculty assist in planning inservice teacher education curriculum	collaborative research involving school & college faculty	on-site (school) courses for preservice teachers
TEXAS **Texas Tech University**						
Bayless Elementary School	no	no	yes	yes	yes	yes
Hutchinson Junior High School	no	no	yes	yes	yes	yes
Lubbock High School	no	no	yes	yes	yes	yes
Mackenzie Junior High School	no	no	yes	yes	yes	yes
Ramirez Elementary School	no	no	yes	yes	yes	yes
Wilson ISD	no	no	yes	yes	yes	yes
TEXAS **University of Houston**						
Ben Milam Professional Development and Technology Center	no	yes	yes	yes	yes	yes
Hamilton Professional Development and Technology Center	no	yes	yes	yes	yes	yes
Kennedy Professional Development and Technology Center	no	yes	yes	yes	yes	yes
Lockhart Professional Development and Technology Center	no	yes	yes	yes	yes	yes

170

Professional Development School Characteristics - Table 1

Professional Development School	College/School Cooperation					Preservice Teachers Program
	school faculty members hold joint school/college teaching appointments	college faculty teach school students	school faculty assist in planning preservice teacher education curriculum	school faculty assist in planning inservice teacher education curriculum	collaborative research involving school & college faculty	on-site (school) courses for preservice teachers
Rufus Cage Professional Development and Technology Center	no	yes	yes	yes	yes	yes
Valley Oaks Professional Development and Technology Center	no	yes	yes	yes	yes	yes
Westwood Professional Development and Technology Center	no	yes	yes	yes	yes	yes
Woodview Professional Development and Technology Center	no	yes	yes	yes	yes	yes
TEXAS University of Houston, Clearlake						
Alvin Junior High School	no	no	yes	yes	yes	yes
Central Middle School	no	no	yes	yes	yes	no
George Washington Carver Elementary School	no	no	yes	yes	yes	yes
TEXAS University of Texas, El Paso						
H.D. Hiley Elementary School	no	no	yes	yes	yes	no
Lamar Elementary School	no	no	yes	yes	yes	no

Professional Development School Characteristics - Table 1

Professional Development School	College/School Cooperation					Preservice Teachers Program
	school faculty members hold joint school/college teaching appointments	college faculty teach school students	school faculty assist in planning preservice teacher education curriculum	school faculty assist in planning inservice teacher education curriculum	collaborative research involving school & college faculty	on-site (school) courses for preservice teachers
Riverside High School	no	no	yes	yes	yes	no
Wiggs Middle School	no	no	yes	yes	yes	no
Ysleta Elementary School	no	no	yes	yes	yes	no
UTAH Brigham-Young University						
Alpine Elementary School	yes	no	yes	yes	yes	yes
Aspen Elementary School	no	no	yes	yes	yes	yes
Barratt Elementary School	yes	no	yes	yes	yes	yes
Canyon Crest Elementary School	no	no	yes	yes	yes	yes
Cascade Elementary School	no	no	yes	yes	no response	no
Copperview Elementary School	no	no	yes	yes	yes	yes
Cottonwood Heights Elementary School	yes	yes	yes	yes	yes	yes
Draper Elementary School	no	no	yes	yes	yes	yes
Edgemont Elementary School	no	no	yes	yes	yes	yes

Professional Development School Characteristics - Table 1

Professional Development School	College/School Cooperation					Preservice Teachers Program
	school faculty members hold joint school/college teaching appointments	college faculty teach school students	school faculty assist in planning preservice teacher education curriculum	school faculty assist in planning inservice teacher education curriculum	collaborative research involving school & college faculty	on-site (school) courses for preservice teachers
Franklin Elementary School	yes	no	no	no response	no response	no
Geneva Elemenntary School	yes	no	yes	yes	no	yes
Goshen Elementary School	no	yes	yes	yes	yes	yes
Grant Elementary School	no	no	yes	yes	yes	yes
Highland Elementary School	yes	no	yes	yes	yes	yes
Jordan Ridge Elementary School	no	no	yes	yes	yes	yes
Larsen Elementary School	yes	no	yes	yes	yes	yes
Lindon Elementary School	no	no	yes	yes	no	yes
Maeser Elementary School	n/a	no	yes	yes	no	yes
Manila Elementary School	yes	no	yes	yes	yes	yes
Mapleton Elementary School	no	yes	yes	yes	yes	yes
Parkview Elementary School	no	no	no	yes	yes	no
Rees Elementary School	no	no	yes	yes	yes	yes

Professional Development School Characteristics - Table 1

Professional Development School	College/School Cooperation					Preservice Teachers Program
	school faculty members hold joint school/college teaching appointments	college faculty teach school students	school faculty assist in planning preservice teacher education curriculum	school faculty assist in planning inservice teacher education curriculum	collaborative research involving school & college faculty	on-site (school) courses for preservice teachers
Rock Canyon Elementary School	no	no	yes	yes	no	yes
Sage Creek Elementary School	no	yes	yes	yes	yes	yes
Salem Elementary School	no	no	yes	yes	yes	yes
Santaquin Elementary School	no	no	yes	yes	yes	yes
Shelley Elementary School	no	no	yes	yes	yes	yes
Southland Elementary School	no	no	yes	yes	yes	yes
Sprucewood Elementary School	no	no	yes	yes	yes	no
Sunrise Elementary School	no	no	yes	yes	yes	yes
Sunset View Elementary School	no	no	yes	yes	no	yes
Taylor Elementary School	no	no response	yes	yes	yes	no
Timpanogos Elementary School	no	no	yes	no response	yes	no response
Westmore Elementary School	no	no	yes	yes	yes	yes
Westridge Elementary School	n/a	yes	yes	yes	yes	yes

Professional Development School Characteristics - Table 1

Professional Development School	College/School Cooperation					Preservice Teachers Program
	school faculty members hold joint school/college teaching appointments	college faculty teach school students	school faculty assist in planning preservice teacher education curriculum	school faculty assist in planning inservice teacher education curriculum	collaborative research involving school & college faculty	on-site (school) courses for preservice teachers
UTAH **University of Utah**						
Willow Canyon Elementary School	no	no	yes	yes	yes	yes
Wilson Elementary School	n/a	no	yes	yes	yes	yes
Bountiful Elementary School	yes	yes	yes	yes	yes	yes
Eisenhower Junior High School	yes	yes	yes	yes	yes	yes
Granger High School	yes	yes	yes	yes	yes	yes
Highland High School	yes	yes	yes	yes	yes	yes
Nibley Park Elementary School	yes	yes	yes	yes	yes	yes
Washington Elementary School- Exemplary Practice School	yes	yes	no	yes	yes	n/a
VIRGINIA **University of Virginia**						
Jackson-Via Elementary School	no response	yes	yes	yes	no response	yes
VIRGINIA **Virginia Commonwealth University**						
Whitcomb Model Elementary School	no	yes	no	no	yes	yes

Professional Development School Characteristics - Table 1

Professional Development School	College/School Cooperation					Preservice Teachers Program
	school faculty members hold joint school/college teaching appointments	college faculty teach school students	school faculty assist in planning preservice teacher education curriculum	school faculty assist in planning inservice teacher education curriculum	collaborative research involving school & college faculty	on-site (school) courses for preservice teachers
WASHINGTON University of Washington						
Adelaide Elementary School	n/a	no	yes	yes	no	n/a
Cedar Wood Elementary School	n/a	no	yes	yes	no	n/a
Clear Creek Elementary School	n/a	no	yes	yes	no	n/a
Juanita Elementary School	n/a	no	yes	yes	no	n/a
Kennydale Elementary School	n/a	no	yes	yes	no	n/a
Maple Hills Elementary School	n/a	no	yes	yes	no	n/a
Meany Middle School Professional Development School	no response	no response	yes	yes	yes	no response
Odle Middle School Professional Development School	no response	no response	yes	yes	yes	no response
WAHINGTON Washington State University						
Lincoln Middle School	no response	yes	yes	yes	yes	yes
WEST VIRGINIA West Virginia University						

176

Professional Development School Characteristics - Table 1

Professional Development School	College/School Cooperation					Preservice Teachers Program
	school faculty members hold joint school/college teaching appointments	college faculty teach school students	school faculty assist in planning preservice teacher education curriculum	school faculty assist in planning inservice teacher education curriculum	collaborative research involving school & college faculty	on-site (school) courses for preservice teachers
Central Elementary School	no	yes	yes	yes	yes	yes
East Dale Elementary School	no	no	yes	yes	yes	yes
Grafton High School	no	no	yes	yes	yes	yes
Morgantown High School	yes	yes	yes	yes	yes	yes
Suncrest Primary School	yes	yes	yes	yes	yes	yes
WISCONSIN University of Wisconsin, Madison						
Lincoln Elementary School	yes	yes	yes	yes	yes	yes

Professional Development School Characteristics - Table 2

Professional Development School	Preservice Teachers Program				Beginning Teachers Program	
	mentor teachers for preservice teachers	clinical supervision of student teachers	each preservice teacher assigned to more than one cooperating teacher	preservice teachers involved in educational research at school site	beginning teacher induction program	mentor teachers for beginning teachers
ARKANSAS University of Arkansas, Fayetteville						
George Elementary School	yes	n/a	yes	no	no	no
Jefferson Elementary School	no response	yes	no response	yes	no response	no response
Woodland Junior High School	no response	yes	no response	no response	no response	no response
CALIFORNIA California State University, Fullerton						
Golden Hill School	yes	yes	yes	yes	yes	no
Highland School	yes	yes	yes	yes	yes	no
Ladera Palma School	yes	yes	yes	yes	yes	no
Linda Vista School	yes	yes	yes	yes	yes	no
Monte Vista School	yes	yes	yes	yes	yes	no
Raymond School	yes	yes	yes	yes	yes	no
Sierra Vista School	yes	yes	yes	yes	yes	no

Professional Development School Characteristics - Table 2

Professional Development School	Preservice Teachers Program				Beginning Teachers Program	
	mentor teachers for preservice teachers	clinical supervision of student teachers	each preservice teacher assigned to more than one cooperating teacher	preservice teachers involved in educational research at school site	beginning teacher induction program	mentor teachers for beginning teachers
Tynes School	yes	yes	yes	yes	yes	no
Vicentia School	yes	yes	yes	yes	yes	no
CALIFORNIA San Diego State University						
Alliance for Excellence	yes		yes	no	no	no
Chula Vista Professional Development School	yes	yes	yes	no	yes	yes
Kennedy Lab School	yes	yes	yes	yes	no	no
Marshall Professional Development School	yes	yes	yes	no	no	no
Model Education Center	yes	yes	yes	no	no	no
Partners in Education	yes	yes	yes	yes	no	no
CALIFORNIA University of California, Riverside						
Ribidoux High School	yes	yes	yes	no response	no response	no response
DELAWARE University of Delaware						

Professional Development School Characteristics - Table 2

Professional Development School	Preservice Teachers Program				Beginning Teachers Program	
	mentor teachers for preservice teachers	clinical supervision of student teachers	each preservice teacher assigned to more than one cooperating teacher	preservice teachers involved in educational research at school site	beginning teacher induction program	mentor teachers for beginning teachers
Thurgood Marshall Elementary School	no	yes	no	no	yes	yes
FLORIDA **University of South Florida**						
Thomas E. Weightman Middle School	yes	yes	yes	yes	yes	yes
GEORGIA **Armstrong State College**						
White Bluff Elementary School	yes	yes	yes	no	no	no
ILLINOIS **DePaul University**						
Glenview Teacher Preparation Program	yes	yes	yes	yes	yes	yes
ILLINOIS **Elmhurst College**						
Brook Park School	yes	yes	yes	no	n/a	n/a
Bryan Junior High School	yes	yes	yes	no	n/a	n/a
Conrad Fischer School	yes	yes	yes	no	n/a	n/a
Early Childhood Education Center	yes	yes	yes	no	n/a	n/a
Emerson School	yes	yes	yes	no	n/a	n/a

Professional Development School Characteristics - Table 2

Professional Development School	Preservice Teachers Program				Beginning Teachers Program	
	mentor teachers for preservice teachers	clinical supervision of student teachers	each preservice teacher assigned to more than one cooperating teacher	preservice teachers involved in educational research at school site	beginning teacher induction program	mentor teachers for beginning teachers
Euclid School	yes	yes	yes	no	n/a	n/a
Field School	yes	yes	yes	no	n/a	n/a
Gower West School	yes	yes	yes	no	n/a	n/a
Grant School	yes	yes	yes	no	n/a	n/a
Hinsdale Central High School	yes	yes	yes	no	n/a	n/a
Indian Trail Junior High School	yes	yes	yes	no	n/a	n/a
Jackson School	yes	yes	yes	no	n/a	n/a
Jefferson School	yes	yes	yes	no	n/a	n/a
Jefferson School	yes	yes	yes	no	n/a	n/a
Lake Park Elementary School	yes	yes	yes	no	n/a	n/a
Leyden High School-East Campus	yes	yes	yes	no	n/a	n/a
Leyden High School-West Campus	yes	yes	yes	no	n/a	n/a
Lincoln Elementary School	yes	yes	yes	no	n/a	n/a

Professional Development School Characteristics - Table 2

Professional Development School	Preservice Teachers Program				Beginning Teachers Program	
	mentor teachers for preservice teachers	clinical supervision of student teachers	each preservice teacher assigned to more than one cooperating teacher	preservice teachers involved in educational research at school site	beginning teacher induction program	mentor teachers for beginning teachers
Lincoln Primary School	yes	yes	yes	no	n/a	n/a
McKinley School	yes	yes	yes	no	n/a	n/a
Queen Bee School	yes	yes	yes	no	n/a	n/a
Reskin School	yes	yes	yes	no	n/a	n/a
Roosevelt Elementary School	yes	yes	yes	no	n/a	n/a
Roosevelt Junior High School	yes	yes	yes	no	n/a	n/a
Sandburg Junior High School	yes	yes	yes	no	n/a	n/a
Schafer School	yes	yes	yes	no	n/a	n/a
Spring Hills School	yes	yes	yes	no	n/a	n/a
Bellwood Preschool	yes	yes	yes	no	n/a	n/a
Stone Park Preschool	yes	yes	yes	no	n/a	n/a
Stone School	yes	yes	yes	no	n/a	n/a
Wesley School	yes	yes	yes	no	n/a	n/a

Professional Development School Characteristics - Table 2

Professional Development School	Preservice Teachers Program				Beginning Teachers Program	
	mentor teachers for preservice teachers	clinical supervision of student teachers	each preservice teacher assigned to more than one cooperating teacher	preservice teachers involved in educational research at school site	beginning teacher induction program	mentor teachers for beginning teachers
Westmore School	yes	yes	no	no	n/a	n/a
York High School	yes	yes	yes	no	n/a	n/a
ILLINOIS National Louis University						
Glenview/Northbrook	yes	yes	no	no	no	no
INDIANA Indiana State University						
Chauncey Rose Middle School	yes	yes	no	yes	yes	yes
Fayette Elementary School	yes	yes	no	yes	yes	yes
Meadows Elementary School	yes	yes	no	yes	yes	yes
Rosedale Elementary School	yes	yes	no	yes	yes	yes
South Vermillion High School	yes	yes	no	yes	yes	yes
Stauton Elementary School	yes	yes	no	yes	yes	yes
Terre Haute North Vigo High School	yes	yes	no	yes	yes	yes
Terre Haute South Vigo High School	yes	yes	no	yes	yes	yes

Professional Development School Characteristics - Table 2

Professional Development School	Preservice Teachers Program				Beginning Teachers Program	
	mentor teachers for preservice teachers	clinical supervision of student teachers	each preservice teacher assigned to more than one cooperating teacher	preservice teachers involved in educational research at school site	beginning teacher induction program	mentor teachers for beginning teachers
INDIANA Indiana University Northwest						
West Vigo High School	yes	yes	no	yes	yes	yes
West Vigo School	yes	yes	yes	yes	yes	yes
Central High School	yes	no	no	no	yes	yes
Eggers Elementary Middle School	yes	yes	no	yes	yes	yes
Franklin Elementary School	yes	n/a	yes	no	n/a	yes
Horace Mann High School	yes	yes	no	no	yes	yes
Lincoln Elementary	yes	yes	yes	no	yes	yes
INDIANA Indiana University Purdue University Indianapolis (IUPUI)						
Arsenal Technical High School	yes	yes	yes	yes	n/a	n/a
Franklin Central High School	yes	yes	yes	yes	n/a	n/a
Franklin Township Middle School	yes	yes	yes	yes	n/a	n/a

Professional Development School Characteristics - Table 2

Professional Development School	Preservice Teachers Program				Beginning Teachers Program	
	mentor teachers for preservice teachers	clinical supervision of student teachers	each preservice teacher assigned to more than one cooperating teacher	preservice teachers involved in educational research at school site	beginning teacher induction program	mentor teachers for beginning teachers
Harcourt Elementary School	yes	yes	yes	yes	n/a	n/a
Indian Creek Elementary School	yes	yes	yes	yes	n/a	n/a
James A. Garfield	yes	yes	yes	yes	n/a	n/a
North Central High School	yes	yes	yes	yes	n/a	n/a
Riverside School	yes	yes	yes	yes	n/a	n/a
Westlane Middle School	yes	yes	yes	yes	n/a	n/a
INDIANA Purdue University						
Klondike Elementary School	no	yes	no	no	no	yes
Lafayette School Corporation	yes	yes	yes	yes	yes	yes
Pine Village School	no	no	no	no	no	no
INDIANA Emporia State University						
Countryside Elementary School	yes	yes	yes	yes	yes	no
Pleasant Ridge Elementary School	yes	yes	yes	yes	yes	no

185

Professional Development School Characteristics - Table 2

Professional Development School	Preservice Teachers Program				Beginning Teachers Program	
	mentor teachers for preservice teachers	clinical supervision of student teachers	each preservice teacher assigned to more than one cooperating teacher	preservice teachers involved in educational research at school site	beginning teacher induction program	mentor teachers for beginning teachers
IOWA **Drake University**						
Moulton Elementary School	yes	yes	yes	yes	yes	
IOWA **Iowa State University**						
Madrid School System	yes	yes	yes	yes	n/a	n/a
Project Opportunity - ISU/Madrid Site	yes	yes	yes	yes	n/a	n/a
IOWA **University of Northern Iowa**						
Malcolm Price Laboratory School	no response	no response	no response	no response	yes	no
KANSAS **Fort Hays State University**						
O'Loughlin Elementary School	yes	yes	no	no	yes	yes
LOUISIANA **University of New Orleans**						
Grace King High School	yes	yes	no	no	yes	yes
H.C. Schaumburg Elementary School	yes	yes	no	yes	yes	yes

Professional Development School Characteristics - Table 2

Professional Development School	Preservice Teachers Program				Beginning Teachers Program	
	mentor teachers for preservice teachers	clinical supervision of student teachers	each preservice teacher assigned to more than one cooperating teacher	preservice teachers involved in educational research at school site	beginning teacher induction program	mentor teachers for beginning teachers
Jefferson Elementary School	yes	no	no	no	yes	yes
John Dibert Elementary School	yes	yes	no	no	no	yes
Paul J. Solis Elementary School	no	yes	no	no	yes	yes
Warren Easton	yes	yes	no	yes	no	yes
MASSACHUSETTS Anna Maria College						
City View Professional Development School	yes	yes	no	no	no	no
Coolidge Professional Development School	yes	yes	no	no	yes	yes
MASSACHUSETTS Assumption College						
Flagg Street School	no	yes	no	yes	yes	no
MASSACHUSETTS University of Massachusetts, Amherst						
East Longmeadow High School	yes	yes	no	no	no	no

Professional Development School Characteristics - Table 2

Professional Development School	Preservice Teachers Program				Beginning Teachers Program	
	mentor teachers for preservice teachers	clinical supervision of student teachers	each preservice teacher assigned to more than one cooperating teacher	preservice teachers involved in educational research at school site	beginning teacher induction program	mentor teachers for beginning teachers
MASSACHUSETTS University of Massachusetts, Lowell						
Reading Memorial High School	yes	yes	yes	yes	yes	yes
MASSACHUSETTS Wheelock College						
Edward Devotion School	yes	yes	yes	no	no	no
MICHIGAN University of Michigan, Dearborn						
Catherine B. White Elementary School	no	no	no	no	no	no
MICHIGAN Western Michigan University						
Battlecreek Central High School	yes	yes	no	yes	no	no
Prairieview Elementary School	yes	yes	no	yes	n/a	n/a
MINNESOTA University of Minnesota						
Patrick Henry Professional Practice School	no	yes	n/a	no	yes	yes

Professional Development School Characteristics - Table 2

Professional Development School	Preservice Teachers Program				Beginning Teachers Program	
	mentor teachers for preservice teachers	clinical supervision of student teachers	each preservice teacher assigned to more than one cooperating teacher	preservice teachers involved in educational research at school site	beginning teacher induction program	mentor teachers for beginning teachers
MISSOURI Harris-Stowe State College						
Shepard Accelerated School Partnership	yes	yes	yes	yes	yes	yes
MISSOURI Maryville University						
South High School	yes	yes	yes	yes	yes	yes
Wilkinson Early Childhood Center	yes	yes	no	yes	yes	yes
MISSOURI Saint Louis University						
Wyman School	yes	yes	no	no	no	no
MISSOURI University of Missouri, Kansas City						
Center Elementary School	yes	yes	yes	no	no	no
Red Bridge Elementary School	yes	yes	no response	yes	yes	yes
MISSOURI University of Missouri, St. Louis						
Chaney Elementary School	yes	yes	n/a	yes	no	no

Professional Development School Characteristics - Table 2

Professional Development School	Preservice Teachers Program				Beginning Teachers Program	
	mentor teachers for preservice teachers	clinical supervision of student teachers	each preservice teacher assigned to more than one cooperating teacher	preservice teachers involved in educational research at school site	beginning teacher induction program	mentor teachers for beginning teachers
Laclede Elementary School	no	yes	no	yes	no	yes
Parkway Central Middle School	yes	yes	no	yes	no	no
Parkway River Bend Elementary School	no	yes	no	no	no	no
MISSOURI **Washington University**						
Kirkwood High School	yes	yes	no	yes	no	no
NEW JERSEY **Rowan College of New Jersey**						
Cooper's Point Professional Development Family School of Excellence	yes	yes	yes	yes	n/a	n/a
Winslow Professional Development District	yes	yes	yes	yes	n/a	n/a
NEW YORK **Buffalo State College**						
Charles Drew Science Magnet School	yes	yes	yes	n/a	n/a	n/a
Como Park Elementary School	yes	n/a	no	n/a	n/a	n/a
Futures Academy	yes	n/a	no	n/a	n/a	n/a

Professional Development School Characteristics - Table 2

Professional Development School	Preservice Teachers Program				Beginning Teachers Program	
	mentor teachers for preservice teachers	clinical supervision of student teachers	each preservice teacher assigned to more than one cooperating teacher	preservice teachers involved in educational research at school site	beginning teacher induction program	mentor teachers for beginning teachers
Hoover Elementary School	no	yes	n/a	yes	no	no
NEW YORK Columbia University						
I.S. 44	yes	yes	no response	no response		yes
P.S. 87	yes	yes	no response	no response	no response	no response
NEW YORK Syracuse University						
Camillus Middle School	yes	yes	yes	no	yes	yes
East Hill Elementary School	yes	yes	yes	yes	yes	yes
Edward Smith Elementary School	yes	yes	yes	yes	yes	yes
Franklin Elementary School	yes	yes	yes	yes	yes	yes
Jamesville Elementary School	yes	yes	yes	n/a	yes	yes
Jamesville-DeWitt High School	yes	yes	yes	n/a	yes	yes
Jamesville-DeWitt Middle School	yes	yes	yes	n/a	yes	yes
Moses-DeWitt Elementary School	yes	yes	yes	n/a	yes	yes

Professional Development School Characteristics - Table 2

Professional Development School	Preservice Teachers Program				Beginning Teachers Program	
	mentor teachers for preservice teachers	clinical supervision of student teachers	each preservice teacher assigned to more than one cooperating teacher	preservice teachers involved in educational research at school site	beginning teacher induction program	mentor teachers for beginning teachers
Onondaga Road Elementary School	yes	yes	yes	yes	yes	yes
Split Rock Elementary School	yes	yes	yes	yes	yes	yes
Stonehedge Elementary School	yes	yes	yes	yes	yes	yes
Tecumseh Elementary School	yes	yes	yes	n/a	yes	yes
Webster Elementary School	yes	yes	yes	yes	yes	yes
West Genesee Middle School	yes	yes	yes	yes	yes	yes
West Genesee Senior High School	yes	yes	yes	yes	yes	yes
NORTH CAROLINA University of North Carolina, Greensboro						
Archer Elementary School	yes	yes	yes	yes	no response	no response
Bluford Elementary School	yes	yes	yes	yes	n/a	n/a
Brightwood Elementary School	yes	yes	yes	yes	n/a	n/a
Global Magnet School	yes	yes	yes	yes	n/a	n/a

Professional Development School Characteristics - Table 2

Professional Development School	Preservice Teachers Program				Beginning Teachers Program	
	mentor teachers for preservice teachers	clinical supervision of student teachers	each preservice teacher assigned to more than one cooperating teacher	preservice teachers involved in educational research at school site	beginning teacher induction program	mentor teachers for beginning teachers
Greene Elementary School	yes	yes	yes	yes	n/a	n/a
Guilford Middle School	yes	yes	yes	yes	no response	no response
Guilford Primary School	yes	yes	yes	yes	no response	no response
Jackson Middle School	yes	yes	yes	yes	n/a	n/a
Jamestown Middle School	yes	yes	yes	yes	n/a	n/a
Jesse Wharton Elementary School	yes	yes	yes	yes	n/a	n/a
Kernersville Elementary School	yes	yes	yes	yes	no response	no response
Kiser Middle School	yes	yes	yes	yes	no response	no response
Mills Road Elementary School	yes	yes	yes	yes	n/a	n/a
Oak Hill Elementary School	yes	yes	yes	yes	n/a	n/a
Oak View Elementary School	yes	yes	yes	yes	no response	no response
Piney Grove Elementary School	yes	yes	yes	yes	n/a	n/a
Rankin Elementary School	yes	yes	yes	yes	no response	no response

Professional Development School Characteristics - Table 2

Professional Development School	Preservice Teachers Program				Beginning Teachers Program	
	mentor teachers for preservice teachers	clinical supervision of student teachers	each preservice teacher assigned to more than one cooperating teacher	preservice teachers involved in educational research at school site	beginning teacher induction program	mentor teachers for beginning teachers
Sedgefield Elementary School	yes	yes	yes	yes	n/a	n/a
Shadybrook Elementary School	yes	yes	yes	yes	n/a	n/a
Western Guilford High School	yes	yes	yes	yes	n/a	n/a
NORTH DAKOTA University of North Dakota						
Lake Agassiz Elementary School	yes	yes	yes	yes	no response	no response
OHIO Ohio State University						
Etna Road Elementary School - Project TEACH	yes	yes	yes	no	no	no
Independence High School - Project TRI	yes	yes	no	no	yes	yes
Northland High School - Northland Teaching Academy	yes	yes	yes	yes	n/a	n/a
Thomas Worthington High School	yes	yes	no response	yes	no	no
PENNSYLVANIA Bloomsburg University						
Danville Elementary School	yes	yes	yes	yes	no response	no response
PENNSYLVANIA Millersville University						

Professional Development School Characteristics - Table 2

Professional Development School	Preserve Teachers Program				Beginning Teachers Program	
	mentor teachers for preservice teachers	clinical supervision of student teachers	each preservice teacher assigned to more than one cooperating teacher	preservice teachers involved in educational research at school site	beginning teacher induction program	mentor teachers for beginning teachers
Conestoga Valley Middle School	yes	yes	no	yes	no	no
Manheim Township Middle School	yes	yes	no	yes	no	no
SOUTH CAROLINA University of South Carolina						
Airport High School	yes	yes	no response	no response	yes	yes
Crayton Middle School	yes	yes	no response	no response		yes
Hood Street School	yes	yes	no response	no response	no response	yes
Horrell Hill Elementary School	yes	yes	no response	yes	no response	no response
Hyatt Park School	yes	yes	no response	no response	no response	yes
Meadowfield Elementary School	yes	no response	no response	no response	yes	no response
Pierce Terrace School	yes	yes	yes	yes	yes	yes
Pinckney Elementary School	yes	yes	no response	no response	no response	yes
Pontiac Elementary School	yes	yes	no response	yes	no response	no response

Professional Development School Characteristics - Table 2

Professional Development School	Preservice Teachers Program				Beginning Teachers Program	
	mentor teachers for preservice teachers	clinical supervision of student teachers	each preservice teacher assigned to more than one cooperating teacher	preservice teachers involved in educational research at school site	beginning teacher induction program	mentor teachers for beginning teachers
Summitt Parkway Middle School	yes	yes	no response	no response	yes	yes
White Knoll Elementary School	yes	yes	no response	yes	no response	no response
TENNESSEE Austin Peay State University						
Burt Elementary School	yes	yes	no	n/a	yes	yes
TENNESSEE Memphis State University						
Campus School	yes	yes	no	no	yes	yes
Coleman Elementary School	yes	yes	yes	no	yes	yes
Dyer County Central Elementary School	yes	yes	yes	no	no	no
Frayser Elementary School	yes	yes	yes	yes	no	no
Lipman School	yes	yes	no	no	yes	yes
Newberry Elementary School	yes	yes	no	yes	yes	yes
Raleigh Egypt Middle School	yes	yes	yes	yes	yes	yes

Professional Development School Characteristics - Table 2

Professional Development School	Preservice Teachers Program				Beginning Teachers Program	
	mentor teachers for preservice teachers	clinical supervision of student teachers	each preservice teacher assigned to more than one cooperating teacher	preservice teachers involved in educational research at school site	beginning teacher induction program	mentor teachers for beginning teachers
TEXAS **Incarnate Word College**						
Ross Elementary	yes	yes	no	no	no	no
Brewer Elementary School	yes	yes	no	no	no	no
Clark High School	yes	yes	no	no	no	no
Connell Middle School	yes	yes	yes	no	no	no
Coronado Escobar Elementary School	yes	yes	no	no	yes	yes
Driscoll Middle School	yes	yes	yes	no	no	no
Emma Frey Elementary School	yes	yes	no	no	no	no
Gadendale Elementary School	yes	yes	no	no	no	no
Hawthorne Elementary School	yes	yes	yes	yes	yes	yes
Hutchins Elementary School	yes	yes	no	no	no	no
Jackson-Keller Elementary School	yes	yes	yes	yes	yes	yes
Kingsborough Middle School	yes	yes	no	no	no	no

Professional Development School Characteristics - Table 2

Professional Development School	Preservice Teachers Program				Beginning Teachers Program	
	mentor teachers for preservice teachers	clinical supervision of student teachers	each preservice teacher assigned to more than one cooperating teacher	preservice teachers involved in educational research at school site	beginning teacher induction program	mentor teachers for beginning teachers
Lamar Elementary School	yes	yes	no	no	no	no
Loma Park Elementary School	yes	n/a	yes	no	n/a	n/a
Mark Twain Middle School	yes	yes	yes	yes	yes	yes
Memorial High School	yes	n/a	yes	no	n/a	n/a
Providence High School	no	no	no	no	no	no
Robert E. Lee High School	yes	yes	yes	yes	yes	yes
Rodriguez Elementary School	yes	yes	yes	yes	no	no
St. Martin Hall	yes	yes	no	no	no	yes
St. Peter Prince of the Apostles	yes	yes	yes	no	no	no
Travis Elementary School	yes	yes	no	no	no	no
Truman Middle School	yes	n/a	yes	yes	n/a	n/a
TEXAS Lubbock Christian University						

Professional Development School Characteristics - Table 2

Professional Development School	Preservice Teachers Program				Beginning Teachers Program	
	mentor teachers for preservice teachers	clinical supervision of student teachers	each preservice teacher assigned to more than one cooperating teacher	preservice teachers involved in educational research at school site	beginning teacher induction program	mentor teachers for beginning teachers
Brown Elementary School	yes	no	no	no	n/a	n/a
Hardwick Elementary School	yes	yes	no	no	n/a	n/a
Parkway Elementary School	yes	yes	no	no	n/a	n/a
TEXAS Southwest Texas State University						
Bowie Elementary School	yes	yes	yes	no	yes	yes
Elgin Middle School	yes	yes	yes	no	yes	yes
Goodnight Junior High School	yes	yes	yes	no	yes	yes
Highland Park Elementary School	yes	yes	yes	no	yes	yes
TEXAS Texas A&M University						
Houston Teaching Academy	yes	yes	yes	yes	yes	yes
TEXAS Texas Tech University						
Bayless Elementary School	no	no	yes	no	no	no

Professional Development School Characteristics - Table 2

Professional Development School	Preservice Teachers Program				Beginning Teachers Program	
	mentor teachers for preservice teachers	clinical supervision of student teachers	each preservice teacher assigned to more than one cooperating teacher	preservice teachers involved in educational research at school site	beginning teacher induction program	mentor teachers for beginning teachers
Hutchinson Junior High School	no	no	yes	no	no	no
Lubbock High School	no	no	yes	no	no	no
Mackenzie Junior High School	no	no	yes	no	no	no
Ramirez Elementary School	no	no	yes	no	no	no
TEXAS University of Houston						
Wilson ISD	no	no	yes	no	no	no
Ben Milam Professional Development and Technology Center	yes	yes	yes	no	no	no
Hamilton Professional Development and Technology Center	yes	yes	yes	no	no	no
Kennedy Professional Development and Technology Center	yes	yes	yes	no	no	no
Lockhart Professional Development and Technology Center	yes	yes	yes	no	no	no
Rufus Cage Professional Development and Technology Center	yes	yes	yes	no	no	no

Professional Development School Characteristics - Table 2

Professional Development School	Preservice Teachers Program				Beginning Teachers Program	
	mentor teachers for preservice teachers	clinical supervision of student teachers	each preservice teacher assigned to more than one cooperating teacher	preservice teachers involved in educational research at school site	beginning teacher induction program	mentor teachers for beginning teachers
Valley Oaks Professional Development and Technology Center	yes	yes	yes	no	no	no
Westwood Professional Development and Technology Center	yes	yes	yes	no	no	no
Woodview Professional Development and Technology Center	yes	yes	yes	no	no	no
TEXAS University of Houston, Clearlake						
Alvin Junior High School	yes	yes	yes	yes	yes	yes
Central Middle School	no	no	no	no	no	no
George Washington Carver Elementary School	yes	yes	yes	yes	yes	yes
TEXAS University of Texas, El Paso						
H.D. Hiley Elementary School	yes	yes	yes	yes	no	yes
Lamar Elementary School	yes	yes	yes	yes	no	yes
Riverside High School	yes	yes	yes	yes	no	yes

Professional Development School Characteristics - Table 2

Professional Development School	Preservice Teachers Program				Beginning Teachers Program	
	mentor teachers for preservice teachers	clinical supervision of student teachers	each preservice teacher assigned to more than one cooperating teacher	preservice teachers involved in educational research at school site	beginning teacher induction program	mentor teachers for beginning teachers
Wiggs Middle School	yes	yes	yes	yes	no	yes
Ysleta Elementary School	yes	yes	yes	yes	no	yes
UTAH Brigham-Young University						
Alpine Elementary School	no	no	no	yes	yes	yes
Aspen Elementary School	yes	yes	yes	yes	yes	yes
Barratt Elementary School	no	yes	yes	no	yes	yes
Canyon Crest Elementary School	yes	yes	no	no	yes	yes
Cascade Elementary School	yes	yes	yes	no	yes	yes
Copperview Elementary School	yes	yes	yes	yes	yes	yes
Cottonwood Heights Elementary School	yes	yes	yes	yes	yes	yes
Draper Elementary School	yes	yes	yes	yes	yes	yes
Edgemont Elementary School	yes	yes	yes	no	yes	yes
Franklin Elementary School	yes	yes	no	no	yes	yes

Professional Development School Characteristics - Table 2

Professional Development School	Preservice Teachers Program				Beginning Teachers Program	
	mentor teachers for preservice teachers	clinical supervision of student teachers	each preservice teacher assigned to more than one cooperating teacher	preservice teachers involved in educational research at school site	beginning teacher induction program	mentor teachers for beginning teachers
Geneva Elemenmtary School	yes	yes	no	no	yes	yes
Goshen Elementary School	yes	yes	yes	no	n/a	n/a
Grant Elementary School	yes	yes	no	yes	yes	yes
Highland Elementary School	yes	yes	no	yes	yes	yes
Jordan Ridge Elementary School	yes	yes	yes	yes	yes	yes
Larsen Elementary School	yes	yes	no	yes	yes	yes
Lindon Elementary School	yes	yes	no	no	yes	yes
Maeser Elementary School	yes	yes	yes	no	yes	yes
Manila Elementary School	yes	yes	yes	no	yes	yes
Mapleton Elementary School	yes	yes	no	yes	yes	yes
Parkview Elementary School	yes	yes	no	no	no	yes
Rees Elementary School	yes	yes	yes	no	yes	yes
Rock Canyon Elementary School	yes	yes	yes	yes	yes	yes

Professional Development School Characteristics - Table 2

Professional Development School	Preservice Teachers Program					Beginning Teachers Program	
		mentor teachers for preservice teachers	clinical supervision of student teachers	each preservice teacher assigned to more than one cooperating teacher	preservice teachers involved in educational research at school site	beginning teacher induction program	mentor teachers for beginning teachers
Sage Creek Elementary School		yes	yes	yes	yes		n/a	yes
Salem Elementary School		yes	yes	n/a	no		no	yes
Santaquin Elementary School		yes	yes	no	no		yes	yes
Shelley Elementary School		yes	yes	no	no		yes	yes
Southland Elementary School		yes	yes	yes	yes		yes	yes
Sprucewood Elementary School		yes	yes	no	no		yes	yes
Sunrise Elementary School		yes	yes	yes	yes		yes	yes
Sunset View Elementary School		yes	yes	yes	n/a		yes	yes
Taylor Elementary School		yes	yes	no	no		yes	yes
Timpanogos Elementary School		yes	yes	yes	yes		yes	yes
Westmore Elementary School		yes	yes	no	yes		yes	yes
Westridge Elementary School		yes	yes	yes	n/a		n/a	yes
Willow Canyon Elementary School		yes	yes	yes	yes		yes	yes

Professional Development School Characteristics - Table 2

Professional Development School	Preservice Teachers Program				Beginning Teachers Program	
	mentor teachers for preservice teachers	clinical supervision of student teachers	each preservice teacher assigned to more than one cooperating teacher	preservice teachers involved in educational research at school site	beginning teacher induction program	mentor teachers for beginning teachers
Wilson Elementary School	yes	yes	yes	yes	yes	yes
UTAH University of Utah						
Bountiful Elementary School	yes	yes	yes	no	no	no
Eisenhower Junior High School	yes	yes	yes	no	no	no
Granger High School	yes	yes	yes	yes	no	no
Highland High School	yes	yes	yes	no	no	no
Nibley Park Elementary School	yes	yes	yes	yes	no	no
Washington Elementary School - Exemplary Practice School	n/a	n/a	n/a	n/a	yes	yes
VIRGINIA University of Virginia						
Jackson-Via Elementary School	yes	yes	no response	yes	no response	no response
VIRGINIA Virginia Commonwealth University						
Whitcomb Model Elementary School	yes	yes	yes	no	no	no

Professional Development School Characteristics - Table 2

Professional Development School	Preservice Teachers Program				Beginning Teachers Program	
	mentor teachers for preservice teachers	clinical supervision of student teachers	each preservice teacher assigned to more than one cooperating teacher	preservice teachers involved in educational research at school site	beginning teacher induction program	mentor teachers for beginning teachers
WASHINGTON University of Washington						
Adelaide Elementary School	n/a	n/a	n/a	n/a	no	no
Cedar Wood Elementary School	n/a	n/a	n/a	n/a	no	no
Clear Creek Elementary School	n/a	n/a	n/a	n/a	no	no
Juanita Elementary School	n/a	n/a	n/a	n/a	no	no
Kennydale Elementary School	n/a	n/a	n/a	n/a	no	no
Maple Hills Elementary School	n/a	n/a	n/a	n/a	no	no
Meany Middle School/Professional Development School	yes	yes	yes	no response	no	no response
Odle Middle School/Professional Development School	yes	yes	yes	no response	no response	no response
WASHINGTON Washington State University						
Lincoln Middle School	yes	yes	yes	yes	no response	yes
WEST VIRGINIA West Virginia University						

Professional Development School Characteristics - Table 2

Professional Development School	Preservice Teachers Program				Beginning Teachers Program	
	mentor teachers for preservice teachers	clinical supervision of student teachers	each preservice teacher assigned to more than one cooperating teacher	preservice teachers involved in educational research at school site	beginning teacher induction program	mentor teachers for beginning teachers
Central Elementary School	yes	yes	no	no	no	no
East Dale Elementary School	yes	yes	no	no	no	no
Grafton High School	yes	yes	no	no	no	no
Morgantown High School	yes	yes	yes	no	no	no
Suncrest Primary School	yes	yes	yes	yes	no	no
WISCONSIN University of Wisconsin, Madison						
Lincoln Elementary School	yes	yes	no	yes	no	no

Professional Development School Characteristics - Table 3

Professional Development School	Beginning Teachers Program	Inservice Teachers Program				
	clinical supervision of beginning teachers	on-site (school) courses for inservice teachers	cooperating teacher training provided to practicing teachers	experienced teachers designated as master teachers	mentor, master, &/or cooperating teachers have reduced course load	mentor, master, &/or cooperating teachers have release time
ARKANSAS University of Arkansas, Fayetteville						
George Elementary School	no	yes	no	no	no	no
Jefferson Elementary School	no response	no response	yes	no response	no response	no response
Woodland Junior High School	no response	no response	no response	no response	no response	no response
CALIFORNIA California State University, Fullerton						
Golden Hill School	no	no	yes	yes	no	yes
Highland School	no	no	yes	yes	no	yes
Ladera Palma School	no	no	yes	yes	no	yes
Linda Vista School	no	no	yes	yes	no	yes
Monte Vista School	no	no	yes	yes	no	yes
Raymond School	no	no	yes	yes	no	yes
Sierra Vista School	no	no	yes	yes	no	yes

Professional Development School Characteristics - Table 3

Professional Development School	Beginning Teachers Program	Inservice Teachers Program				
	clinical supervision of beginning teachers	on-site (school) courses for inservice teachers	cooperating teacher training provided to practicing teachers	experienced teachers designated as master teachers	mentor, master, &/or cooperating teachers have reduced course load	mentor, master, &/or cooperating teachers have release time
Tynes School	no	no	yes	yes	no	yes
Vicentia School	no	no	yes	yes	no	yes
CALIFORNIA **San Diego State University**						
Alliance for Excellence	no	yes	no	yes	no	no
Chula Vista Professional Development School	yes	yes	no	yes	no	no
Kennedy Lab School	no	yes	no	yes	no	no
Model Education Center	no	no	no	yes	no	no
Marshall Professional Development School	no	yes	no	yes	no	no
Partners in Education	no	yes	no	yes	no	no
CALIFORNIA **University of California, Riverside**						
Ribidoux High School	no response	yes	yes	no response	no response	yes
DELAWARE **University of Delaware**						
Thurgood Marshall Elementary School	yes	yes	yes	yes	yes	yes

Professional Development School Characteristics - Table 3

Professional Development School	Beginning Teachers Program	Inservice Teachers Program				
	clinical supervision of beginning teachers	on-site (school) courses for inservice teachers	cooperating teacher training provided to practicing teachers	experienced teachers designated as master teachers	mentor, master, &/or cooperating teachers have reduced course load	mentor, master, &/or cooperating teachers have release time
FLORIDA **University of South Florida**						
Thomas E. Weightman Middle School	yes	yes	yes	no	no	
GEORGIA **Armstrong State College**						
White Bluff Elementary School	no	yes	yes	no	no	no
ILLINOIS **DePaul University**						
Glenview Teacher Preparation Program	yes	no	yes	yes	no	yes
ILLINOIS **Elmhurst College**						
Brook Park School	n/a	n/a	yes	yes	no	no
Bryan Junior High School	n/a	n/a	yes	yes	no	no
Conrad Fischer School	n/a	n/a	yes	yes	no	no
Early Childhood Education Center	n/a	n/a	yes	yes	no	no
Emerson School	n/a	n/a	yes	yes	no	no
Euclid School	n/a	n/a	yes	yes	no	no

Professional Development School Characteristics - Table 3

Professional Development School	Beginning Teachers Program	clinical supervision of beginning teachers	Inservice Teachers Program	on-site (school) courses for inservice teachers	cooperating teacher training provided to practicing teachers	experienced teachers designated as master teachers	mentor, master, &/or cooperating teachers have reduced course load	mentor, master, &/or cooperating teachers have release time
Field School		n/a		n/a	yes	yes	no	no
Gower West School		n/a		n/a	yes	yes	no	no
Grant School		n/a		n/a	yes	yes	no	no
Hinsdale Central High School		n/a		n/a	yes	yes	no	no
Indian Trail Junior High School		n/a		n/a	yes	yes	no	no
Jackson School		n/a		n/a	yes	yes	no	no
Jefferson School		n/a		n/a	yes	yes	no	no
Jefferson School		n/a		n/a	yes	yes	no	no
Lake Park Elementary School		n/a		n/a	yes	yes	no	no
Leyden High School-East Campus		n/a		n/a	yes	yes	no	no
Leyden High School-West Campus		n/a		n/a	yes	yes	no	no
Lincoln Elementary School		n/a		n/a	yes	yes	no	no
Lincoln Primary School		n/a		n/a	yes	yes	no	no

Professional Development School Characteristics - Table 3

Professional Development School	Beginning Teachers Program		Inservice Teachers Program			
	clinical supervision of beginning teachers		on-site (school) courses for inservice teachers	cooperating teacher training provided to practicing teachers	experienced teachers designated as master teachers	mentor, master, &/or cooperating teachers have reduced course load
McKinley School		n/a		n/a	yes	yes
Queen Bee School		n/a		n/a	yes	yes
Reskin School		n/a		n/a	yes	yes
Roosevelt Elementary School		n/a		n/a	yes	yes
Roosevelt Junior High School		n/a		n/a	yes	yes
Sandburg Junior High School		n/a		n/a	yes	yes
Schafer School		n/a		n/a	yes	yes
Spring Hills School		n/a		n/a	yes	yes
Bellwood Preschool		n/a		n/a	yes	yes
Stone Park Preschool		n/a		n/a	yes	yes
Stone School		n/a		n/a	yes	yes
Wesley School	n/a		n/a		yes	yes
Westmore School	n/a		n/a		yes	yes

(Additional columns:) cooperating teacher training provided to practicing teachers = yes (all rows); experienced teachers designated as master teachers = yes (all rows); mentor, master, &/or cooperating teachers have reduced course load = no (all rows); mentor, master, &/or cooperating teachers have release time = no (all rows).

Professional Development School Characteristics - Table 3

Professional Development School	Beginning Teachers Program	Inservice Teachers Program			
	clinical supervision of beginning teachers	on-site (school) courses for inservice teachers	cooperating teacher training provided to practicing teachers	experienced teachers designated as master teachers	mentor, master, &/or cooperating teachers have reduced course load	mentor, master, &/or cooperating teachers have release time
ILLINOIS National Louis University						
York High School	n/a	n/a	yes	yes	no	no
Glenview/Northbrook	no	yes	yes	no	no	no
INDIANA Indiana State University						
Chauncey Rose Middle School	yes	yes	yes	no	no	no
Fayette Elementary School	yes	yes	yes	no	no	no
Meadows Elementary School	yes	yes	yes	no	no	no
Rosedale Elementary School	yes	yes	yes	no	no	no
South Vermillion High School	yes	yes	yes	no	no	no
Stauton Elementary School	yes	yes	yes	no	no	no
Terre Haute North Vigo High School	yes	yes	yes	no	no	no
Terre Haute South Vigo High School	yes	yes	yes	no	no	no
West Vigo High School	yes	yes	yes	no	no	no

Professional Development School Characteristics - Table 3

Professional Development School	Beginning Teachers Program	Inservice Teachers Program				
	clinical supervision of beginning teachers	on-site (school) courses for inservice teachers	cooperating teacher training provided to practicing teachers	experienced teachers designated as master teachers	mentor, master, &/or cooperating teachers have reduced course load	mentor, master, &/or cooperating teachers have release time
West Vigo School	yes	yes	yes	no	no	no
INDIANA Indiana University Northwest						
Central High School	no	no	yes	no	yes	no
Eggers Elementary Middle School	yes	no	yes	no	no	no
Franklin Elementary School	no	yes	yes	no	no	no
Horace Mann High School	yes	no	no	yes	no	no
Lincoln Elementary	yes	yes	yes	yes	no	no
INDIANA Indiana University Purdue University Indianapolis (IUPUI)						
Arsenal Technical High School	n/a	yes	yes	no	no	no
Franklin Central High School	n/a	yes	yes	no	no	no
Franklin Township Middle School	n/a	yes	yes	no	no	no
Harcourt Elementary School	n/a	yes	yes	no	no	no

Professional Development School Characteristics - Table 3

Professional Development School	Beginning Teachers Program	Inservice Teachers Program	cooperating teacher training provided to practicing teachers	experienced teachers designated as master teachers	mentor, master, &/or cooperating teachers have reduced course load	mentor, master, &/or cooperating teachers have release time
	clinical supervision of beginning teachers	on-site (school) courses for inservice teachers				
Indian Creek Elementary School	n/a	yes	yes	no	no	no
James A. Garfield	n/a	yes	yes	no	no	no
North Central High School	n/a	yes	yes	no	no	no
Riverside School	n/a	yes	yes	no	no	no
Westlane Middle School	n/a	yes	yes	no	no	no
INDIANA Purdue University						
Klondike Elementary School	no	no	no	yes	no	no
Lafayette School Corporation	yes	yes	yes	no	no	yes
Pine Village School	no	no	no	no	no	no
INDIANA Emporia State University						
Countryside Elementary School	no	yes	yes	yes	no	no
Pleasant Ridge Elementary School	no	yes	yes	yes	no	no
IOWA Drake University						

Professional Development School Characteristics - Table 3

Professional Development School	Beginning Teachers Program	Inservice Teachers Program				
	clinical supervision of beginning teachers	on-site (school) courses for inservice teachers	cooperating teacher training provided to practicing teachers	experienced teachers designated as master teachers	mentor, master, &/or cooperating teachers have reduced course load	mentor, master, &/or cooperating teachers have release time
IOWA Iowa State University						
Moulton Elementary School	yes	yes	yes	yes	no	no
Madrid School System	n/a	no	yes	yes	no	no
Project Opportunity - ISU/Madrid Site	n/a	yes	yes	yes	n/a	no
IOWA University of Northern Iowa						
Malcolm Price Laboratory School	yes	yes	yes	n/a	n/a	n/a
KANSAS Fort Hays State University						
O'Loughlin Elementary School	yes	yes	yes	yes	no	no
LOUISIANA University of New Orleans						
Grace King High School	no	no	yes	yes	no	no
H.C. Schaumburg Elementary School	no	yes	yes	no	no	no
Jefferson Elementary School	no response	no	yes	yes	no	no
John Dibert Elementary School	no	no	yes	yes	no	yes

Professional Development School Characteristics - Table 3

Professional Development School	Beginning Teachers Program		Inservice Teachers Program				
		clinical supervision of beginning teachers		on-site (school) courses for inservice teachers	cooperating teacher training provided to practicing teachers	experienced teachers designated as master teachers	mentor, master, &/or cooperating teachers have reduced course load	mentor, master, &/or cooperating teachers have release time
Paul J. Solis Elementary School		no		no	no	yes	no	no
Warren Easton		yes		no response	no	no	no	no
MASSACHUSETTS Anna Maria College								
City View Professional Development School		no		no	no	no	no	no
Coolidge Professional Development School		no		no	no	yes	yes	yes
MASSACHUSETTS Assumption College								
Flagg Street School		yes		yes	yes	no	no	yes
MASSACHUSETTS University of Massachusetts, Amherst								
East Longmeadow High School		no		yes	yes	no	no	no
MASSACHUSETTS University of Massachusetts, Lowell								
Reading Memorial High School		yes		yes	yes	no	no	no
MASSACHUSETTS Wheelock College								

Professional Development School Characteristics - Table 3

Professional Development School	Beginning Teachers Program	Inservice Teachers Program				
	clinical supervision of beginning teachers	on-site (school) courses for inservice teachers	cooperating teacher training provided to practicing teachers	experienced teachers designated as master teachers	mentor, master, &/or cooperating teachers have reduced course load	mentor, master, &/or cooperating teachers have release time
Edward Devotion School	no	no	yes	no	yes	yes
MICHIGAN University of Michigan, Dearborn						
Catherine B. White Elementary School	no	yes	yes	no	no	no
MICHIGAN Western Michigan University						
Battlecreek Central High School	no	no	yes	no	no	yes
Prairieview Elementary School	n/a	yes	yes	yes	no	yes
MINNESOTA University of Minnesota						
Patrick Henry Professional Practice School	yes	no	no	no	yes	yes
MISSOURI Harris-Stowe State College						
Shepard Accelerated School Partnership	yes	yes	yes	yes	no	yes
MISSOURI Maryville University						
South High School	yes	yes	yes	yes	no	no

Professional Development School Characteristics - Table 3

Professional Development School	Beginning Teachers Program		Inservice Teachers Program				
		clinical supervision of beginning teachers		on-site (school) courses for inservice teachers	cooperating teacher training provided to practicing teachers	experienced teachers designated as master teachers	mentor, master, &/or cooperating teachers have reduced course load	mentor, master, &/or cooperating teachers have release time
MISSOURI Saint Louis University							
Wilkinson Early Childhood Center		yes		yes	yes	no	no	no
Wyman School		no		no	no	no	no	yes
MISSOURI University of Missouri, Kansas City							
Center Elementary School		no		yes	no	yes	no	no
Red Bridge Elementary School		no response		no response	no response	no response	no response	no response
MISSOURI University of Missouri, St. Louis							
Chaney Elementary School		yes		yes	yes	no	no	yes
Laclede Elementary School		yes		yes	yes	yes	no	no
Parkway Central Middle School		yes		no	no	yes	no	no
MISSOURI Washington University							
Parkway River Bend Elementary School		yes		yes	no	no	no	no

Professional Development School Characteristics - Table 3

Professional Development School	Beginning Teachers Program	Inservice Teachers Program				
	clinical supervision of beginning teachers	on-site (school) courses for inservice teachers	cooperating teacher training provided to practicing teachers	experienced teachers designated as master teachers	mentor, master, &/or cooperating teachers have reduced course load	mentor, master, &/or cooperating teachers have &/or release time
Kirkwood High School	no	yes	yes	yes	no	yes
NEW JERSEY **Rowan College of New Jersey**						
Cooper's Point Professional Development Family School of Excellence	n/a	yes	yes	n/a	n/a	yes
Winslow Professional Development District	n/a	yes	yes	n/a	n/a	yes
NEW YORK **Buffalo State College**						
Charles Drew Science Magnet School	n/a	yes	no	no	no	no
Como Park Elementary School	n/a	n/a	yes	no	no	no
Futures Academy	n/a	n/a	yes	no	no	no
Hoover Elementary School	no	no	no	no	no	no
NEW YORK **Columbia University**						
I.S. 44	no response	no response	no response	yes	no response	yes
P.S. 87	no response	yes	no response	yes	no response	yes

Professional Development School Characteristics - Table 3

Professional Development School	Beginning Teachers Program	Inservice Teachers Program				
	clinical supervision of beginning teachers	on-site (school) courses for inservice teachers	cooperating teacher training provided to practicing teachers	experienced teachers designated as master teachers	mentor, master, &/or cooperating teachers have reduced course load	mentor, master, &/or cooperating teachers have release time
NEW YORK Syracuse University						
Camillus Middle School	yes	yes	yes	no	no	no
East Hill Elementary School	no	yes	yes	no	no	no
Edward Smith Elementary School	yes	no	yes	no	no	no
Franklin Elementary School	yes	yes	yes	yes	no	no
Jamesville Elementary School	yes	yes	yes	yes	no	no
Jamesville-DeWitt High School	yes	yes	yes	yes	no	no
Jamesville-DeWitt Middle School	yes	yes	yes	no	no	no
Moses-DeWitt Elementary School	yes	yes	yes	no	no	no
Onondaga Road Elementary School	no	yes	yes	yes	no	no
Split Rock Elementary School	yes	yes	yes	yes	no	no
Stonehedge Elementary School	yes	yes	yes	yes	no	no
Tecumseh Elementary School	yes	yes	yes	no	no	no

221

Professional Development School Characteristics - Table 3

Professional Development School	Beginning Teachers Program — clinical supervision of beginning teachers	Inservice Teachers Program — on-site (school) courses for inservice teachers	cooperating teacher training provided to practicing teachers	experienced teachers designated as master teachers	mentor, master, &/or cooperating teachers have reduced course load	mentor, master, &/or cooperating teachers have release time
Webster Elementary School	yes	no	yes	no	no	no
West Genesee Middle School	yes	yes	yes	yes	no	no
West Genesee Senior High School	yes	yes	yes	yes	no	no
NORTH CAROLINA University of North Carolina, Greensboro						
Archer Elementary School	no response	no response	no response	no response	no response	no response
Bluford Elementary School	n/a	no	yes	no	no	no
Brightwood Elementary School	n/a	no	yes	no	no	no
Global Magnet School	n/a	no	yes	no	no	no
Greene Elementary School	n/a	no	yes	no	no	no
Guilford Middle School	no response	no response	no response	no response	no response	no response
Guilford Primary School	no response	no response	no response	no response	no response	no response
Jackson Middle School	n/a	no	yes	no	no	no
Jamestown Middle School	n/a	no	yes	no	no	no

222

Professional Development School Characteristics - Table 3

Professional Development School	Beginning Teachers Program	Inservice Teachers Program				
	clinical supervision of beginning teachers	on-site (school) courses for inservice teachers	cooperating teacher training provided to practicing teachers	experienced teachers designated as master teachers	mentor, master, &/or cooperating teachers have reduced course load	mentor, master, &/or cooperating teachers have release time
Jesse Wharton Elementary School	n/a	no	yes	no	no	no
Kernersville Elementary School	no response	no response	no response	no response	no response	no response
Kiser Middle School	no response	no response	no response	no response	no response	no response
Oak Hill Elementary School	n/a	no	yes	no	no	no
Mills Road Elementary School	n/a	no	yes	no	no	no
Oak View Elementary School	no response	no response	no response	no response	no response	no response
Piney Grove Elementary School	n/a	no	yes	no	no	no
Rankin Elementary School	no response	no response	no response	no response	no response	no response
Sedgefield Elementary School	n/a	no	yes	no	no	no
Shadybrook Elementary School	n/a	no	yes	no	no	no
Western Guilford High School	n/a	no	yes	no	no	no
NORTH DAKOTA **University of North Dakota**						
Lake Agassiz Elementary School	no response	no response	yes	no response	no response	no response

Professional Development School Characteristics - Table 3

Professional Development School	Beginning Teachers Program	Inservice Teachers Program				
	clinical supervision of beginning teachers	on-site (school) courses for inservice teachers	cooperating teacher training provided to practicing teachers	experienced teachers designated as master teachers	mentor, master, &/or cooperating teachers have reduced course load	mentor, master, &/or cooperating teachers have release time
OHIO Ohio State University						
Etna Road Elementary School - Project TEACH	no	yes	no	yes	no	
Independence High School - Project TRI	yes	yes	yes	no	no	no
Northland High School - Northland Teaching Academy	n/a	no	yes	no	no	no
Thomas Worthington High School	no	yes	no	no response	no	no
PENNSYLVANIA Bloomsburg University						
Danville Elementary School	no response	no response	no response	no response	no response	yes
PENNSYLVANIA Millersville University						
Conestoga Valley Middle School	no	no	yes	yes	no	no
Manheim Township Middle School	no	yes	yes	yes	no	no
SOUTH CAROLINA University of South Carolina						
Airport High School	yes	yes	no response	no response	no response	no response
Crayton Middle School	no response	no response	no response	no response	no response	no response

Professional Development School Characteristics - Table 3

Professional Development School	Beginning Teachers Program	Inservice Teachers Program				
	clinical supervision of beginning teachers	on-site (school) courses for inservice teachers	cooperating teacher training provided to practicing teachers	experienced teachers designated as master teachers	mentor, master, &/or cooperating teachers have reduced course load	mentor, master, &/or cooperating teachers have release time
Hood Street School	yes	no response	no response	no response	yes	no response
Horrell Hill Elementary School	no response	yes	yes	no response	no response	no response
Hyatt Park School	yes	no response	yes	no response	yes	yes
Meadowfield Elementary School	no response	no response	yes	no response	no response	no response
Pierce Terrace School	yes	yes	yes	yes	no response	no response
Pinckney Elementary School	yes	yes	yes	yes	yes	yes
Pontiac Elementary School	no response	yes	no response	no response	no response	no response
Summit Parkway Middle School	yes	yes	no response	no response	no response	no response
White Knoll Elementary School	no response	yes	no response	no response	no response	no response
TENNESSEE Austin Peay State University						
Burt Elementary School	yes	yes	yes	n/a	n/a	n/a
TENNESSEE Memphis State University						
Campus School	yes	no	yes	yes	no	no

225

Professional Development School Characteristics - Table 3

Professional Development School	Beginning Teachers Program		Inservice Teachers Program			
	clinical supervision of beginning teachers		on-site (school) courses for inservice teachers	cooperating teacher training provided to practicing teachers	experienced teachers designated as master teachers	mentor, master, &/or cooperating teachers have reduced course load	mentor, master, &/or cooperating teachers have release time
Coleman Elementary School	yes		yes	yes	yes	n/a	yes
Dyer County Central Elementary School	no		yes	no	no	no	no
Frayser Elementary School	no		yes	no	no	no	yes
Lipman School	yes		no	yes	no	no	no
Newbery Elementary School	yes		yes	yes	no	no	no
Raleigh Egypt Middle School	yes		yes	yes	yes	n/a	yes
Ross Elementary	yes		yes	yes	yes	no	no
TEXAS **Incarnate Word College**							
Brewer Elementary School	no		yes	yes	no	no	no
Clark High School	no		yes	yes	no	no	no
Connell-Middle School	no		no	yes	no	no	yes
Coronado Escobar Elementary School	no		yes	yes	yes	no	no
Driscoll Middle School	no		no	yes	no	no	yes

Professional Development School Characteristics - Table 3

Professional Development School	Beginning Teachers Program	Inservice Teachers Program				
	clinical supervision of beginning teachers	on-site (school) courses for inservice teachers	cooperating teacher training provided to practicing teachers	experienced teachers designated as master teachers	mentor, master, &/or cooperating teachers have reduced course load	mentor, master, &/or cooperating teachers have release time
Emma Frey Elementary School	no	yes	no	no	no	no
Gadendale Elementary School	no	yes	no	no	no	no
Hawthorne Elementary School	yes	no	yes	yes	no	no
Hutchins Elementary School	no	yes	no	no	no	no
Jackson-Keller Elementary School	yes	no	yes	yes	no	no
Kingsborough Middle School	no	yes	yes	no	no	no
Lamar Elementary School	no	yes	yes	no	no	no
Loma Park Elementary School	n/a	no	yes	yes	no	no
Mark Twain Middle School	yes	no	yes	yes	no	no
Memorial High School	n/a	no	yes	yes	no	no
Providence High School	no	yes	no	no	no	no
Robert E. Lee High School	yes	no	yes	yes	no	no
Rodriguez Elementary School	no	no	yes	no	no	no

Professional Development School Characteristics - Table 3

Professional Development School	Beginning Teachers Program		Inservice Teachers Program			
	clinical supervision of beginning teachers	on-site (school) courses for inservice teachers	cooperating teacher training provided to practicing teachers	experienced teachers designated as master teachers	mentor, master, &/or cooperating teachers have reduced course load	mentor, master, &/or cooperating teachers have release time
St. Martin Hall	no	yes	yes	yes	no	no
St. Peter Prince of the Apostles	no	no	yes	no	yes	yes
Travis Elementary School	no	yes	yes	no	no	no
Truman Middle School	n/a	no	yes	yes	no	no
TEXAS Lubbock Christian University						
Brown Elementary School	n/a	yes	yes	no	no	no
Hardwick Elementary School	n/a	yes	yes	no	no	no
Parkway Elementary School	n/a	yes	yes	no	no	no
TEXAS Southwest Texas State University						
Bowie Elementary School	yes	no	yes	no	no	yes
Elgin Middle School	yes	no	yes	no	no	yes
Goodnight Junior High School	yes	no	yes	no	no	yes

Professional Development School Characteristics - Table 3

Professional Development School	Beginning Teachers Program	Inservice Teachers Program				
	clinical supervision of beginning teachers	on-site (school) courses for inservice teachers	cooperating teacher training provided to practicing teachers	experienced teachers designated as master teachers	mentor, master, &/or cooperating teachers have reduced course load	mentor, master, &/or cooperating teachers have release time
Highland Park Elementary School	yes	no	yes	no	no	yes
TEXAS Texas A&M University						
Houston Teaching Academy	yes	yes	yes	yes	no response	yes
TEXAS Texas Tech University						
Bayless Elementary School	no	yes	no	no	no	no
Hutchinson Junior High School	no	yes	no	no	no	no
Lubbock High School	no	yes	no	no	no	no
Mackenzie Junior High School	no	yes	no	no	no	no
Ramirez Elementary School	no	yes	no	no	no	no
Wilson ISD	no	yes	no	no	no	no
TEXAS University of Houston						
Ben Milam Professional Development and Technology Center	no	yes	yes	yes	no	no

Professional Development School Characteristics - Table 3

Professional Development School	Beginning Teachers Program — clinical supervision of beginning teachers	Inservice Teachers Program — on-site (school) courses for inservice teachers	cooperating teacher training provided to practicing teachers	experienced teachers designated as master teachers	mentor, master, &/or cooperating teachers have reduced course load	mentor, master, &/or cooperating teachers have release time
Hamilton Professional Development and Technology Center	no	yes	yes		no	no
Kennedy Professional Development and Technology Center	no	yes	yes		no	no
Lockhart Professional Development and Technology Center	no	yes	yes		no	no
Rufus Cage Professional Development and Technology Center	no	yes	yes	yes	no	no
Valley Oaks Professional Development and Technology Center	no	yes	yes	yes	no	no
Westwood Professional Development and Technology Center	no	yes	yes	yes	no	no
Woodview Professional Development and Technology Center	no	yes	yes	yes	no	no
TEXAS University of Texas, El Paso						
Alvin Junior High School	no	yes	yes	yes	no	no
Central Middle School	no	no	no	no	no	no

Professional Development School Characteristics - Table 3

Professional Development School	Beginning Teachers Program	Inservice Teachers Program				
	clinical supervision of beginning teachers	on-site (school) courses for inservice teachers	cooperating teacher training provided to practicing teachers	experienced teachers designated as master teachers	mentor, master, &/or cooperating teachers have reduced course load	mentor, master, &/or cooperating teachers have release time
George Washington Carver Elementary School	no	yes	yes	yes	no	no
H.D. Hiley Elementary School	yes	no	yes	yes	no	no
Lamar Elementary School	yes	no	yes	yes	no	no
Riverside High School	yes	no	yes	yes	no	no
Wiggs Middle School	yes	no	yes	yes	no	no
Ysleta Elementary School	yes	no	yes	yes	no	no
UTAH Brigham-Young University						
Alpine Elementary School	no	yes	yes	yes	no	no
Aspen Elementary School	yes	yes	yes	yes	yes	yes
Barratt Elementary School	yes	yes	yes	yes	no	no
Canyon Crest Elementary School	yes	yes	yes	yes	yes	yes
Cascade Elementary School	yes	yes	yes	yes	no	no
Copperview Elementary School	yes	yes	no	no	no	no

Professional Development School Characteristics - Table 3

Professional Development School	Beginning Teachers Program	clinical supervision of beginning teachers	Inservice Teachers Program	on-site (school) courses for inservice teachers	cooperating teacher training provided to practicing teachers	experienced teachers designated as master teachers	mentor, master, &/or cooperating teachers have reduced course load	mentor, master, &/or cooperating teachers have release time
Cottonwood Heights Elementary School		yes		yes	yes	yes	no	yes
Draper Elementary School		yes		yes	no response	no response	no	no
Edgemont Elementary School		yes		yes	yes	yes	no	yes
Franklin Elementary School		yes		no	no	yes	yes	yes
Geneva Elememtary School		yes		yes	no	yes	no	yes
Goshen Elementary School		n/a		no	yes	yes	yes	yes
Grant Elementary School		yes		yes	yes	yes	yes	yes
Highland Elementary School		yes		yes	yes	yes	no	no
Jordan Ridge Elementary School		yes		yes	yes	yes	yes	yes
Larsen Elementary School		yes		yes	yes	yes	yes	yes
Lindon Elementary School		yes		yes	yes	no	no	no
Maeser Elementary School		yes		yes	no	no	no	yes
Manila Elementary School		yes		yes	yes	no	no	no

232

Professional Development School Characteristics - Table 3

Professional Development School	Beginning Teachers Program	Inservice Teachers Program				
	clinical supervision of beginning teachers	on-site (school) courses for inservice teachers	cooperating teacher training provided to practicing teachers	experienced teachers designated as master teachers	mentor, master, &/or cooperating teachers have reduced course load	mentor, master, &/or cooperating teachers have release time
Mapleton Elementary School	yes	yes	no	yes	yes	yes
Parkview Elementary School	yes	no	yes	yes	no	no
Rees Elementary School	yes	yes	yes	yes	yes	yes
Rock Canyon Elementary School	yes	yes	yes	yes	no	yes
Sage Creek Elementary School	yes	yes	yes	yes	no	no
Salem Elementary School	yes	yes	yes	yes	no	no
Santaquin Elementary School	yes	no response	yes	no	yes	yes
Shelley Elementary School	yes	yes	yes	no	no	yes
Southland Elementary School	yes	yes	yes	yes	yes	yes
Sprucewood Elementary School	no	yes	yes	yes	no	no
Sunrise Elementary School	yes	yes	yes	yes	no	no
Sunset View Elementary School	yes	yes	yes	yes	no	no
Taylor Elementary School	yes	yes	yes	yes	no	no response

233

Professional Development School Characteristics - Table 3

Professional Development School	Beginning Teachers Program	Inservice Teachers Program				
	clinical supervision of beginning teachers	on-site (school) courses for inservice teachers	cooperating teacher training provided to practicing teachers	experienced teachers designated as master teachers	mentor, master, &/or cooperating teachers have reduced course load	mentor, master, &/or cooperating teachers have release time
Timpanogos Elementary School	yes	yes	yes	no	no	yes
Westmore Elementary School	yes	yes	yes	yes	no	yes
Westridge Elementary School	yes	yes	yes	no	yes	yes
Willow Canyon Elementary School	yes	yes	yes	yes	yes	yes
Wilson Elementary School	yes	yes	yes	yes	yes	yes
UTAH **University of Utah**						
Bountiful Elementary School	no	yes	yes	no	no	no
Eisenhower Junior High School	no	yes	yes	no	yes	yes
Granger High School	no	yes	yes	no	yes	yes
Highland High School	no	yes	yes	no	yes	yes
Nibley Park Elementary School	no	yes	yes	no	yes	yes
Washington Elementary School - Exemplary Practice School	yes	yes	n/a	n/a	yes	yes
VIRGINIA **University of Virginia**						

234

Professional Development School Characteristics - Table 3

Professional Development School	Beginning Teachers Program		Inservice Teachers Program		cooperating teacher training provided to practicing teachers	experienced teachers designated as master teachers	mentor, master, &/or cooperating teachers have reduced course load	mentor, master, &/or cooperating teachers have release time
		clinical supervision of beginning teachers		on-site (school) courses for inservice teachers				
Jackson-Via Elementary School		no response		yes	yes	no response	no response	no response
VIRGINIA **Virginia Commonwealth University**								
Whitcomb Model Elementary School		no		yes	no	no	no	no
WASHINGTON **University of Washington**								
Adelaide Elementary School		no		no	yes	yes	n/a	n/a
Cedar Wood Elementary School		no		no	yes	yes	n/a	n/a
Clear Creek Elementary School		no		no	yes	yes	n/a	n/a
Juanita Elementary School		no		no	yes	yes	n/a	n/a
Kennydale Elementary School		no		no	yes	yes	n/a	n/a
Maple Hills Elementary School		no		no	yes	yes	n/a	n/a
Meany Middle School/Professional Development School		no response		yes	yes	no response	yes	no response
Odle Middle School/Professional Development School		no response		yes	yes	no response	yes	yes

Professional Development School Characteristics - Table 3

Professional Development School	Beginning Teachers Program	Inservice Teachers Program				
	clinical supervision of beginning teachers	on-site (school) courses for inservice teachers	cooperating teacher training provided to practicing teachers	experienced teachers designated as master teachers	mentor, master, &/or cooperating teachers have reduced course load	mentor, master, &/or cooperating teachers have release time
WASHINGTON **Washington State University**						
Lincoln Middle School	yes	yes	yes	yes	no response	no response
WEST VIRGINIA **West Virginia University**						
Central Elementary School	no	yes	yes	yes	no	no
East Dale Elementary School	no	yes	yes	yes	no	no
Grafton High School	no	yes	yes	yes	no	no
Morgantown High School	no	yes	yes	yes	no	no
Suncrest Primary School	no	yes	yes	yes	no	no
WISCONSIN **University of Wisconsin, Madison**						
Lincoln Elementary School	yes	yes	yes	no	no	no

Professional Development School	Inservice Teachers Program cont'd.			Multicultural Issues			
	practicing teachers involved in curriculum development	practicing teachers actively involved in decision making with regard to organizational/ structural changes within the school	inservice teachers involved in educational research conducted at the school site	preservice teachers participate in structured learning experiences that address issues related to educating minority group students	inservice teachers participate in structured learning experiences that address issues related to educating minority group students	approximate percentage of student enrollment from minority groups	approximate percentage of teacher interns (preservice teachers) from minority groups
ARKANSAS University of Arkansas, Fayetteville							
Woodland Junior High School	yes	yes	yes	no response	no response	0-19%	0-19%
Jefferson Elementary School	yes	yes	yes	yes	yes	20-39%	no response
George Elementary School	yes	yes	yes	yes	yes	0-19%	0-19%
CALIFORNIA California State University, Fullerton							
Golden Hill School	yes	n/a	no	yes	n/a	40-59%	0-19%
Highland School	yes	n/a	no	yes	n/a	0-19%	0-19%
Ladera Palma School	yes	n/a	no	yes	n/a	40-59%	0-19%
Linda Vista School	yes	n/a	no	yes	n/a	0-19%	0-19%
Monte Vista School	yes	n/a	no	yes	n/a	no response	80-100%
Raymond School	yes	n/a	no	yes	n/a	40-59%	0-19%
Sierra Vista School	yes	n/a	no	yes	n/a	40-59%	0-19%
Tynes School	yes	n/a	no	yes	n/a	40-59%	0-19%
Vicentia School	yes	n/a	no	yes	n/a	0-19%	0-19%

Professional Development School Characteristics - Table 4

Professional Development School	Inservice Teachers Program cont'd.			Multicultural Issues			
	practicing teachers involved in curriculum development	practicing teachers actively involved in decision making with regard to organizational/structural changes within the school	inservice teachers involved in educational research conducted at the school site	preservice teachers participate in structured learning experiences that address issues related to educating minority group students	inservice teachers participate in structured learning experiences that address issues related to educating minority group students	approximate percentage of student enrollment from minority groups	approximate percentage of teacher interns (preservice teachers) from minority groups
CALIFORNIA **San Diego State University**							
Alliance for Excellence	yes	yes	yes	yes	yes	40-59%	20-39%
Chula Vista Professional Development School	yes	yes	yes	yes	yes	60-79%	20-39%
Kennedy Lab School	no	yes	no	yes	yes	80-100%	20-39%
Marshall Professional Development School	yes	yes	no	yes	yes	80-100%	20-39%
Model Education Center	yes	yes	no	yes	yes	60-79%	20-39%
Partners in Education	yes	yes	no	yes	yes	40-59%	20-39%
CALIFORNIA **University of California, Riverside**							
Ribidoux High School	yes	yes	yes	yes	yes	40-59%	no response
DELAWARE **University of Delaware**							
Thurgood Marshall Elementary School	yes	yes	yes	yes	yes	20-39%	no response
FLORIDA **University of South Florida**							

Professional Development School Characteristics - Table 4

Professional Development School	Inservice Teachers Program cont'd.			Multicultural Issues			
	practicing teachers involved in curriculum development	practicing teachers actively involved in decision making with regard to organizational/structural changes within the school	inservice teachers involved in educational research conducted at the school site	preservice teachers participate in structured learning experiences that address issues related to educating minority group students	inservice teachers participate in structured learning experiences that address issues related to educating minority group students	approximate percentage of student enrollment from minority groups	approximate percentage of teacher interns (preservice teachers) from minority groups
Thomas E. Weightman Middle School	yes	yes	yes	yes	yes	20-39%	0-19%
GEORGIA **Armstrong State College**							
White Bluff Elementary School	yes	yes	yes	yes	no	40-59%	40-59%
ILLINOIS **DePaul University**							
Glenview Teacher Preparation Program	yes	yes	yes	yes	yes	0-19%	0-19%
ILLINOIS **Elmhurst College**							
Brook Park School	n/a	n/a	n/a	yes	yes	0-19%	0-19%
Bryan Junior High School	n/a	n/a	n/a	yes	yes	0-19%	0-19%
Conrad Fischer School	n/a	n/a	n/a	yes	yes	20-39%	0-19%
Early Childhood Education Center	n/a	n/a	n/a	yes	yes	0-19%	0-19%
Emerson School	n/a	n/a	n/a	yes	yes	0-19%	0-19%
Euclid School	n/a	n/a	n/a	yes	yes	40-59%	0-19%
Field School	n/a	n/a	n/a	yes	yes	0-19%	0-19%

Professional Development School Characteristics - Table 4

Professional Development School	Inservice Teachers Program con'd.			Multicultural Issues			
	practicing teachers involved in curriculum development	practicing teachers actively involved in decision making with regard to organizational/structural changes within the school	inservice teachers involved in educational research conducted at the school site	preservice teachers participate in structured learning experiences that address issues related to educating minority group students	inservice teachers participate in structured learning experiences that address issues related to educating minority group students	approximate percentage of student enrollment from minority groups	approximate percentage of teacher interns (preservice teachers) from minority groups
Gower West School	n/a	n/a	n/a	yes	yes	20-39%	0-19%
Grant School	n/a	n/a	n/a	yes	yes	80-100%	0-19%
Hinsdale Central High School	n/a	n/a	n/a	yes	yes	0-19%	0-19%
Indian Trail Junior High School	n/a	n/a	n/a	yes	yes	20-39%	0-19%
Jackson School	n/a	n/a	n/a	yes	yes	0-19%	0-19%
Jefferson School	n/a	n/a	n/a	yes	yes	0-19%	0-19%
Jefferson School	n/a	n/a	n/a	yes	yes	80-100%	0-19%
Lake Park Elementary School	n/a	n/a	n/a	yes	yes	20-39%	0-19%
Leyden High School-East Campus	n/a	n/a	n/a	yes	yes	20-39%	0-19%
Leyden High School-West Campus	n/a	n/a	n/a	yes	yes	20-39%	0-19%
Lincoln Elementary School	n/a	n/a	n/a	yes	yes	80-100%	0-19%
Lincoln Primary School	n/a	n/a	n/a	yes	yes	80-100%	0-19%
McKinley School	n/a	n/a	n/a	yes	yes	80-100%	0-19%
Queen Bee School	n/a	n/a	n/a	yes	yes	0-19%	0-19%
Reskin School	n/a	n/a	n/a	yes	yes	20-39%	0-19%

Professional Development School Characteristics - Table 4

Professional Development School	Inservice Teachers Program cont'd. practicing teachers involved in curriculum development	practicing teachers actively involved in decision making with regard to organizational/structural changes within the school	inservice teachers involved in educational research conducted at the school site	Multicultural Issues preservice teachers participate in structured learning experiences that address issues related to educating minority group students	inservice teachers participate in structured learning experiences that address issues related to educating minority group students	approximate percentage of student enrollment from minority groups	approximate percentage of teacher interns (preservice teachers) from minority groups
Roosevelt Elementary School	n/a	n/a	n/a	yes	yes	80-100%	0-19%
Roosevelt Junior High School	n/a	n/a	n/a	yes	yes	80-100%	0-19%
Sandburg Junior High School	n/a	n/a	n/a	yes	yes	0-19%	0-19%
Schafer School	n/a	n/a	n/a	yes	yes	20-39%	0-19%
Spring Hills School	n/a	n/a	n/a	yes	yes	0-19%	0-19%
Bellwood Preschool	n/a	n/a	n/a	yes	yes	80-100%	0-19%
Stone Park Preschool	n/a	n/a	n/a	yes	yes	80-100%	0-19%
Stone School	n/a	n/a	n/a	yes	yes	0-19%	0-19%
Wesley School	n/a	n/a	n/a	yes	yes	0-19%	0-19%
Westmore School	n/a	n/a	n/a	yes	yes	0-19%	0-19%
York High School	n/a	n/a	n/a	yes	yes	0-19%	0-19%
ILLINOIS National Louis University							
Glenview/Northbrook	yes	no	no	no	no	0-19%	0-19%
INDIANA Indiana State University							
Chauncey Rose Middle School	yes	yes	yes	yes	yes	0-19%	0-19%

Professional Development School Characteristics - Table 4

Professional Development School	Inservice Teachers Program cont'd.			Multicultural Issues			
	practicing teachers involved in curriculum development	practicing teachers actively involved in decision making with regard to organizational/ structural changes within the school	inservice teachers involved in educational research conducted at the school site	preservice teachers participate in structured learning experiences that address issues related to educating minority group students	inservice teachers participate in structured learning experiences that address issues related to educating minority group students	approximate percentage of student enrollment from minority groups	approximate percentage of teacher interns (preservice teachers) from minority groups
Fayette Elementary School	yes	yes	yes	yes	yes	0-19%	0-19%
Meadows Elementary School	yes	yes	yes	yes	yes	0-19%	0-19%
Rosedale Elementary School	yes	yes	yes	yes	yes	0-19%	0-19%
South Vermillion High School	yes	yes	yes	yes	yes	0-19%	0-19%
Stauton Elementary School	yes	yes	yes	yes	yes	0-19%	0-19%
Terre Haute North Vigo High School	yes	yes	yes	yes	yes	0-19%	0-19%
Terre Haute South Vigo High School	yes	yes	yes	yes	yes	0-19%	0-19%
West Vigo High School	yes	yes	yes	yes	yes	0-19%	0-19%
West Vigo School	yes	yes	yes	yes	yes	0-19%	0-19%
INDIANA Indiana University Northwest							
Central High School	no	yes	no	yes	yes	80-100%	20-39%
Eggers Elementary Middle School	yes	yes	yes	yes	yes	40-59%	60-79%
Franklin Elementary School	yes	no	no	no	yes	80-100%	80-100%
Horace Mann High School	yes	no	no	yes	yes	80-100%	60-79%

Professional Development School Characteristics - Table 4

Professional Development School	Inservice Teachers Program cont'd.	practicing teachers involved in curriculum development	practicing teachers actively involved in decision making with regard to organizational/ structural changes within the school	inservice teachers involved in educational research conducted at the school site	Multicultural Issues: preservice teachers participate in structured learning experiences that address issues related to educating minority group students	inservice teachers participate in structured learning experiences that address issues related to educating minority group students	approximate percentage of student enrollment from minority groups	approximate percentage of teacher interns (preservice teachers) from minority groups
Lincoln Elementary		yes	no	no	yes	yes	80-100%	40-59%
INDIANA Indiana University Purdue University Indianapolis (IUPU)								
Arsenal Technical High School		yes	yes	yes	yes	yes	20-39%	0-19%
Franklin Central High School		yes	yes	yes	yes	yes	20-39%	0-19%
Franklin Township Middle School		yes	yes	yes	yes	yes	20-39%	0-19%
Harcourt Elementary School		yes	yes	yes	yes	yes	20-39%	0-19%
Indian Creek Elementary School		yes	yes	yes	yes	yes	20-39%	0-19%
James A. Garfield		yes	yes	yes	yes	yes	20-39%	0-19%
North Central High School		yes	yes	yes	yes	yes	20-39%	0-19%
Riverside School		yes	yes	yes	yes	yes	20-39%	0-19%
Westlane Middle School		yes	yes	yes	yes	yes	20-39%	0-19%
INDIANA Purdue University								
Klondike Elementary School		yes	yes	no	no	no	0-19%	0-19%

243

Professional Development School Characteristics - Table 4

Professional Development School	Inservice Teachers Program cont'd.			Multicultural Issues			
	practicing teachers involved in curriculum development	practicing teachers actively involved in decision making with regard to organizational/ structural changes within the school	inservice teachers involved in educational research conducted at the school site	preservice teachers participate in structured learning experiences that address issues related to educating minority group students	inservice teachers participate in structured learning experiences that address issues related to educating minority group students	approximate percentage of student enrollment from minority groups	approximate percentage of teacher interns (preservice teachers) from minority groups
Lafayette School Corporation	yes	yes	yes	yes	yes	0-19%	0-19%
Pine Village School	yes	yes	no	no	no	0-19%	0-19%
INDIANA Emporia State University							
Countryside Elementary School	yes	yes	yes	yes	yes	no response	0-19%
Pleasant Ridge Elementary School	yes	yes	yes	yes	yes	no response	0-19%
IOWA Drake University							
Moulton Elementary School	yes	yes	yes	yes	yes	40-59%	0-19%
IOWA Iowa State University							
Madrid School System	yes	yes	yes	yes	no	0-19%	0-19%
Project Opportunity - ISU/Madrid Site	yes	yes	yes	yes	yes	0-19%	0-19%
IOWA University of Northern Iowa							
Malcolm Price Laboratory School	yes	yes	yes	no	no	0-19%	0-19%

Professional Development School Characteristics - Table 4

Professional Development School	Inservice Teachers Program cont'd.			Multicultural Issues			
	practicing teachers involved in curriculum development	practicing teachers actively involved in decision making with regard to organizational/structural changes within the school	inservice teachers involved in educational research conducted at the school site	preservice teachers participate in structured learning experiences that address issues related to educating minority group students	inservice teachers participate in structured learning experiences that address issues related to educating minority group students	approximate percentage of student enrollment from minority groups	approximate percentage of teacher interns (preservice teachers) from minority groups
KANSAS Fort Hays State University							
O'Loughlin Elementary School	yes	yes	yes	yes	yes	0-19%	0-19%
LOUISIANA University of New Orleans							
H.C. Schaumburg Elementary School	yes	yes	yes	yes	yes	80-100%	60-79%
Grace King High School	yes	yes	no	no	no	20-39%	0-19%
Jefferson Elementary School	yes	no	no	yes	yes	20-39%	0-19%
John Dibert Elementary School	yes	yes	yes	yes	yes	60-79%	0-19%
Paul J. Solis Elementary School	yes	yes	no	no	yes	40-59%	0-19%
Warren Easton School	yes	yes	no	yes	yes	80-100%	20-39%
MASSACHUSETTS Anna Maria College							
City View Professional Development School	yes	yes	no	yes	yes	40-59%	0-19%
Coolidge Professional Development School	yes	yes	no	yes	yes	0-19%	0-19%

Professional Development School Characteristics - Table 4

Professional Development School	Inservice Teachers Program cont'd.			Multicultural Issues			
	practicing teachers involved in curriculum development	practicing teachers actively involved in decision making with regard to organizational/ structural changes within the school	inservice teachers involved in educational research conducted at the school site	preservice teachers participate in structured learning experiences that address issues related to educating minority group students	inservice teachers participate in structured learning experiences that address issues related to educating minority group students	approximate percentage of student enrollment from minority groups	approximate percentage of teacher interns (preservice teachers) from minority groups
MASSACHUSETTS Assumption College							
Flagg Street School	yes	yes	yes	yes	yes	20-39%	0-19%
MASSACHUSETTS University of Massachusetts, Amherst							
East Longmeadow High School	yes	no	no	no	yes	0-19%	0-19%
MASSACHUSETTS University of Massachusetts, Lowell							
Reading Memorial High School	yes	yes	yes	no	no	0-19%	0-19%
MASSACHUSETTS Wheelock College							
Edward Devotion School	yes	yes	yes	yes	yes	40-59%	0-19%
MICHIGAN University of Michigan, Dearborn							
Catherine B. White Elementary School	yes	yes	no	yes	yes	80-100%	no response

Professional Development School Characteristics - Table 4

Professional Development School	Inservice Teachers Program cont'd.			Multicultural Issues			
	practicing teachers involved in curriculum development	practicing teachers actively involved in decision making with regard to organizational/structural changes within the school	inservice teachers involved in educational research conducted at the school site	preservice teachers participate in structured learning experiences that address issues related to educating minority group students	inservice teachers participate in structured learning experiences that address issues related to educating minority group students	approximate percentage of student enrollment from minority groups	approximate percentage of teacher interns (preservice teachers) from minority groups
MICHIGAN **Western Michigan University**							
Battlecreek Central High School	yes	yes	yes	yes	yes	0-19%	0-19%
Prairieview Elementary School	yes	yes	yes	yes	yes	0-19%	0-19%
MINNESOTA **University of Minnesota**							
Patrick Henry Professional Practice School	yes	yes	yes	yes	yes	40-59%	0-19%
MISSOURI **Harris-Stowe State College**							
Shepard Accelerated School Partnership	no	yes	yes	yes	yes	60-79%	60-79%
MISSOURI **Maryville University**							
South High School	yes	yes	no	yes	no	20-39%	0-19%
Wilkinson Early Childhood Center	yes	yes	yes	yes	yes	40-59%	0-19%
MISSOURI **Saint Louis University**							
Wyman School	yes	yes	no	yes	yes	80-100%	0-19%

Professional Development School Characteristics - Table 4

Professional Development School	Inservice Teachers Program cont'd.			Multicultural Issues			
	practicing teachers involved in curriculum development	practicing teachers actively involved in decision making with regard to organizational/ structural changes within the school	inservice teachers involved in educational research conducted at the school site	preservice teachers participate in structured learning experiences that address issues related to educating minority group students	inservice teachers participate in structured learning experiences that address issues related to educating minority group students	approximate percentage of student enrollment from minority groups	approximate percentage of teacher interns (preservice teachers) from minority groups
MISSOURI University of Missouri, Kansas City							
Center Elementary School	no	no	no	yes	yes	40-59%	0-19%
MISSOURI University of Missouri, St. Louis							
Red Bridge Elementary School	no response	no response	no response	no response	no response	no response	no response
Chaney Elementary School	yes	yes	yes	yes	yes	40-59%	0-19%
Laclede Elementary School	yes	yes	yes	yes	yes	80-100%	0-19%
Parkway Central Middle School	yes	yes	yes	yes	yes	0-19%	0-19%
Parkway River Bend Elementary School	yes	yes	yes	yes	yes	0-19%	0-19%
MISSOURI Washington University							
Kirkwood High School	yes	yes	yes	yes	yes	20-39%	0-19%
NEW JERSEY Rowan College of New Jersey							

248

Professional Development School Characteristics - Table 4

Professional Development School	Inservice Teachers Program cont'd.			Multicultural Issues			
	practicing teachers involved in curriculum development	practicing teachers actively involved in decision making with regard to organizational/ structural changes within the school	inservice teachers involved in educational research conducted at the school site	preservice teachers participate in structured learning experiences that address issues related to educating minority group students	inservice teachers participate in structured learning experiences that address issues related to educating minority group students	approximate percentage of student enrollment from minority groups	approximate percentage of teacher interns (preservice teachers) from minority groups
Cooper's Point Professional Development Family School of Excellence	yes	yes	yes	yes	yes	80-100%	0-19%
Winslow Professional Development District	yes	yes	yes	yes	yes	20-39%	0-19%
NEW YORK Buffalo State College							
Charles Drew Science Magnet School	yes	yes	n/a	yes	yes	80-100%	40-59%
Como Park Elementary School	yes	yes	n/a	yes	yes	0-19%	0-19%
Futures Academy	yes	yes	n/a	yes	yes	80-100%	40-59%
Hoover Elementary School	yes	yes	n/a	yes	yes	0-19%	0-19%
NEW YORK Columbia University							
I.S. 44	yes	yes	yes	yes	yes	80-100%	80-100%
P.S. 87	yes	yes	yes	yes	yes	40-59%	40-59%
NEW YORK Syracuse University							
Camillus Middle School	yes	yes	yes	yes	yes	0-19%	0-19%
East Hill Elementary School	yes	yes	no	yes	yes	0-19%	0-19%

Professional Development School Characteristics - Table 4

Professional Development School	Inservice Teachers Program cont'd.			Multicultural Issues			
	practicing teachers involved in curriculum development	practicing teachers actively involved in decision making with regard to organizational/ structural changes within the school	inservice teachers involved in educational research conducted at the school site	preservice teachers participate in structured learning experiences that address issues related to educating minority group students	inservice teachers participate in structured learning experiences that address issues related to educating minority group students	approximate percentage of student enrollment from minority groups	approximate percentage of teacher interns (preservice teachers) from minority groups
Edward Smith Elementary School	yes	yes	yes	yes	yes	60-79%	60-79%
Franklin Elementary School	yes	yes	yes	yes	yes	no response	60-79%
Jamesville Elementary School	yes	yes	yes	yes	no	0-19%	0-19%
Jamesville-DeWitt High School	yes	yes	yes	yes	no	0-19%	0-19%
Jamesville-DeWitt Middle School	yes	yes	yes	yes	no	0-19%	0-19%
Moses-DeWitt Elementary School	yes	yes	yes	yes	no	0-19%	0-19%
Onondaga Road Elementary School	yes	yes	no	yes	yes	0-19%	0-19%
Split Rock Elementary School	yes	yes	yes	yes	yes	0-19%	0-19%
Stonehedge Elementary School	yes	yes	yes	yes	yes	0-19%	0-19%
Tecumseh Elementary School	yes	yes	yes	yes	yes	0-19%	0-19%
Webster Elementary School	yes	yes	yes	yes	yes	0-19%	0-19%
West Genesee Middle School	yes	yes	no	yes	yes	0-19%	0-19%
West Genesee Senior High School	yes	yes	yes	yes	yes	0-19%	0-19%

Professional Development School Characteristics - Table 4

Professional Development School	Inservice Teachers Program cont'd.			Multicultural Issues			
	practicing teachers involved in curriculum development	practicing teachers actively involved in decision making with regard to organizational/structural changes within the school	inservice teachers involved in educational research conducted at the school site	preservice teachers participate in structured learning experiences that address issues related to educating minority group students	inservice teachers participate in structured learning experiences that address issues related to educating minority group students	approximate percentage of student enrollment from minority groups	approximate percentage of teacher interns (preservice teachers) from minority groups
NORTH CAROLINA University of North Carolina, Greensboro							
Archer Elementary School	no response	no response	no response	yes	no	20-39%	0-19%
Bluford Elementary School	yes	n/a	yes	yes	no	20-39%	0-19%
Brightwood Elementary School	yes	n/a	yes	yes	no	20-39%	0-19%
Global Magnet School	yes	n/a	yes	yes	no	20-39%	0-19%
Greene Elementary School	yes	n/a	yes	yes	no	20-39%	0-19%
Guilford Middle School	no response	no response	no response	yes	no	20-39%	0-19%
Guilford Primary School	no response	no response	no response	yes	no	20-39%	0-19%
Jackson Middle School	yes	n/a	yes	yes	no	20-39%	0-19%
Jamestown Middle School	yes	n/a	yes	yes	no	20-39%	0-19%
Jesse Wharton Elementary School	yes	n/a	yes	yes	no	20-39%	0-19%
Kernersville Elementary School	no response	no response	no response	yes	no	20-39%	0-19%
Kiser Middle School	no response	no response	no response	yes	no	20-39%	0-19%
Mills Road Elementary School	yes	n/a	yes	yes	no	20-39%	0-19%

Professional Development School Characteristics - Table 4

Professional Development School	Inservice Teachers Program cont'd.			Multicultural Issues			
	practicing teachers involved in curriculum development	practicing teachers actively involved in decision making with regard to organizational/structural changes within the school	inservice teachers involved in educational research conducted at the school site	preservice teachers participate in structured learning experiences that address issues related to educating minority group students	inservice teachers participate in structured learning experiences that address issues related to educating minority group students	approximate percentage of student enrollment from minority groups	approximate percentage of teacher interns (preservice teachers) from minority groups
Oak Hill Elementary School	yes	n/a	yes	no	no	20-39%	0-19%
Oak View Elementary School	no response	no response	no response	yes	no	20-39%	0-19%
Piney Grove Elementary School	yes	n/a	yes	yes	no	20-39%	0-19%
Rankin Elementary School	no response	no response	no response	yes	no	20-39%	0-19%
Sedgefield Elementary School	yes	n/a	yes	yes	no	20-39%	0-19%
Shadybrook Elementary School	yes	n/a	yes	yes	no	20-39%	0-19%
Western Guilford High School	yes	n/a	yes	yes	no	20-39%	0-19%
NORTH DAKOTA University of North Dakota							
Lake Agassiz Elementary School	yes	yes	yes	no response	no response	0-19%	0-19%
OHIO Ohio State University							
Etna Road Elementary School - Project TEACH	yes	yes	yes	no	yes	20-39%	0-19%
Independence High School - Project TRI	yes	yes	yes	yes	yes	60-79%	20-39%
Northland High School - Northland Teaching Academy	yes	yes	n/a	yes	yes	40-59%	40-59%

Professional Development School Characteristics - Table 4

Professional Development School	Inservice Teachers Program cont'd.			Multicultural Issues			
	practicing teachers involved in curriculum development	practicing teachers actively involved in decision making with regard to organizational/structural changes within the school	inservice teachers involved in educational research conducted at the school site	preservice teachers participate in structured learning experiences that address issues related to educating minority group students	inservice teachers participate in structured learning experiences that address issues related to educating minority group students	approximate percentage of student enrollment from minority groups	approximate percentage of teacher interns (preservice teachers) from minority groups
Thomas Worthington High School	yes	no	yes	no	no	0-19%	0-19%
PENNSYLVANIA Bloomsburg University							
Danville Elementary School	yes	yes	yes	no response	no response	0-19%	0-19%
PENNSYLVANIA Millersville University							
Conestoga Valley Middle School	yes	no	no	yes	no	0-19%	0-19%
SOUTH CAROLINA University of South Carolina							
Manheim Township Middle School	yes	no	no	yes	no	0-19%	0-19%
Airport High School	no response	no response	yes	yes	yes	0-19%	0-19%
Crayton Middle School	no response	no response	no response	yes	no response	40-59%	0-19%
Hood Street School	no response	no response	no response	yes	no response	0-19%	0-19%
Horrell Hill Elementary School	yes	yes	yes	yes	yes	20-39%	0-19%
Hyatt Park School	yes	yes	no response	yes	yes	0-19%	0-19%
Meadowfield Elementary School	no response	no response	no response	yes	no response	40-59%	0-19%

Professional Development School Characteristics - Table 4

Professional Development School	Inservice Teachers Program cont'd.			Multicultural Issues			
	practicing teachers involved in curriculum development	practicing teachers actively involved in decision making with regard to organizational/ structural changes within the school	inservice teachers involved in educational research conducted at the school site	preservice teachers participate in structured learning experiences that address issues related to educating minority group students	inservice teachers participate in structured learning experiences that address issues related to educating minority group students	approximate percentage of student enrollment from minority groups	approximate percentage of teacher interns (preservice teachers) from minority groups
Pierce Terrace School	yes	yes	yes	no response	no response	60-79%	40-59%
Pinckney Elementary School	yes	yes	yes	yes	yes	60-79%	40-59%
Pontiac Elementary School	yes	yes	no response	yes	yes	0-19%	0-19%
Summitt Parkway Middle School	no response	no response	yes	yes	yes	20-39%	0-19%
White Knoll Elementary School	yes	yes	no response	yes	yes	0-19%	0-19%
TENNESSEE Austin Peay State University	yes	n/a	n/a	yes	yes	40-59%	20-39%
Burt Elementary School	yes			yes	yes	40-59%	20-39%
TENNESSEE Memphis State University							
Campus School	yes	no	no	yes	yes	20-39%	20-39%
Coleman Elementary School	yes	no	yes	yes	yes	60-79%	0-19%
Dyer County Central Elementary School	yes	yes	yes	no	no	40-59%	0-19%
Frayser Elementary School	yes	yes	yes	yes	yes	80-100%	40-59%
Lipman School	yes	no	no	yes	yes	20-39%	20-39%
Newberry Elementary School	yes	yes	yes	yes	yes	80-100%	0-19%

254

Professional Development School Characteristics - Table 4

Professional Development School	Inservice Teachers Program cont'd.			Multicultural Issues			
	practicing teachers involved in curriculum development	practicing teachers actively involved in decision making with regard to organizational/ structural changes within the school	inservice teachers involved in educational research conducted at the school site	preservice teachers participate in structured learning experiences that address issues related to educating minority group students	inservice teachers participate in structured learning experiences that address issues related to educating minority group students	approximate percentage of student enrollment from minority groups	approximate percentage of teacher interns (preservice teachers) from minority groups
Ross Elementary	yes	yes	no	yes	no	20-39%	0-19%
Raleigh Egypt Middle School	yes	no	yes	yes	yes	60-79%	0-19%
TEXAS **Incarnate Word College**							
Brewer Elementary School	no	yes	no	yes	yes	80-100%	20-39%
Clark High School	no	yes	no	yes	yes	80-100%	20-39%
Connell Middle School	yes	yes	no	yes	yes	80-100%	60-79%
Coronado Escobar Elementary School	no	yes	no	no	no	80-100%	40-59%
Driscoll Middle School	yes	yes	no	yes	yes	20-39%	60-79%
Emma Frey Elementary School	no	yes	no	yes	yes	80-100%	20-39%
Gadendale Elementary School	no	yes	no	yes	yes	80-100%	20-39%
Hawthorne Elementary School	yes	yes	yes	yes	yes	80-100%	20-39%
Hutchins Elementary School	no	yes	no	yes	yes	80-100%	20-39%
Jackson-Keller Elementary School	yes	yes	yes	yes	yes	60-79%	20-39%
Kingsborough Middle School	no	yes	no	yes	yes	80-100%	20-39%
Lamar Elementary School	no	yes	no	yes	yes	80-100%	20-39%

Professional Development School Characteristics - Table 4

Professional Development School	Inservice Teachers Program cont'd.			Multicultural Issues			
	practicing teachers involved in curriculum development	practicing teachers actively involved in decision making with regard to organizational/ structural changes within the school	inservice teachers involved in educational research conducted at the school site	preservice teachers participate in structured learning experiences that address issues related to educating minority group students	inservice teachers participate in structured learning experiences that address issues related to educating minority group students	approximate percentage of student enrollment from minority groups	approximate percentage of teacher interns (preservice teachers) from minority groups
Loma Park Elementary School	yes	no	no	yes	yes	60-79%	60-79%
Mark Twain Middle School	yes	yes	yes	yes	yes	20-39%	80-100%
Memorial High School	yes	no	no	yes	yes	80-100%	60-79%
Providence High School	no	no	no	no	no	80-100%	0-19%
Robert E. Lee High School	yes	yes	yes	yes	yes	60-79%	20-39%
Rodriguez Elementary School	yes	no	yes	yes	no	80-100%	80-100%
St. Martin Hall	no	no	yes	yes	no	80-100%	80-100%
St. Peter Prince of the Apostles	yes	yes	no	yes	yes	40-59%	60-79%
Travis Elementary School	no	yes	no	yes	yes	80-100%	20-39%
Truman Middle School	yes	yes	no	yes	yes	80-100%	60-79%
TEXAS LubbockChristian University							
Brown Elementary School	yes	yes	no	yes	yes	80-100%	0-19%
Hardwick Elementary School	yes	yes	no	yes	yes	0-19%	0-19%
Parkway Elementary School	yes	yes	no	yes	yes	0-19%	80-100%
TEXAS Southwest Texas State University							

Professional Development School Characteristics - Table 4

Professional Development School	Inservice Teachers Program cont'd.			Multicultural Issues			
	practicing teachers involved in curriculum development	practicing teachers actively involved in decision making with regard to organizational/ structural changes within the school	inservice teachers involved in educational research conducted at the school site	preservice teachers participate in structured learning experiences that address issues related to educating minority group students	inservice teachers participate in structured learning experiences that address issues related to educating minority group students	approximate percentage of student enrollment from minority groups	approximate percentage of teacher interns (preservice teachers) from minority groups
Bowie Elementary School	yes	yes	yes	yes	yes	60-79%	20-39%
Elgin Middle School	yes	yes	yes	yes	yes	60-79%	20-39%
Goodnight Junior High School	yes	yes	yes	yes	yes	60-79%	20-39%
Highland Park Elementary School	yes	yes	yes	yes	yes	60-79%	20-39%
TEXAS Texas A&M University							
Houston Teaching Academy	yes	yes	yes	yes	yes	80-100%	0-19%
TEXAS Texas Tech University							
Bayless Elementary School	yes	yes	yes	no	no	40-59%	0-19%
Hutchinson Junior High School	yes	yes	yes	no	no	40-59%	0-19%
Lubbock High School	yes	yes	yes	no	no	40-59%	0-19%
Mackenzie Junior High School	yes	yes	yes	no	no	40-59%	0-19%
Ramirez Elementary School	yes	yes	yes	no	no	40-59%	0-19%
Wilson ISD	yes	yes	yes	no	no	40-59%	0-19%
TEXAS University of Houston							

Professional Development School Characteristics - Table 4

Professional Development School	Inservice Teachers Program cont'd.			Multicultural Issues			
	practicing teachers involved in curriculum development	practicing teachers actively involved in decision making with regard to organizational/ structural changes within the school	inservice teachers involved in educational research conducted at the school site	preservice teachers participate in structured learning experiences that address issues related to educating minority group students	inservice teachers participate in structured learning experiences that address issues related to educating minority group students	approximate percentage of student enrollment from minority groups	approximate percentage of teacher interns (preservice teachers) from minority groups
Ben Milam Professional Development and Technology Center	yes	no	no	yes	yes	0-19%	20-39%
Hamilton Professional Development and Technology Center	yes	no	no	yes	yes	0-19%	20-39%
Kennedy Professional Development and Technology Center	yes	no	no	yes	yes	0-19%	20-39%
Lockhart Professional Development and Technology Center	yes	no	no	yes	yes	0-19%	20-39%
Rufus Cage Professional Development and Technology Center	yes	no	no	yes	yes	0-19%	20-39%
Valley Oaks Professional Development and Technology Center	yes	no	no	yes	yes	0-19%	20-39%
Westwood Professional Development and Technology Center	yes	no	no	yes	yes	0-19%	20-39%
Woodview Professional Development and Technology Center	yes	no	no	yes	yes	0-19%	20-39%

Professional Development School Characteristics - Table 4

Professional Development School	Inservice Teachers Program cont'd.			Multicultural Issues			
	practicing teachers involved in curriculum development	practicing teachers actively involved in decision making with regard to organizational/ structural changes within the school	inservice teachers involved in educational research conducted at the school site	preservice teachers participate in structured learning experiences that address issues related to educating minority group students	inservice teachers participate in structured learning experiences that address issues related to educating minority group students	approximate percentage of student enrollment from minority groups	approximate percentage of teacher interns (preservice teachers) from minority groups
TEXAS University of Houston, Clearlake							
Alvin Junior High School	yes	yes	yes	yes	yes	20-39%	0-19%
Central Middle School	yes	yes	no	no	yes	60-79%	0-19%
George Washington Carver Elementary School	yes	yes	yes	yes	yes	60-79%	0-19%
TEXAS University of Texas, El Paso							
H.D. Hiley Elementary School	yes	yes	yes	yes	yes	80-100%	60-79%
Lamar Elementary School	yes	yes	yes	yes	yes	80-100%	60-79%
Riverside High School	yes	yes	yes	yes	yes	80-100%	60-79%
Wiggs Middle School	yes	yes	yes	yes	yes	80-100%	60-79%
Ysleta Elementary School	yes	yes	yes	yes	yes	80-100%	60-79%
UTAH Brigham-Young University							
Alpine Elementary School	yes	yes	yes	n/a	n/a	0-19%	0-19%
Aspen Elementary School	no	no	yes	no	no	0-19%	0-19%

Professional Development School Characteristics - Table 4

Professional Development School	Inservice Teachers Program cont'd.			Multicultural Issues			
	practicing teachers involved in curriculum development	practicing teachers actively involved in decision making with regard to organizational/ structural changes within the school	inservice teachers involved in educational research conducted at the school site	preservice teachers participate in structured learning experiences that address issues related to educating minority group students	inservice teachers participate in structured learning experiences that address issues related to educating minority group students	approximate percentage of student enrollment from minority groups	approximate percentage of teacher interns (preservice teachers) from minority groups
Barratt Elementary School	yes	no	yes	yes	no	0-19%	0-19%
Canyon Crest Elementary School	yes	yes	yes	no	no	0-19%	0-19%
Cascade Elementary School	yes	yes	yes	no	no	0-19%	0-19%
Copperview Elementary School	yes	yes	no	no	no	40-59%	0-19%
Cottonwood Heights Elementary School	yes	yes	no	no	yes	no response	0-19%
Draper Elementary School	yes	no	yes	no	no	0-19%	0-19%
Edgemont Elementary School	yes	yes	no	no	yes	no response	0-19%
Franklin Elementary School	yes	yes	no	yes	yes	0-19%	0-19%
Geneva Elemenntary School	yes	no	n/a	no	no	0-19%	0-19%
Goshen Elementary School	yes	yes	yes	no	no	0-19%	0-19%
Grant Elementary School	yes	yes	no	no	no	0-19%	0-19%
Highland Elementary School	yes	yes	yes	n/a	n/a	0-19%	0-19%
Jordan Ridge Elementary School	yes	yes	yes	n/a	n/a	0-19%	0-19%
Larsen Elementary School	yes	yes	yes	n/a	n/a	0-19%	0-19%

Professional Development School Characteristics - Table 4

Professional Development School	Inservice Teachers Program cont'd.			Multicultural Issues			
	practicing teachers involved in curriculum development	practicing teachers actively involved in decision making with regard to organizational/ structural changes within the school	inservice teachers involved in educational research conducted at the school site	preservice teachers participate in structured learning experiences that address issues related to educating minority group students	inservice teachers participate in structured learning experiences that address issues related to educating minority group students	approximate percentage of student enrollment from minority groups	approximate percentage of teacher interns (preservice teachers) from minority groups
Lindon Elementary School	yes	yes	yes	no	no	0-19%	0-19%
Maeser Elementary School	yes	yes	yes	yes	yes	20-29%	0-19%
Manila Elementary School	yes	yes	yes	yes	yes	0-19%	0-19%
Mapleton Elementary School	yes	yes	yes	no	no	0-19%	0-19%
Parkview Elementary School	yes	yes	no	no	no	0-19%	0-19%
Rees Elementary School	yes	yes	yes	no	no	0-19%	0-19%
Rock Canyon Elementary School	yes	yes	no	yes	yes	0-19%	0-19%
Sage Creek Elementary School	yes	yes	no	no	no	0-19%	0-19%
Salem Elementary School	yes	yes	yes	no	no	0-19%	0-19%
Santaquin Elementary School	yes	yes	no	no	no	0-19%	0-19%
Shelley Elementary School	yes	yes	yes	yes	yes	0-19%	0-19%
Southland Elementary School	yes	yes	yes	n/a	n/a	0-19%	0-19%
Sprucewood Elementary School	yes	yes	yes	n/a	n/a	0-19%	0-19%
Sunrise Elementary School	yes	no	yes	no	no	0-19%	0-19%
Sunset View Elementary School	yes	yes	n/a	yes	yes	0-19%	0-19%

Professional Development School Characteristics - Table 4

Professional Development School	Inservice Teachers Program cont'd.			Multicultural Issues			
	practicing teachers involved in curriculum development	practicing teachers actively involved in decision making with regard to organizational/ structural changes within the school	inservice teachers involved in educational research conducted at the school site	preservice teachers participate in structured learning experiences that address issues related to educating minority group students	inservice teachers participate in structured learning experiences that address issues related to educating minority group students	approximate percentage of student enrollment from minority groups	approximate percentage of teacher interns (preservice teachers) from minority groups
Taylor Elementary School	yes	yes	yes	no	no	0-19%	0-19%
Timpanogos Elementary School	yes	yes	yes	no response	no response	20-39%	0-19%
Westmore Elementary School	yes	yes	no	no	no	0-19%	0-19%
Westridge Elementary School	yes	yes	yes	n/a	yes	20-39%	0-19%
Willow Canyon Elementary School	yes	yes	yes	n/a	n/a	0-19%	0-19%
Wilson Elementary School	yes	yes	no response	yes	yes	0-19%	0-19%
UTAH **University of Utah**							
Bountiful Elementary School	yes	yes	yes	yes	yes	0-19%	0-19%
Eisenhower Junior High School	yes	yes	yes	yes	yes	0-19%	0-19%
Granger High School	yes	yes	yes	yes	yes	0-19%	0-19%
Highland High School	yes	yes	yes	yes	yes	0-19%	0-19%
Nibley Park Elementary School	yes	yes	yes	yes	yes	0-19%	0-19%
Washington Elementary School - Exemplary Practice School	yes	yes	yes	n/a	yes	40-59%	no response

Professional Development School Characteristics - Table 4

Professional Development School	Inservice Teachers Program cont'd.			Multicultural Issues			
	practicing teachers involved in curriculum development	practicing teachers actively involved in decision making with regard to organizational/structural changes within the school	inservice teachers involved in educational research conducted at the school site	preservice teachers participate in structured learning experiences that address issues related to educating minority group students	inservice teachers participate in structured learning experiences that address issues related to educating minority group students	approximate percentage of student enrollment from minority groups	approximate percentage of teacher interns (preservice teachers) from minority groups
VIRGINIA University of Virginia							
Jackson-Via Elementary School	yes	yes	no response	yes	yes	20-39%	0-19%
VIRGINIA Virginia Commonwealth University							
Whitcomb Model Elementary School	yes	yes	no	yes	yes	80-100%	40-59%
WASHINGTON University of Washington							
Adelaide Elementary School	yes	yes	no	n/a	no	0-19%	no response
Cedar Wood Elementary School	yes	yes	no	no response	no	0-19%	no response
Clear Creek Elementary School	yes	yes	no	no response	no	0-19%	no response
Juanita Elementary School	yes	yes	no	no response	no	0-19%	no response
Kennydale Elementary School	yes	yes	no	no response	no	20-39%	no response
Maple Hills Elementary School	yes	yes	no	n/a	no	0-19%	no response
Meany Middle School/Professional Development School	yes	yes	no response	yes	yes	40-59%	0-19%

Professional Development School Characteristics - Table 4

Professional Development School	practicing teachers involved in curriculum development	practicing teachers actively involved in decision making with regard to organizational/ structural changes within the school	inservice teachers involved in educational research conducted at the school site	preservice teachers participate in structured learning experiences that address issues related to educating minority group students	inservice teachers participate in structured learning experiences that address issues related to educating minority group students	approximate percentage of student enrollment from minority groups	approximate percentage of teacher interns (preservice teachers) from minority groups
Inservice Teachers Program cont'd.				**Multicultural Issues**			
Odle Middle School/Professional Development School	yes	yes	yes	yes	yes	0-19%	0-19%
WASHINGTON Washington State University							
Lincoln Middle School	yes	yes	yes	yes	yes	0-19%	0-19%
WEST VIRGINIA West Virginia University							
Central Elementary School	yes	yes	yes	yes	yes	20-39%	0-19%
East Dale Elementary School	yes	yes	yes	yes	yes	0-19%	0-19%
Grafton High School	yes	yes	yes	yes	yes	0-19%	0-19%
Morgantown High School	yes	yes	yes	yes	yes	0-19%	0-19%
Suncrest Primary School	yes	yes	yes	yes	yes	0-19%	0-19%
WISCONSIN University of Wisconsin, Madison							
Lincoln Elementary School	yes	yes	yes	yes	yes	40-59%	0-19%

Appendices

Appendix 1: Data Collection Form 267

Appendix 2: College and University Partners Profiled in This
Directory 269

Appendix 3: Professional Development School Sites 271

Appendix 4: Bibliography 278

Appendix 5: The Clinical Schools Clearinghouse 282

Appendix 6: Publications on Professional Development Schools
from the Clinical Schools Clearinghouse, ERIC
Clearinghouse on Teaching and Teacher Education,
and AACTE 283

1. **Contact:** Name, Institution
    Address, Phone, Fax, E-mail
    _____
    _____
    _____
    _____
    _____
    _____

2. **PDS collaborative part-
    ners:**
    Institution(s) - School,
    College, Department of
    Education
    _____
    _____
    _____

    School District(s)
    _____
    _____
    _____

    Union(s)/Others
    _____
    _____

3. **Organization or foundation
    sponsor or affiliation** (e.g.,
    National Network for
    Educational Renewal, AT&T
    Teachers for Tomorrow)
    _____
    _____

4. **Funding sources** (e.g., school
    district, foundation, univer-
    sity)
    _____
    _____

5. **Starting date**
    _____

For items 6 - 13, please check the response that best describes the PDS program at your institution.

	yes	no	n/a
6. Preservice teachers assigned to PDSs in cohorts	___	___	___
7. College funding for PDS program from grants, discretionary funds, or other types of "soft money"	___	___	___
8. Release time, reduced course load, or other related arrangement made for college faculty actively involved with PDS sites	___	___	___

9. Computer technology used in PDS teacher education program **to facilitate instruction** &/or staff development:

	yes	no	n/a
telecommunications (e.g., E-Mail, bulletin boards)	___	___	___
computer-assisted instruction	___	___	___
interactive video	___	___	___
desktop publishing	___	___	___

10. Computer technology used **to facilitate collaboration** among PDS partners:

	yes	no	n/a
telecommunications (e.g., E-Mail, bulletin boards)	___	___	___
computer-assisted instruction	___	___	___
interactive video	___	___	___
desktop publishing	___	___	___

11. Computer technology included in **subject matter** of teacher education &/or staff development curriculum of PDS participants:

	yes	no	n/a
telecommunications (e.g., E-Mail, bulletin boards)	___	___	___
computer assisted instruction	___	___	___
interactive video	___	___	___
programming	___	___	___
authoring systems	___	___	___
desktop publishing	___	___	___

12. Policies of college, with regard to hiring, tenure, pro-motion, or other aspects of col-lege's reward structure, acknow-lege PDS-related work   ___ ___ ___

13. Approximate percentage of department faculty who participate in PDS-related work (planning or implementation)
    ___ 0-19% ___ 20-39% ___ 40-59%
    ___ 60-79% ___ 80-100%

14. Name & title of person completing this form (please type or print) _____
    Address _____
    Phone _____ Date _____

Section II

Professional Development School Checklist

Please complete a separate PDS Checklist for __each__ PDS affiliated with your collaborative. You may photocopy this checklist.

1. PDS Name _____
2. Address _____
3. City, State, Zip _____
4. Phone, Fax, & E-mail _____
5. Site Coordinator (Name & Title) _____
6. Starting Date _____

7. Grade level (check one):
   _____ K-6
   _____ 7-9
   _____ 10-12
   _____ other (specify):_____

8. School type (check one):
   ____ clinical school
   ____ professional development school
   ____ professional practice school
   ____ partner school
   ____ other (specify):_____

Please check the response that best describes the PDS listed above.

.

C. College/School Cooperation

	yes	no	n/a
1. school faculty members hold joint school/college teaching appointments	—	—	—
2. college faculty teach school students	—	—	—
3. school faculty assist in planning preservice teacher education curriculum	—	—	—
4. school faculty assist in planning inservice teacher education curriculum	—	—	—
5. collaborative research involving school & college faculty	—	—	—

D. Preservice Teachers Program

	yes	no	n/a
6. on-site (school) courses for preservice teachers	—	—	—
7. mentor teachers for preservice teachers	—	—	—
8. clinical supervision of student teachers	—	—	—
9. each preservice teacher assigned to more than one cooperating teacher	—	—	—
10. preservice teachers involved in educational research conducted at the school site	—	—	—

E. Beginning Teachers Program

	yes	no	n/a
11. beginning teacher induction program	—	—	—
12. mentor teachers for beginning teachers	—	—	—
13. clinical supervision of beginning teachers	—	—	—

F. Inservice Teachers Program

	yes	no	n/a
14. on-site (school) courses for inservice teachers	—	—	—

	yes	no	n/a
15. cooperating teacher training provided to practicing teachers	—	—	—
16. experienced teachers designated as master teachers	—	—	—
17. mentor, master, and/or cooperating teachers have reduced course load	—	—	—
18. mentor, master, and/or cooperating teachers have release time	—	—	—
19. practicing teachers involved in curriculum development	—	—	—
20. practicing teachers actively involved in decision making with regard to organizational/structural changes within the school	—	—	—
21. inservice teachers involved in educational research conducted at the school site	—	—	—

G. Multicultural Issues

	yes	no	n/a
22. preservice teachers participate in structured learning experiences that address issues related to educating minority group students	—	—	—
23. inservice teachers participate in structured learning experiences that address issues related to educating minority group students	—	—	—

24. approximate percentage of student enrollment from minority groups (check one):
   ___0-19%   ___20-39%   ___40-59%
   ___60-79%   ___80-100%

25. approximate percentage of teacher interns (preservice teachers) from minority groups (check one):
   ___0-19%   ___20-39%   ___40-59%
   ___60-79%   ___80-100%

268

APPENDIX 2

**College and University Partners
Profiled in This Directory***

Abilene Christian University (see McMurray University)
Anna Maria College
Armstrong State College
Assumption College
Austin Peay State University
Bloomsburg University
Brigham-Young University
Buffalo State College
California State University - Fullerton
Columbia University
DePaul University
Drake University
Elmhurst College
Emporia State University
Fort Hays State University
Hardin-Simmons University (see McMurray University)
Harris-Stowe State College
Houston Baptist University (see University of Houston)
Howard Payne University (see McMurray University)
Incarnate Word College
Indiana State University
Indiana University - Northwest
Indiana University Purdue University Indianapolis (IUPUI)
Iowa State University
Laredo Community College (see Texas A&M International University)
Lubbock Christian University
Maryville University
McMurray University
Memphis State University
Michigan State University (see Western Michigan University)
Millersville University
National Louis University
Ohio State University, The
Our Lady of the Lake University (see Incarnate Word College)
Purdue University
Rowan College of New Jersey
Saint Louis University
San Diego State University
Simmons College (see Wheelock College)
Southwest Texas State University
St. Mary's University (see Incarnate Word College)
Syracuse University
Temple University
Texas A&M International University
Texas A&M University
Texas Tech University
Trinity University (see Incarnate Word College)
University of Arkansas - Fayetteville
University of California - Riverside
University of Delaware
University of Houston (see also Texas A&M University)
University of Houston - Clear Lake
University of Kansas
University of Massachusetts - Amherst

** In some instances, a PDS partner-
ship may include more than one university or college partner. In such
cases, only one partnership profile
is given in the profiles section of
this directory although each college
or university partner is listed in the
"Partners" section of the profile. On
this list of college and university
partners, the profile for an institution that is referenced in parenthe-
ses will include information on the
listed college or university.*

**College and University Partners
Profiled in This Directory***

University of Massachusetts - Lowell
University of Michigan - Dearborn
University of Minnesota
University of Missouri - Kansas City
University of Missouri - St.Louis
University of New Orleans
University of North Carolina - Greensboro
University of North Dakota
University of Northern Iowa
University of South Carolina
University of South Florida
University of St. Thomas (see University of Houston)
University of Texas - El Paso
University of Texas - San Antonio (see Incarnate Word College)
University of Utah
University of Virginia
University of Washington
University of Wisconsin - Madison
Virginia Commonwealth University
Washington State University
Washington University
West Virginia University
Western Michigan University
Wheelock College

**Professional Development School
Sites**

Arkansas
Jefferson Elementary School, Fayetteville
Woodland Junior High School, Fayetteville
George Elementary School, Springdale

California
Vicentia School, Corona
Golden Hill School, Fullerton
Raymond School, Fullerton
Ladera Palma School, La Habra
Sierra Vista School, La Habra
Highland School, Norco
Tynes School, Placentia
Ribidoux High School, Riverside
Alliance for Excellence, San Diego
Chula Vista Professional Development School, San Diego
Kennedy Lab School, San Diego
Marshall Professional Development School, San Diego
Model Education Center, San Diego
Partners in Education, San Diego
Monte Vista School, Santa Ana
Linda Vista School, Yorba Linda

Delaware
Thurgood Marshall Elementary School, Newark

Florida
Thomas E. Weightman Middle School, Zephyrhills

Georgia
White Bluff Elementary School, Savannah

Illinois
Indian Trail Junior High School, Addison
Lake Park Elementary School, Addison
Stone School, Addison
Wesley School, Addison
Jefferson School, Bellwood
Lincoln Elementary School, Bellwood
Lincoln Primary School, Bellwood
McKinley School, Bellwood
Roosevelt Junior High School, Bellwood
Roosevelt Elementary School, Bellwood
Glenview Teacher Preparation Program, Chicago
Bryan Junior High School, Elmhurst
Conrad Fischer School, Elmhurst
Emerson School, Elmhurst
Field School, Elmhurst
Jackson School, Elmhurst
Jefferson School, Elmhurst
Sandburg Junior High School, Elmhurst
York High School, Elmhurst
Glenview/Northbrook, Evanston
Leyden High School-East Campus, Franklin Park

Professional Development School Sites

Leyden High School-West Campus, Franklin Park
Queen Bee School, Glendale Heights
Reskin School, Glendale Heights
Hinsdale Central High School, Hinsdale
Brook Park School, La Grange Park
Schafer School, Lombard
Westmore School, Lombard
Grant School, Melrose Park
Euclid School, Mt. Prospect
Spring Hills School, Roselle
Bellwood Preschool, Stone Park
Stone Park Preschool, Stone Park
Gower West School, Willowbrook
Early Childhood Education Center, Wood Dale

Indiana
South Vermillion High School, Clinton
Central High School, East Chicago
Lincoln Elementary, East Chicago
Franklin Elementary School, Gary
Horace Mann High School, Gary
Eggers Elementary Middle School, Hammond
Arsenal Technical High School, Indianapolis
Franklin Central High School, Indianapolis
Franklin Township Middle School, Indianapolis
Harcourt Elementary School, Indianapolis
Indian Creek Elementary School, Indianapolis
James A. Garfield, Indianapolis
North Central High School, Indianapolis
Riverside School, Indianapolis
Westlane Middle School, Indianapolis
Lafayette School Corporation, Lafayette
Pine Village School, Pine Village
Rosedale Elementary School, Rosedale
Stauton Elementary School, Stauton
Chauncey Rose Middle School, Terre Haute
Meadows Elementary School, Terre Haute
Terre Haute North Vigo High School, Terre Haute
Terre Haute South Vigo High School, Terre Haute
Fayette Elementary School, West Terre Haute
Klondike Elementary School, West Lafayette
West Vigo High School, West Terre Haute
West Vigo School, West Terre Haute

Iowa
Project Opportunity, Ames
Malcolm Price Laboratory School, Cedar Falls
Moulton Elementary School, Des Moines
Madrid Community School System, Madrid

Kansas
O'Loughlin Elementary School, Hays
Countryside Elementary School, Olathe
Pleasant Ridge Elementary School, Overland Park

272

Professional Development School Sites

Louisiana
Paul J. Solis Elementary School, Gretna
Jefferson Elementary School, Jefferson
J.J. Audubon, Kenner
Grace King High School, Metairie
H.C. Schaumburg Elementary School, New Orleans
John Dibert Elementary School, New Orleans
Warren Easton, New Orleans

Massachusetts
Edward Devotion School, Brookline
East Longmeadow High School, East Longmeadow
Reading Memorial High School, Reading
Coolidge Professional Development School, Shrewsbury
City View Professional Development School, Worcester
Flagg Street School, Worcester

Michigan
Battlecreek Central High School, Battlecreek
Prairieview Elementary School, Battlecreek
Catherine B. White Elementary School, Detroit

Minnesota
Patrick Henry Professional Practice School, Minneapolis

Missouri
Parkway Central Middle School, Chesterfield
Parkway River Bend Elementary School, Chesterfield
Center Elementary School, Kansas City
Red Bridge Elementary School, Kansas City
Kirkwood High School, Kirkwood,
Chaney Elementary School, Richmond Heights,
Laclede Elementary School, St. Louis
Shepard Accelerated School Partnership, St. Louis
South High School, St. Louis
Wilkinson Early Childhood Center, St. Louis
Wyman School, St. Louis

New Jersey
Winslow Professional Development District, Blue Anchor
Cooper's Point Professional Development Family School of Excellence, Camden

New York
Charles Drew Science Magnet School, Buffalo
Futures Academy, Buffalo
Camillus Middle School, Camillus
East Hill Elementary School, Camillus
Split Rock Elementary School, Camillus
Stonehedge Elementary School, Camillus
West Genesee Senior High School, Camillus
West Genesee Middle School, Camillus
Jamesville-DeWitt High School, DeWitt
Jamesville Elementary School, Jamesville
Jamesville-DeWitt Middle School, Jamesville

Professional Development School Sites

Tecumseh Elementary School, Jamesville
Hoover Elementary School, Kenmore
Como Park Elementary School, Lancaster
I.S. 44, New York
P.S. 87, New York
Edward Smith Elementary School, Syracuse
Franklin Elementary School, Syracuse
Moses-DeWitt Elementary School, Syracuse
Onondaga Road Elementary School, Syracuse
Webster Elementary School, Syracuse

North Carolina
Archer Elementary School, Greensboro
Bluford Elementary School, Greensboro
Brightwood Elementary School, Greensboro
Global Magnet School, Greensboro
Greene Elementary School, Greensboro
Guilford Middle School, Greensboro
Guilford Primary School, Greensboro
Jackson Middle School, Greensboro
Jesse Wharton Elementary School, Greensboro
Kiser Middle School, Greensboro
Rankin Elementary School, Greensboro
Sedgefield Elementary School, Greensboro
Western Guilford High School, Greensboro
Oak Hill Elementary School, High Point
Oak View Elementary School, High Point
Shadybrook Elementary School, High Point
Jamestown Middle School, Jamestown
Mills Road Elementary School, Jamestown
Kernersville Elementary School, Kernersville
Piney Grove Elementary School, Kernersville

North Dakota
Lake Agassiz Elementary School, Grand Forks

Ohio
Independence High School - Project TRI, Columbus
Northland High School - Northland Teaching Academy, Columbus
Etna Road Elementary School - Project TEACH, Whitehall
Thomas Worthington High School, Worthington

Pennsylvania
Danville Elementary School, Danville
Manheim Township Middle School, Lancaster
Conestoga Valley Middle School, Leola

South Carolina
Crayton Middle School, Columbia
Hood Street School, Columbia
Hyatt Park School, Columbia
Meadowfield Elementary School, Columbia
Pierce Terrace School, Columbia
Pinckney Elementary School, Columbia

Professional Development School Sites

Summitt Parkway Middle School, Columbia
Pontiac Elementary School, Elgin
Horrell Hill Elementary School, Hopkins
Airport High School, W. Columbia
White Knoll Elementary School, W. Columbia

Tennessee
Burt Elementary School, Clarksville
Dyer County Central Elementary School, Dyersburg
Campus School, Memphis
Coleman Elementary School, Memphis
Frayser Elementary School, Memphis
Lipman School, Memphis,
Newberry Elementary School, Memphis
Raleigh Egypt Middle School, Memphis
Ross Elementary, Memphis

Texas
Alvin Junior High School, Alvin
Highland Park Elementary School, Austin
George Washington Carver Elementary School, Baytown
H.D. Hiley Elementary School, El Paso
Lamar Elementary School, El Paso
Riverside High School, El Paso
Wiggs Middle School, El Paso
Ysleta Elementary School, El Paso
Elgin Middle School, Elgin
Central Middle School, Galveston
Ben Milam Professional Development and Technology Center, Houston
Hamilton Professional Development and Technology Center, Houston
Houston Teaching Academy, Houston
Kennedy Professional Devlopment and Technology Center, Houston
Lockhart Professional Development and Technology Center, Houston
Rufus Cage Professional Development and Technology Center, Houston
Valley Oaks Professional Development and Technology Center, Houston
Westwood Professional Development and Technology Center, Houston
Woodview Professional Development and Technology Center, Houston
Bayless Elementary School, Lubbock
Brown Elementary School, Lubbock
Hardwick Elementary School, Lubbock
Hutchinson Junior High School, Lubbock
Lubbock High School, Lubbock
Mackenzie Junior High School, Lubbock
Parkway Elementary School, Lubbock
Ramirez Elementary School, Lubbock
Brewer Elementary School, San Antonio
Clark High School, San Antonio
Connell Middle School, San Antonio
Coronado Escobar Elementary School, San Antonio
Driscoll Middle School, San Antonio
Emma Frey Elementary School, San Antonio
Gadendale Elementary School, San Antonio
Hawthorne Elementary School, San Antonio
Hutchins Elementary School, San Antonio

275

Professional Development School Sites

Jackson-Keller Elementary School, San Antonio
Kingsborough Middle School, San Antonio
Lamar Elementary School, San Antonio
Loma Park Elementary School, San Antonio
Mark Twain Middle School, San Antonio
Memorial High School, San Antonio
Providence High School, San Antonio
Robert E. Lee High School, San Antonio
Rodriguez Elementary School, San Antonio
St. Peter Prince of the Apostles, San Antonio
St. Martin Hall, San Antonio
Travis Elementary School, San Antonio
Truman Middle School, San Antonio
Bowie Elementary School, San Marcos
Goodnight Junior High School, San Marcos
Wilson ISD, Wilson

Utah

Alpine Elementary School, Alpine
Barratt Elementary School, American Fork
Shelley Elementary School, American Fork
Bountiful Elementary School, Bountiful
Draper Elementary School, Draper
Goshen Elementary School, Goshen
Highland Elementary School, Highland
Lindon Elementary School, Lindon
Mapleton Elementary School, Mapleton
Copperview Elementary School, Midvale
Aspen Elementary School, Orem
Cascade Elementary School, Orem
Geneva Elemenmtary School, Orem
Westmore Elementary School, Orem
Parkview Elementary School, Payson
Taylor Elementary School, Payson
Wilson Elementary School, Payson
Manila Elementary School, Pleasant Grove
Canyon Crest Elementary School, Provo
Edgemont Elementary School, Provo
Franklin Elementary School, Provo
Maeser Elementary School, Provo
Rock Canyon Elementary School, Provo
Sunset View Elementary School, Provo
Timpanogos Elementary School, Provo
Westridge Elementary School, Provo
Southland Elementary School, Riverton
Salem Elementary School, Salem
Cottonwood Heights Elementary School, Salt Lake City
Eisenhower Junior High School, Salt Lake City
Highland High School, Salt Lake City
Nibley Park Elementary School, Salt Lake City
Washington Elementary School - Exemplary Practice School, Salt Lake City
Sprucewood Elementary School, Sandy
Sunrise Elementary School, Sandy
Willow Canyon Elementary School, Sandy

Professional Development School Sites

Santaquin Elementary School, Santaquin
Jordan Ridge Elementary School, South Jordan
Larsen Elementary School, Spanish Fork
Rees Elementary School, Spanish Fork
Grant Elementary School, Springville
Sage Creek Elementary School, Springville
Granger High School, West Valley City

Virginia
Jackson-Via Elementary School, Charlottesville
Whitcomb Model Elementary School, Richmond

Washington
Odle Middle School/Professional Development School, Bellevue
Cedar Wood Elementary School, Bothell
Adelaide Elementary School, Federal Way
Juanita Elementary School, Kirkland
Lincoln Middle School, Pullman
Kennydale Elementary School, Renton
Maple Hills Elementary School, Renton
Meany Middle School/Professional Development School, Seattle
Clear Creek Elementary School, Silverdale

West Virginia
East Dale Elementary School, Fairmont
Grafton High School, Grafton
Central Elementary School, Morgantown
Morgantown High School, Morgantown
Suncrest Primary School, Morgantown

Wisconsin
Lincoln Elementary School, Madison

Bibliography

This bibliography features selected references related to some of the professional development school (PDS) programs included in this directory. Many of the listed references were submitted by survey respondents; others came to the attention of the Clinical Schools Clearinghouse staff through its acquisition efforts. This is by no means an exhaustive list of PDS references that focus on specific programs, either the programs profiled in this directory or others.

Abstracts of references followed by an accession number, which begins with either **ED** or **EJ**, can be found in the ERIC database. References followed by an **SP** number were being processed for the ERIC database at the time of publication.

Brigham Young University
Green, E. E., & Harris, R. C. (1990). Creating long-term collaboration: The BYU/public school partnership experience. *Tech Trends, 35*(1), 12-16.

Harris, R. C. (1991). Educational renewal: Not by remote control--Work of a university professor in a partner school. *Metropolitan Universities, 2*(1), 61-71.

Harris, R. C., & Harris, M. F. (1991). Symbiosis on trial in educational renewal. *Researcher, 7*(2), 15-27. ED325482

Harris, R. C., & Harris, M. F. (1992a). Glasser comes to a rural school. *Educational Leadership, 50*(3), 18-21. EJ454321

Harris, R. C., & Harris, M. F. (1992b). Partner schools: Places to solve teacher preparation problems. *Action in Teacher Education, 14*(4), 1-8. EJ482514

Harris, R. C., & Harris, M. F. (1992c). Preparing teachers for literacy education: University/school collaboration. *Journal of Reading, 35*(7), 572-579. EJ440918

Harris, R. C., & Harris, M. F. (1993). Renewing teacher education & public schooling via university/school collaboration. *Contemporary Education, 64*(4), 234-238. EJ485710

California State University, Fullerton
Guillaume, A. M., & Yopp, H. K. (In press). Professional portfolios for student teachers. *Teacher Education Quarterly.*

Yopp, H. K., Guillaume, A., & Savage, T. (1993-1994). Collaboration at the grass roots: Implementing the professional development school concept. *Action in Teacher Education, 15*(4), 29-35. EJ492181

Elmhurt College
Tusin, L. F. (1993a). The satellite program: A collaboration for clinical experiences in teacher education. *Critical Issues in Teacher Education, 3,* 1-12.

Tusin, L. F. (Ed.). (1993b). *Satellite program handbook* (rev. ed.). Elmhurst, IL: Elmhurst College, Department of Education. ED374083

Bibliography

Indiana State University

Andrews, S. V., & Smith, P. G. (1994, February). *Multiple levels of collaboration in professional development schools: A continuum of professional development.* Paper presented at the annual meeting of the American Association of Colleges for Teacher Education, Chicago, IL. ED374082

Contemporary Education, 64(4), (1993, Summer). This theme issue includes 14 articles related to professional development schools. Indiana State University (ISU) publishes this journal and many of the articles in this theme issue are written by individuals associated with ISU's professional development schools. EJ485704 - EJ485717

Memphis State University

Morris, V. G., & Nunnery, J. A. (1993). Teacher empowerment in a professional development school collaborative: Pilot assessment. (Technical Report 931101). Memphis, TN: College of Education, Center for Research in Educational Policy. ED368678

Morris, V. G., & Nunnery, J. A. (1994). *A case study of teacher empowerment in a professional development school.* (Technical Report 940101). Memphis, TN: College of Education, Center for Research in Educational Policy. SP035037

Michigan State University

Forrest, L., Putnam, J., Narusis, E. M., & Peeke, P. (1993). *Win/win restructuring. Counseling psychology collaboration with teacher education in professional development schools.* Unpublished manuscript, Michigan State University, Department of Counseling Psychology & Department of Teacher Education, East Lansing, Michigan. ED370889

Putnam, J. (1990). *Professional development schools: Emerging changes in the professional community.* Unpublished manuscript, Michigan State University, Department of Teacher Education, East Lansing, Michigan. ED370890

Putnam, J. (1991, April). *Initiating conversation at a professional development school.* Paper presented at the annual meeting of the American Educational Research Association, Chicago, IL. ED370891

Ohio State University

Ohio State University, College of Education. (1993). *Anatomy of a professional development school initiative.* Paper presented at the annual meeting of the American Association of Colleges for Teacher Education, San Diego, CA.

Building Bridges (newsletter). College of Education, Ohio State University, Columbus, OH 43210-1172.

Presentations, papers, and projects developed by PDS co-coordinators. 1994. Columbus, OH: Ohio State University, College of Education. This bibliography was compiled for a PDS Mini-Conference on Inquiry, January 25, 1994, Columbus, OH. It includes approximately 100 citations, annotations, and abstracts of publications, presentations, and writing-in-progress by school and college faculty and students associated with the university's network of professional development schools.

San Diego State University
Billings, L., Harding, K., & Hovenic, G. (1992, November). *The Chula Vista Professional Development School.* Paper presented at the National Council of States Seventeenth Annual National Conference, San Diego, CA.

Mehaffy, G. L. (1993a, February). *Collaboration in the development and implementation of professional development schools: Lessons learned.* Paper presented at the annual meeting of the Association of Teacher Educators, Los Angeles, CA.

Mehaffy, G. L. (1993b, February). *Professional development schools: Glimpses of practice. The San Diego experience.* Paper presented at the annual meeting of the American Association of Colleges for Teacher Education, San Diego, CA.

Syracuse University
P.D.S. Bulletin (newsletter). West Genesee Teaching Center, Camillus Middle School, Ike Dixon Road, Camillus, NY 13031.

Teaching Center. West Genesee/Syracuse University statement of agreement and policy handbook. (revised 1991). Unpublished document. Camillus, NY: West Genesee Teaching Center, Camillus Middle School.

Teachers College, Columbia University.
Fager, P., Andrews, T., Shepherd, M. J., & Quinn, E. (1993). Teamed to teach: Integrating teacher training through cooperative teaching at an urban professional development school. *Teacher Education and Special Education, 16*(1), 51-59. EJ468864

Texas A&M University
Stallings, J. (1991). *Connecting preservice teacher education and inservice professional development: A professional development school.* Paper presented at the Annual Meeting of the American Educational Research Association. ED339682

Stallings, J., & Quinn, L. F. (1991). Learning how to teach in the inner city. *Educational Leadership, 25-27.* EJ435740

Texas Tech University
Smith, C. W. (1993, April). *A collaborative agenda: Linking school and teacher education renewal with research through professional development schools.* Paper presented at the annual meeting of the American Educational Research Association, Atlanta, GA. ED367588

University of Massachusetts - Amherst
Schneider, H., Seidman, I., & Cannone, P. (1994). Ten steps to collaboration: The story of a professional development school. *Teaching & Learning: The Journal of Natural Inquiry, 8*(2), 21-33. EJ492201

Bibliography

University of Northern Iowa
Selke, M. J., & Kueter, R. A. (1994, February). *School/university partner-ships and the UNI Teaching Associates Cadre model: Professional benefits to Pre-K-12 educators.* Paper presented at the annual meeting of the American Association of Colleges for Teacher Education, Chicago, IL. ED369728

University of South Carolina
Gottesman, B., Graham, P., & Nogy, C. (1993). *South Carolina Center for the Advancement of Teaching and School Leadership: Professional development schools.* Rock Hill, SC: Winthrop College, South Carolina Center for the Advancement of Teaching and School Leadership. ED366549

University of Washington
Shen, J. (1994, February). *A study in contrast: Visions of preservice teacher education in the context of a professional development school.* Paper presented at the annual meeting of the American Association of Colleges for Teacher Education, Chicago, IL. ED368677

University of Wisconsin - Madison
Gomez, M., & Abt-Perkins, D. (1993). *Using narrative to prepare preservice teachers for diverse classrooms.* Paper presented at the annual meeting of the American Educational Research Association, Atlanta, GA.

Gomez, M., & Tabachnick, B. R. (1991). *Preparing prospective teachers for diverse learners.* Paper presented at the annual meeting of the American Educational Research Association, Chicago, IL.

Western Michigan University
Woloszyk, C. A., & Hill, R. (1994, February). *Restructuring teacher preparation: Seminar and related activities within a secondary professional development school.* Paper presented at the annual meeting of the Association of Teacher Educators, Atlanta, GA. ED374076

Wheelock College
Boles, K., & Troen, V. (1992). How teachers make restructuring happen. *Educational Leadership, 49*(5) 53-56. EJ439286

Boles, K., & Troen, V. (1993, 3 November). Teacher leadership: How to make it more than a catch phrase (Commentary). *Education Week, 27.*

Boles, K., & Troen, V. (1994, April). *Teacher leadership in a professional development school.* Paper presented at the annual meeting of the American Educational Research Association, New Orleans, LA. ED375103

**The Clinical Schools
Clearinghouse**

Purposes

❑ Provides a source of information on clinical schools, professional development schools, professional practice schools, partner schools, and similar institutions.

❑ Acquires, abstracts, and processes literature on clinical schools for the ERIC database.

❑ Produces bibliographies, periodic papers, digests, and other material on issues related to clinical schools.

❑ Conducts research on clinical schools.

❑ Functions as the Adjunct ERIC Clearinghouse on Clinical Schools.

Professional Development School Database

The Clinical Schools Clearinghouse (CSC) maintains a searchable database containing information on professional development schools (PDSs), clinical schools, professional practice schools, partner schools, and similar institutions. The database has records on more than 300 individual K-12 PDS sites and the more than 70 partnerships that manage these PDSs. In addition to location and contact information, records include data on program features, funding, affiliation, and partners.

❑ To include PDS sites and partnerships in the CSC database, contact CSC and request a Data Collection Form.

❑ To obtain information from the database, contact CSC.

Call for Literature

The Clinical Schools Clearinghouse is seeking literature on topics related to clinical schools, professional development schools, professional practice schools, partner schools, and similar institutions. The clearinghouse facilitates dissemination of this material via the ERIC database and CSC publications. CSC welcomes:

❑ Research Reports
❑ Project Descriptions
❑ Conference Papers
❑ Practice-Oriented Materials
❑ State Laws and Regulations
❑ Audiovisual Materials
❑ Institutional Agreements Establishing Collaboratives

❑ Course Descriptions
❑ Curriculum Guides
❑ Literature Reviews
❑ Journal Articles
❑ Bibliographies
❑ Other Related Information

To submit documents, order publications, or request information, contact:
Ismat Abdal-Haqq, Coordinator
Clinical Schools Clearinghouse
American Association of Colleges for Teacher Education
One Dupont Circle NW, Suite 610
Washington, DC 20036-1186
(202) 293-2450; (800) 822-9229; fax: (202) 457-8095
Internet Address: iabdalha@inet.ed.gov or iah@aacte.nche.edu

Appendix 6

Publications on Professional Development Schools from the Clinical Schools Clearinghouse, ERIC Clearinghouse on Teaching and Teacher Education, and AACTE

Professional Development School Projects, Mini-Bibliography No. 1 (1991). Free

Collaboration Within the Context of Professional Development Schools, Mini-Bibliography No. 2 (1991). Free

Professional Development Schools: Principles and Concepts, Mini-Bibliography No. 3 (1991). Free

Teacher Education and Professional Development Schools, Mini-Bibliography No. 4 (1992). Free

Professional Development Schools and Educational Reform: Concepts and Concerns, ERIC Digest 91-2 (1991). Free

Professionalizing Teaching: Is There a Role for Professional Development Schools? ERIC Digest 91-3 (1992). Free

Professional Development Schools: Toward a New Relationship for Schools and Universities, Trends and Issues Paper No. 3, Raphael O. Nystrand (1991). $14.50 prepaid

Resources on Professional Development Schools: An Annotated Bibliography (1993). More than 100 annotations and abstracts on literature related to professional development schools. Literature includes research reports, project descriptions, handbooks, conference papers, journal articles, and other published and unpublished material. Additional resources listed in this guide include newsletters, audiovisual material, and organizations. $14.50 prepaid

Professional Development Schools: A Directory of Projects in the United States (1992). This directory contains information on more than 125 professional development schools, professional practice schools, and clinical schools; including individual profiles of 80 elementary and secondary schools nationwide. Data are reported from a national survey of professional development schools:

❑ Collaborative partners and activities
❑ Preservice, beginning, & inservice teachers programs
❑ Multicultural issues
❑ Network or consortium affiliations
❑ Address, grade level, site coordinators, starting date
❑ Funding sources

$20 prepaid (AACTE members) $23 prepaid (nonmembers)

Voices of Change: A Report of the Clinical Schools Project, C. Raymond Anderson, Ed. (1992). This monograph reports observations, experiences, and outcomes from the seven clinical sites that participated in the Ford Foundation Clinical Schools Project. $20 prepaid

**Publications on Professional
Development Schools from the
Clinical Schools Clearinghouse,
ERIC Clearinghouse on Teaching
and Teacher Education, and
AACTE**

New Publications

*Professional Development Schools: A Directory of Projects in the United
States. Second Edition* (1995). This directory is an expanded, updated
edition of the popular 1992 CSC directory of PDSs. Profiles of over 300 K-
12 PDS sites and more than 65 partnerships are included. Findings from
the second national CSC survey of PDSs are presented. Contact information
and data on program features are included. $25 prepaid

*Teachers for Tomorrow. A Symposium: Outcomes & Implications of a
Clinical Schools Demonstration Project* (1994). Video: 120 minutes.
Teams of teacher education students and school & college faculty from the
five urban sites of the AT&T Teachers for Tomorrow program engage in a
reflective conversation about the features, activities, and outcomes of this 3-
year demonstration project. Topics include recruitment & retention of
teachers for urban schools, institutionalization, portfolio assessment, school
& college faculty roles, & student teacher cohorts. $30 prepaid

All prices include shipping & handling. To order contact the Clinical
Schools Clearinghouse.

Clinical Schools Clearinghouse
One Dupont Circle NW, Suite 610
Washington, DC 20036-1186
(202) 293-2450
(800) 822-9229
Internet: iabdalha@inet.ed.gov **or** iah@aacte.nche.edu